LANDLORDS AND TENANTS

A Complete Guide
to the
Residential Rental Relationship

LANDLORDS AND TENANTS

A Complete Guide
to the
Residential Rental Relationship

Jerome G. Rose
Rutgers University

Transaction Books
New Brunswick, New Jersey
Distributed by E.P. Dutton & Company

Printed in the United States of America
Library of Congress Catalog Number: 72-82194
ISBN 0-87855-042-9 (cloth)
0-87855-538-2 (paper)

This volume was prepared for the Center for Urban Policy Research
Rutgers—the State University of New Jersey,
New Brunswick, New Jersey

This book is dedicated to

In whose domain I willingly entrust
all my worldly possessions,
my quest for happiness
and my love

Acknowledgements

Many people were helpful in the preparation of this book. I am particularly indebted to Dr. George Sternlieb who encouraged me to undertake the study and who was a continuing source of information and insight. A number of students helped in the research and preliminary editing. I want to acknowledge the contribution of Lynn Sagalyn, G. Jeffrey Pancza, Jonathan Bernstein and Robert Jacobs.

Mary Picarella was a great help in obtaining information and coordinating the details of manuscript preparation. Nancy Rosenthal performed far beyond the call of duty in typing the many drafts. Dominic Salluce assisted in the proofreading. Transaction Books provided the services of two talented and professional staff members, editorial director, Mary Curtis, and marketing manager, Nat Bodian, who took a personal interest in the preparation for publication. I want to express my gratitude to Vera Lee for tending to my other administrative duties so that I could devote my time to this study, and to Gerald Schorr and Linda Toth of Transaction, who prepared the index.

Financial support for this study was provided by the Center for Urban Policy Research, Rutgers University, from a grant from the New Jersey Department of Community Affairs.

Contents

1 Legal and Economic Perspectives on the Landlord-Tenant Relationship

1

MALADJUSTMENT OF LANDLORD-TENANT LAW

1.1   The legal relationship between landlords and tenants is an outmoded, unworkable and mischievous anachronism that is dangerously maladjusted to the social, economic and political needs of an urban democracy, for it is a relationship that was created to meet the needs of an agrarian and feudal society. The judicial application of legal principles that are now socially irrelevant has prevented the adaptation of the landlord-tenant relationship to the momentous social and economic changes that have evolved since its creation.

1.2   The landlord-tenant relationship survives today, albeit precariously, in a state of rapid deterioration. Symptoms of this pathology are: blatant tenant hostility towards landlords, manifested at best in militant tenant organization action and at worst in wanton destruction of landlords' property; widespread neglect and wholesale abandonment of properties by landlords; increasing reluctance of investors and lenders to become enmeshed in the aggravation-frought maze; and a critical shortage of housing accommodations for low- and moderate-income tenants.

1.3   This book will show that most of the statutory proposals for landlord-tenant reform are mere palliatives that will only postpone the ultimate demise of the landlord-tenant relationship. This is not to demean proposals for the interim improvement of the landlord-tenant relationship but only to point up the short-range impact of the remedies thus far proposed. Long-range reform requires fundamental changes in the underlying economic, social and political causes of maladjustment.

ECONOMIC CAUSES OF MALADJUSTMENT

1.4   Tenants have little economic incentive to preserve, protect and maintain the premises. All increases in the value of the property and other advantages of investment, if any, accrue to the landlord. With no entrepreneural interest in the property and with no assurance of long-range tenure, tenants are unwilling to provide funds for long-range maintenance.

1.5   The incentive of landlords to spend money on maintenance depends upon their ability to recover these expenditures from rental receipts. Increases in rent, however, force the poorest tenants to vacate and create attitudes of hostility in those who remain.

1.6 Construction of rental units requires capital from financiers whose primary interest is the return on their investment. Increases in risk and decreases in return from investments diminish the capital available for apartment construction. Tenant hostility also tends to discourage the capital investment required to remedy the underlying problem of an inadequate housing supply.

SOCIAL CAUSES OF MALADJUSTMENT

1.7 When the individual lacks wealth or other attributes of social status, tenancy connotes a low social position. Tenants may adopt the social psychology of "have-nots" in a society. Not having a proprietary stake in the community tends to diminish the tenant's willingness to support and preserve the existing social structure.

1.8 The status of tenant is in fundamental contradiction to man's innate quest for secure shelter and to his territorial instincts. The insecurity that arises from the threat of eviction and the family calamity that may result create feelings of anguish and hostility towards the landlord who commands such summary and devastating power.

POLITICAL CAUSES OF MALADJUSTMENT

1.9 The growing awareness of the inequities of a legal system that favors property rights over fundamental social needs undermines political support for the legal and governmental structure. The inadequacy of short-term remedies causes further disappointment and frustration, and only exacerbates dissatisfaction with the political system.

1.10 The tenant organization movement, designed to exert political influence for changes in landlord-tenant law, has produced only minimal reform, and has even evoked counterproductive responses. Landlords and investors have become fearful of the potential power of tenant constituencies to bring legal changes that may threaten their control over their investment and diminish their return. Such fears tend to drive capital away from housing investments.

CONSEQUENCES OF MALADJUSTMENT

1.11 The Courts seem to be beginning to recognize that landlord-tenant law is poorly adapted to evolving principles of an urban democracy,[1] but the cumulative effect of centuries of judicial reinforcement of archaic concepts is not easily purged. The charge that the law is "more often than not unjust in its preference for the cause of the landlord . . ."[2] is difficult to dispute. The legal principles that comprise the body of landlord-tenant law conspire to: deprive tenants of reasonable expectation of continuing in possession of the premises; perpetuate unhabitable conditions; deny the relationship between the tenant's obligation to pay rent and the landlord's obligation to maintain the premises; provide landlords with drastic and summary remedies for tenants' defaults; and deny tenants adequate remedies for landlords' defaults.

THE INSECURITY OF TENANCY

1.12   The law relating to the creation and duration of a tenancy provides tenants with few rights in the initial selection of a dwelling and fewer guarantees to its uninterrupted possession.

No Standards for Refusal To Rent
1.13   A landlord is under virtually no legal obligation to rent to any applicant for an apartment. A landlord may establish and administer his own standards of eligibility to determine whether the applicant will be able to pay the rent and will behave in an acceptable manner. Thus, a landlord may refuse to rent to a prospective tenant to whom he objects for purely irrational reasons (see 2.17-2.19).

Insecurity of a Month-to-Month Tenancy
1.14   If a tenant receives a lease for one year or another specified term, he may be reasonably assured of uninterrupted possession for that time. However, owners of substandard housing commonly offer no lease at all but instead establish a month-to-month tenancy. Under this form of tenancy the tenant has no assurance that he may continue to live there beyond one month. The landlord may, upon one month's notice, evict a tenant for any reason whatsoever (see 2.35). Tenancies which arise by implication of law, such as tenancies-at-will, similarly give the landlord the right of summary eviction upon short notice (see 2.38, 2.39).

Landlord's Right of Forfeiture
1.15   Leases frequently provide that a tenancy terminates when certain terms and conditions are violated. The standard lease usually provides that the tenant's failure to comply with all rules and regulations gives the landlord the right to terminate the tenancy, known as the right of "forfeiture" (see 2.53). This harsh rule gives the landlord power to threaten to evict tenants for unintentional or inconsequential violation of ambiguous terms of the lease. In addition, the lease may give the landlord the right to terminate the tenancy if the tenant sublets the premises without consent (see 2.56), uses the premises in an unauthorized manner (see 2.57), or fails to repair and maintain the apartment (see 2.58).

PERPETUATION OF UNHABITABLE CONDITIONS

1.16   The underlying cause of housing deterioration arises out of dysfunctions in the *economic* rather than the *legal* system. Landlords of deteriorating units may attempt to maximize their personal return out of current rental receipts and thereby reduce the funds available for repair. This "cash flow profit taking" decreases the value of the property and reduces the landlord's incentive to make further capital investments in repair and rehabilitation (see 3.1).

1.17   Once the economic incentive to spend money on repairs is removed, only legal sanctions may force the landlord to maintain minimum standards of habitability. One may argue that it is unreasonable to expect the legal system to resolve the problems of the housing industry. It does not, however, appear to be unreasonable to expect that landlord-tenant law, as it appears in the common law, lease provisions and housing codes, should work to ameliorate rather than perpetuate our deteriorating housing supply.

Anachronisms of the Common Law
1.18   *Conditions at the beginning of the tenancy.* At common law the landlord had no obligation to deliver the premises to the tenant in a habitable condition (see 3.2). The courts established the principle that in the absence of an express agreement there was no implied warranty that the premises were safe or fit for habitation. Like a buyer, to whom the doctrine of *caveat emptor* was applied (see 3.4, 3.5) a tenant took the property for better or worse. With a few exceptions, this anachronism is still the law today.

1.19   *Conditions arising during the tenancy.* At common law the obligation to repair and maintain belonged to whoever had immediate control over the premises. Once the landlord conveyed possession and control, the tenant was obliged to maintain the property so that he could return it in substantially the same condition (see 3.9). Although today a tenant has no control over and little ability to maintain his premises, the courts, with only a few exceptions (see 3.11), continue to impose the duty of repair upon him.

Inequities of Lease Provisions
1.20   The acute shortage of housing in most urban areas gives the landlord a superior bargaining position and enables him to rent his units without agreeing to repair or maintain the premises. A tenant rarely is able to negotiate a lease that contains a landlord's covenant to repair. On the contrary, the printed lease form that is usually imposed upon the tenant contains provisions by which he agrees to keep the premises in repair and to comply with statutes and ordinances that prescribe standards of habitability (see 3.22). Such provisions confirm the shift of responsibility for maintenance from the landlord, who should reasonably be expected to fulfill this obligation, to the tenant, who lacks the knowledge and ability to perform these duties. This contractual obligation is enforced by the courts because of the judicial myth, inconsistent with economic reality, that the parties have voluntarily agreed to the terms, and consequently it is improper for the courts to rewrite their agreement.

The Failure of Housing Code Enforcement

1.21   Housing codes are supposed to protect the health, safety and welfare of tenants and to prevent or delay the deterioration of housing to substandard or slum condition. Detailed and extensive prescriptions of minimum standards of habitability have been set forth in housing codes, but the governmental agencies charged with enforcing them have been unable to achieve the codes objectives (see 3.43-3.52). Explanations for this failure have included insufficient financial support, fragmented municipal authority, political opposition, and lax judicial enforcement (see 3.43-3.47).

1.22   One could argue that housing code enforcement has failed for political and financial reasons rather than legal reasons. It is true that the courts have been slow to adopt legal principles that aid in achieving housing code objectives. For example, in spite of judicial precedent, most courts have denied the tenant the right to recover the costs of repairs made because of the landlord's failure to comply with housing code provisions (see 3.53, 3.54). Furthermore, most courts have been unwilling to apply the well-established principle of contract law that a contract is illegal and unenforceable if it violates statutory declarations of public policy (see 3.57, 3.58). Except for isolated cases, most courts have continued to enforce the landlord's claim for rent payment even though the premises are in flagrant violation of the housing code.

RENT AND HABITABILITY

1.23   Feudal principles of property law have been combined with leases favoring landlords to establish and protect the landlord's right to rent even if the premises are in an unhabitable condition (see 4.22-4.31).

Common Law Principles

1.24   At common law, the tenant was obliged to continue to pay rent, at the risk of eviction, regardless of the condition of the premises. This obligation was based on the following established common law principles: first, that in the absence of express agreement a lease does not contain any implied warranty of fitness or habitability; second, that the person in possession of premises has the obligation to repair and maintain; and third, that a lease conveys an interest in real estate rather than binds one to mutual obligations. Once having conveyed the property the landlord's right to rent was unconditional. Thus even if he made an express agreement to repair, the landlord's right to rent remained independent of his promise to repair. This doctrine, known as the "independence of covenants," required the tenant to continue to pay rent or risk eviction, and to bring a separate action against the landlord for damages resulting from his breach of agreement to repair (see 4.26).

Lease Provisions

1.25   The continuing obligation of the tenant to pay rent in spite of the premises' condition may be established by agreement of the parties. The lease will usually not state the agreement in such blatantly onerous terms but will include a provision by which the tenant assumes all obligations of repair and maintenance. Once he agrees to repair the premises himself, the tenant relinquishes his right to withhold rent as a means of requiring the landlord to maintain the property (see 4.26).

LANDLORDS' LEGAL REMEDIES

1.26   Common law practices, statutory procedures and lease provisions provide landlords with an effective arsenal of legal remedies to protect their right to rent and possession of the leased premises. Among the possible remedies are: self-help evictions; liens, distraint and attachment; summary eviction proceedings; legal action for rent; and security deposits.

Self-help Evictions

1.27   At common law a landlord was permitted to remove a tenant from the premises when the tenancy terminated, without using legal process if the eviction could be accomplished peacefully (see 5.44). Among the legal questions that arise with the use of this remedy, still available in many states, are, first: Does the landlord have a right of reentry? The answer to this question frequently depends upon disputed questions of fact relating to the landlord's right to terminate the tenancy (see 5.45). A second question is: Was the eviction accomplished peacefully? Although landlords may not evict tenants by force or fear, most courts permit landlords to wait until tenants leave the premises and then change the lock after removing the tenant's belongings (see 5.47, 5.48).

Liens, Distraint and Attachment

1.28   Common law precedent and statutory and lease provisions have created a number of legal mechanisms by which a landlord may claim the tenant's household goods and other property as security in lieu of unpaid rent (see 4.44). The landlord's legal remedies against a defaulting tenant include: *liens,* a legal claim upon the tenant's property as security for the payment of an obligation; *distraint,* a common law self-help right of the landlord to seize the tenant's property; *attachment,* a legal procedure established by statute to seize the tenant's property for the payment of rent. In some states all three techniques are available to the landlord. In other states, distraint and liens have been superseded by a statutory procedure of attachment (see 4.52-4.59).

Summary Eviction Proceedings

1.29   To discourage the hazardous and sometimes violent consequences of a landlord's self-help eviction, all states have enacted some form of summary eviction proceedings to provide a speedy, inexpensive and equitable method for the landlord to recover possession of his property (see 5.1). Such proceedings are known by different names in differ-

7

ent states, including summary proceedings, dispossessory warrant proceedings and landlord-tenant proceedings. Although the details of the statutes vary widely among the states, most contain provisions dealing with the following subjects:

1. *Grounds for eviction.* The usual grounds for eviction are holding over after expiration of the lease, nonpayment of rent and breach of agreement (see 5.2). Most summary proceedings are brought for nonpayment of rent.

2. *Procedure for instituting and conducting the proceedings.* Proceedings are usually started through one of a number of alternate methods of service (see 5.10). Although the methods of service were designed to protect the tenant by insuring that he is informed of the proceedings, process servers, particularly those in high-crime areas, sometimes do not actually serve the process. Frequently, the tenant does not learn about the proceedings until the sheriff or marshal arrives with an order to evict (see 5.13).

3. *Defenses and counterclaims.* One of the most significant current issues of landlord-tenant law is the question of the extent to which a tenant may defend himself, in a proceeding for nonpayment of rent, on the grounds of the defective condition of the premises. In recent years, courts and legislatures have begun to permit defense on grounds that the landlord has failed to maintain the premises in livable condition (see 5.21, 5.22).

4. *Enforcement of judgment.* If the verdict or decision is in favor of the landlord, a judgment will be entered awarding him possession of the premises. It is common practice for the judgment to include a stay of execution for a short period of time. At the expiration of the stay, the landlord may obtain a warrant of eviction that authorizes an officer to evict the tenant. The traditional method of eviction is to remove all of the tenant's property from the premises and to place it on the sidewalk in front of the building (see 5.34).

5. *Appeals from the judgment.* Most states authorize an appeal of a judgment in a dispossess proceeding. Requirements of appeal usually include timely notice and application, and the filing of a bond. Such requirements usually create effective deterrents to appeal by low-income tenants. Some states expressly limit the opportunity for and scope of appeals (see 5.23).

Actions for Rent

1.30   In addition to the special summary proceedings for recovery of possession of the premises, a landlord may bring an action to recover a sum of money for rent owed him (see 4.44). In some states the landlord must bring a separate action for the recovery of rent. In other states he may obtain a judgment for rent as well as possession in summary eviction proceedings. If a landlord decides to seek a money judgment rather than eviction, he must elect either to bring suit for each installment of rent as it becomes due or to bring one suit for all rent due at the expiration of the term. To avoid this dilemma, landlords often include an acceleration clause in the lease that makes the rent for the entire term due and payable upon default in the payment of a single installment (see 4.46, 4.47). If the tenant has abandoned the premises and the landlord has not relet them, the amount of money the landlord recovers will depend upon whether he is required to make a reasonable effort to relet the premises. The courts are divided on this issue (see 4.49).

Security Deposits

1.31   At common law, the landlord relied upon his right of distraint as a means of enforcing the payment of rent. Although most states enacted a form of statutory lien or distraint, the inconvenience, delay and cost of enforcing the statutory remedies resulted in the practice of requiring the tenant to deposit money with the landlord to secure the payment of rent (see 4.77). Security deposits are intended to protect a landlord from various losses that may result from a tenant's default: a period of vacancy after a tenant's abandonment, costs of reletting or costs of repair (see 4.77). One cause of tenant hostility is the practice by some landlords of withholding the security deposit and making a unilateral determination of the amount of the deposit to be applied to the repair of alleged damages to the premises. Tenant hostility is aggravated by the lack of clear and definite standards of determining the validity of the landlord's claim and by the inadequacy of remedies to regain the deposit from an obstinate or unreasonable landlord (see 4.94).

TENANTS' LEGAL REMEDIES

1.32   In recent years, the courts and legislatures have begun to respond, although timidly, to the need to adapt landlord-tenant law to the needs of an urban democracy. Numerous programs and techniques have been devised to improve tenant's rights and living conditions. Although the adoption of these remedies is a hopeful sign, the programs have proven to be less than effective in accomplishing their objectives. Among the new tenant remedies are rent abatement, rent escrow, receivership, tenant right to repair and deduct, tenant unions and protection against landlord retaliation (see Chapter 6).

Rent Abatement

1.33   At common law the obligation of the tenant to pay rent was suspended only when he was actually evicted. Thus, the tenant had no right to refuse to pay rent on the grounds that the premises were unhabitable or below minimum standards of decency. In recent years, the right of tenants to refuse to pay rent for substandard premises has been granted by a few courts and by legislatures in some states (see 6.3). The judicial creation of a tenant right of rent abatement has been based upon such diverse legal principles as: the implied warrant of habitability created by housing codes (see 6.5, 6.6); constructive eviction (see 6.7);

illegal contract (see 6.10); and partial failure of consideration (see 6.11, 6.12). In spite of the judicial development of a tenant's right to rent abatement for unhabitable premises, most courts have chosen not to adopt this principle on the grounds that it involves policy judgment that is more appropriate for legislative authority. The legislatures of some states have adopted programs of statutory rent abatement. However, the procedures and conditions prescribed in such programs have been so restrictive that the statutory remedies have not been effective (see 6.13, 6.14).

Rent Escrow
1.34　　The difference between tenant remedies of rent abatement and rent escrow is that rent abatement suspends the tenant's obligation to pay, but rent escrow provides a procedure by which rent is paid into a fund to be used for the repair and improvement of the premises (see 6.16). The rent escrow program has not developed into an effective remedy, however, for a number of reasons. First, the program is useful only when the defective condition affects the entire building (see 6.22, 6.23). Second, the courts have had difficulty finding an administrator willing and capable of using the funds in a productive and efficient manner (see 6.24). A third reason is that the rental income has not been sufficient to pay for repairs and maintenance (see 6.25, 6.26).

Housing Receivership
1.35　　The ineffectiveness of rent escrow points up the need for a legal apparatus by which a court-appointed administrator may finance the long-term repayment of expenditures for substantial repairs. Housing receivership is designed to accomplish this by providing for the appointment of a receiver who is authorized to secure a long-term loan to be applied to the costs of repair by offering a mortgage that is superior to existing mortgages (see 6.27). Without such security, lenders are unwilling to make loans for repair. Housing receivership has been ineffective, however, for a number of reasons:

1. *Legal problems.* The original receivership program was declared unconstitutional on the grounds that the law deprived the existing mortgagee of substantive and procedural due process and also impaired the obligation of his contract in violation of the United States Constitution (see 6.28-6.30). Subsequent statutory modifications of this law appears to have overcome these objections (see 6.28-6.30).
2. *Economic problems.* Experience with the program has shown that the mere transfer of control and management from the landlord to a receiver does not in any way resolve the problem of insufficient rental income to pay for repairs (see 6.31).
3. *Political problems.* Once the building is taken into receivership the landlord loses all financial incentive to recover the property. The city becomes the owner-manager of increasing numbers of problem-

ridden slum properties at a time when tenants are becoming more vocal about their dissatisfactions (see 6.32).

Tenants' Right To Repair and Deduct

1.36   The landlord is not obliged to keep the premises in repair or to pay any of the costs of repair assumed by the tenant unless the lease or the law specifies otherwise (see 6.33, 6.34). Although housing codes impose the obligation of repair upon the landlord, the courts are divided on whether the codes give the tenant the right to make the repairs they require (see 6.35). When the lease contains an agreement by the landlord to keep the premises in repair and he fails to do so, the tenant may make the repairs himself and may deduct the costs from the rent (see 6.36). However, landlords rarely consent to include such an agreement in the lease. Some states have granted tenants legal authority to deduct the costs of repair from the rent (see 6.40). However, such statutes have been ineffective because the tenant can still waive his rights by lease provision and because the amount of expenditures authorized is usually limited to an insignificant sum (see 6.41, 6.42).

Tenant Unions

1.37   The willingness of tenants to submit to substandard housing conditions and onerous lease provisions reflect the individual tenant's limited bargaining power against the landlord in a housing market characterized by a great demand for, and limited supply of, low-cost housing. Tenant unions are a device by which a tenant may increase his limited economic power by collective bargaining (see 6.48). In spite of the potential advantages of a tenant union, organization of tenants has been slow and difficult. Many distrust organizations; others have been embittered by their labor union experience or resent the payment of union dues, without which the organization cannot function effectively; many fear landlord retaliation. Landlords frequently respond to tenant organization by threatening to terminate services or to abandon the building. If the property is worth preserving, the landlord may undermine the support for a tenant union by improving the condition of the building. Once this concession is made, many tenants lose interest in the union and withdraw their support (see 6.53).

Protection Against Landlord Retaliation

1.38   A tenant who arouses the antipathy of his landlord places himself in a vulnerable position. Most tenants of substandard apartments occupy those premises without a lease and without a fixed term of residence. Without a lease to limit the amount of rent and assure a period of habitation, the landlord is free to raise the rent or terminate the tenancy upon 30 days notice (see 6.64, 6.65). Tenant remedies have only limited usefulness if the landlord can use his power to raise rent or to evict in retaliation for a tenant's exercise of those remedies. In recent years a few courts and some state legislatures have recognized the need

11

to protect tenants against landlord retaliation. In one landmark decision (see 6.66-6.69) a United States Court of Appeals held that proof of a retaliatory motive is a good defense against eviction. The court held that the tenant must prove that the landlord sought to evict him because he had reported violations of the housing code. Subsequent decisions have left other questions unanswered. How long may the tenant remain in possession after a court's refusal to evict because of retaliatory motives? What are the rights of a landlord if the complaints are unfounded or the result of tenant abuse of the property? The answers to such questions could be provided with greater precision by state legislatures. The few states that have enacted antiretaliatory legislation have failed to deal with the problem in a comprehensive manner (see 6.70-6.72).

NOTES

1.   *See* Reste Realty Corporation v. Cooper, 53 N.J. 444, 251 A2d 268 (1969); Marini v. Ireland, 56 N.J. 130, 265 A2d 526 (1970).

2.   Quinn and Phillips, *The Law of Landlord-Tenant: A Critical Evaluation of the Past with Guidelines for the Future,* 38 Ford. L. Rev. 225 (1969).

2 The Period of Tenancy

CREATION OF A TENANCY

2.1   A landlord-tenant relationship is created when the owner (or someone entitled to possession) of real estate lets another use the property. The person who lets the property is called the landlord or lessor. The person who hires the use of the property is called the tenant

14

or lessee. The interest of the tenant in the property is called a lease-hold. The interest of the landlord is called a reversion.

2.2   The obligations of the parties to each other are based upon the agreement between them. This agreement may be oral, in writing, or may arise by implication. A landlord and tenant may create a legally enforceable contract for the rental of a premises by an oral agreement if the term of the tenancy is limited. In most states such an agreement is enforceable if the period of tenancy is one year or less. In most states, the Statute of Frauds requires a lease for more than one year (or three years in some states) to be in writing. If a tenant remains after the agreed term of his tenancy has expired, a new tenancy is created, the terms of which are determined by law, and vary from state to state.

2.3   A lease is an agreement by which the landlord conveys the right to use the property for a specified period of time in exchange for the tenant's agreement to pay rent. The lease is both an *instrument of conveyance* of an interest in real estate and a *contract* that sets forth the terms of agreement between the parties. Many of the problems of the landlord-tenant relationship result from the legal implications that arise from this dual function. To the extent that the lease is treated merely as a conveyance, the landlord's obligation is satisfied, once and for all, by the transfer of the right of possession to the tenant (see 4.22). To the extent that a lease is treated as a contract, one can argue that the continuing obligation of the tenant to pay rent is dependent upon the continuing obligation of the landlord to provide maintenance and services (see 4.22).

REQUIREMENTS OF A VALID LEASE

2.4   A lease need not be in any prescribed form to be valid, but it must contain a number of essential elements.

Contractual Capacity of the Parties
2.5   Both landlord and tenant must have the legal capacity to enter into a binding agreement. If either party is under legal age (18 or 21 years of age in most states), or is mentally incompetent, or is induced to enter the agreement by fraud or duress, the lease will not be binding.

Agreement To Let and Take
2.6   The lease should contain a statement that the landlord agrees to give the tenant possession of the property and that the tenant agrees to take possession of it.

Description of the Premises
2.7   The premises should be described with sufficient detail to eliminate any question about the extent of the tenant's rights of poses-sion. An apartment may be described by an apartment number and street address. The lease should also describe the extent of the tenant's right

15

to use other parts of the building, such as storage space in the basement, recreation rooms, television aerials, clothes washing facilities, driveways and parking lots.

Term of the Lease

2.8   The parties may agree to any period of time, called the term of the lease, during which the tenant has the right of possession of the premises. A few states have statutes limiting the term of leases to under 100 years.[1] For this reason, long-term leases, in these and other states as well, are usually written for a term of not more than 99 years. If the lease does not specify the period of tenancy, the court will consider it to be a tenancy at will. At the expiration of the specified term the tenant's right to possession terminates. If the lease does not contain an option to renew, the tenant has no right to remain or to demand a renewal of the lease. If the tenant remains in the premises after the expiration of the term, he may become a tenant from year to year, from month to month or a tenant at will (see 5.3).

The Payment of Rent

2.9   For his use of the property, the tenant agrees to make periodic payments of rent. At common law, in an agrarian society, rent was due and payable at the end of the rental period, to enable the tenant to pay the rent from the profits and proceeds of the land. Today, however, leases provide for an annual rental, payable monthly in advance, on the first day of each month.

The Rights and Duties of the Parties

2.10   The lease contains provisions that describe the rights and obligations of the parties. Some of the subjects covered by lease provisions are: limitations on the tenant's use of the property; landlord and/or tenant obligations to repair; landlord's right to enter and inspect; rights of the parties upon damage to, or destruction of, the premises; the right to make alterations; the tenant's right to sublet; liability of the parties for injuries sustained on the premises; rights of the parties relating to security deposits; rights of the parties upon taking of the property by governmental action; landlord's rights upon tenant's abandonment; rights of either party to terminate upon default; landlord's rights of eviction. Each of these subjects will be discussed later.

Execution of the Lease

2.11   The formalities required for the proper execution of a lease vary from state to state. Some of the issues that may arise follow.

2.12   *Signature of the parties.* Since a lease conveys an interest in real estate, the landlord's signature is essential. The tenant's signature is usually required but is not essential to the validity of the lease as long as the tenant takes possession of the premises under the terms of the lease.

2.13   *Witnesses.* In most states the execution of the lease by the parties need not be witnessed, but in a few states, long-term leases require one or two witnesses.

2.14   *Acknowledgments.* In most states, a lease is valid without the formal acknowledgement of its execution before a notary public, but in a few states,[2] long-term leases must be acknowledged. If the lease is to be recorded, the recording statutes of most states require acknowledgment before a notary public.

2.15   *Delivery and acceptance.* A lease does not become an operative legal instrument until it is delivered by the landlord and accepted by the tenant. Because of the unequal bargaining position of the parties, it is not uncommon for an unscrupulous landlord to obtain the signature of the tenant and then fail to deliver a signed copy of the lease to him. The tenant considers himself bound to a lease for a specified term while the landlord has the option of establishing a tenancy at will because he has not delivered the lease.

THE REQUIREMENT OF MUTUAL CONSENT

2.16   Whether the landlord-tenant relationship is created by written lease, oral agreement or by implication from the landlord's consent to the tenant's possession, some form of agreement by the landlord to let, and agreement by the tenant to take possession of, the premises is necessary. This requirement of mutual consent of the parties has profound consequences. In theory, it means that in a democratic society, the place where a person resides is not assigned to him by governmental fiat. Each person is free to move about the country at will, to select any place of residence of his choice within his financial means, and to negotiate the terms and conditions of his use with the owner. The requirement of mutual consent also means that the landlord is under virtually no obligation to let his premises to any prospective tenant. The landlord may establish his own standards to determine whether a particular applicant is willing and able to fulfill the conditions and obligations of the tenancy, and whether the applicant will become a "desirable tenant," within the landlord's definition of that term. Thus, the requirement of mutual consent means that a landlord may refuse to accept a prospective tenant for many reasons.

Insufficient Income
2.17   A landlord may reject a prospective tenant if the amount and stability of the tenant's income appears to be insufficient to meet the continuing obligations of the rental payments. The significance of this criterion as a basis for the disqualification of tenants has been made clear in *The Report of the President's Committee on Urban Housing:*

> About 7.8 million American families—one in every eight—cannot now afford to pay the market price for standard housing that would cost no

17

more than 20 percent of their total incomes. (The average ratio of housing costs to gross income for the total population is 15 percent.) About half of these 7.8 million families are surviving on less than $3,000 a year—the Federal poverty level.

The study projected the size of this gap ten years from now, assuming no marked changes in current economic trends, national policies and priorities among federal programs. The projection showed that the prevalence of poverty can be expected to decline only slightly. In 1978, about 7.5 million families—one in every ten—would still be unable to afford standard housing.[3]

Social Criteria

2.18   From a landlord's experience and point of view, a number of social characteristics make some tenants less desirable than others. Tenants with children tend to cause greater expenditures for repair and maintenance than childless couples. On the other hand, some young single adults are not as stable, quiet and dependable as their married counterparts. A landlord is under no legal obligation to offer the premises to any tenant in spite of the fact that the basis for rejection is not any violation of legal or moral standards of behavior. There is even less basis for complaint against the landlord when he refuses to rent an apartment to someone whom he suspects of drug addiction, alcoholism, poor housekeeping standards, lack of furniture, irregular work history or illegitimate children.

Irrational Prejudices

2.19   The requirement of mutual consent means that a landlord may refuse to rent his apartment to someone for reasons that are completely irrational. A tenant may be rejected because he has "shifty eyes," "an effeminate manner," "long straggly hair," a "floozy" or "sharp" appearance, a "smart-aleck" attitude or any other subjective, personal or irrational reason given by the landlord. Except for fair housing laws prohibiting discrimination on the grounds of race, religion or national origin, there is no legal requirement that a landlord be "fair" in the selection of his tenants. The constitutional requirements of a due process fair hearing are not applicable to the business relations of private individuals. On the other hand, if the landlord is a public agency[4] (see 8.34-8.81), or if there is a sufficiently close relationship between the private landlord and a governmental agency, then the landlord must establish tenant eligibility on the basis of standards and procedures that will satisfy the constitutional requirements of due process and equal protection of the laws.

Race, Religion or National Origin

2.20   A landlord may not refuse to enter into a landlord-tenant relationship with a person on the grounds of race, religion or national origin. Discrimination in the leasing or rental of housing accommoda-

18

tions is prohibited by federal legislation and, in some states, by state statute and local ordinance.

2.21 *Federal legislation.* There are two important federal laws that prohibit discrimination on the grounds of race. The Civil Rights Act of 1866 provides that

> All citizens of the United States shall have the same right, in every State and Territory, as is enjoyed by White citizens thereof to inherit, purchase, lease, sell, hold and convey real and personal property.[5]

Although the validity of this law had been in question for over 100 years, in 1968, in the case of *Jones v. Mayer,* the United States Supreme Court upheld the Civil Rights Act as a valid exercise of the Thirteenth Amendment.[6] The court held that the law prohibits private as well as governmental discrimination on the grounds of race in the sale or resale of property.

2.22 Title VIII of the Civil Rights Act of 1968 is much more comprehensive than the 1866 statute. The more recent federal legislation prohibits discrimination in the sale or rental of most housing on the grounds of race, color, religion or national origin. The law makes it illegal for a landlord to discriminate by: refusing to rent; discriminating in the rental terms; discriminating by advertising that an apartment is available only to persons of certain race, color, religion or national origin; or denying that an apartment is available for inspection or rental when it really is available. Three different methods of enforcement are provided. The tenant may bring a court action for injunction or damages, including up to $1,000 punitive damages. Or, he may complain to the Department of Housing and Urban Development, which will attempt to obtain compliance. A third option is to complain to the Attorney General of the United States, who will take action if there is reasonable evidence of a pattern or practice of discrimination.[7] The 1968 Fair Housing Law does not cover the rental of single-family houses where no broker is used or the rental of units in owner-occupied dwellings for two to four families, if discriminatory advertising is not used.

2.23 *State and local legislation.* Most states and many municipalities have fair housing laws that make it illegal for a landlord to discriminate against a prospective tenant on the grounds of race, religion or national origin. Most of these statutes create a state or municipal commission to enforce the provisions. Generally, the commission has only limited power to effect a conciliation between the parties, and in most instances, has insufficient enforcement power to enforce compliance in time to be of real benefit to the tenant.[8]

2.24 On the other hand, it must be noted that even states that have enacted fair housing laws at the same time permit their local governments to enact zoning ordinances that prohibit multiple dwelling and inexpensive one- and two-family houses, and thereby discourage the construction of housing for low-income families and racial minorities.[9]

DURATION OF A TENANCY

2.25   Once a landlord agrees to let the premises, and a tenant agrees to take possession, the parties must decide upon the duration of the tenancy. They may agree to bind each other to a definite period of time, or if they fail to agree or if there is ambiguity about their agreement, the duration of the tenancy will be determined by the application of one of a number of principles of law created by the courts and legislatures to resolve this question.

TENANCY FOR AN AGREED PERIOD OF TIME

2.26   A written lease should prescribe the agreed duration of the term. A typical lease provision will contain language such as: "The within premises are hereby rented for a period of two years, commencing September 15, 1972 and terminating September 14, 1974." During the described period the tenant has the exclusive right to use the premises, and must vacate without any further notice by the landlord, upon the termination of the period.

Options To Extend or Renew

2.27   The lease may contain a provision giving the tenant the option to extend the term for another specified period, which may be either longer or shorter than the original term. The lease should also set forth the manner in which the tenant must notify the landlord of his intention to extend. The failure of the tenant to notify the landlord of his intention to exercise his option to extend the term can cause doubt and ambiguity. In some states, the continued possession of the premises by the tenant and the payment of rent constitutes intention to exercise his option to extend the term for the period specified in the lease. In other states, the tenant will not be entitled to a renewal for the specified period unless he gives notice in accordance with the lease provisions.

2.28   An option to extend differs from an option to renew in that an extension takes effect upon giving notice, whereas an option to renew obligates the parties to enter into a new lease for the specified period. In most states the courts will ignore this distinction and will treat an extension and a renewal as being synonymous. The words will be used interchangeably in this book.

Automatic Extension Provisions

2.29   A lease may contain a provision calling for an automatic extension for a specified period unless either party gives written notice to the other party that he intends to terminate. In some states this provision is made inoperative by laws that require the landlord to notify the tenant that the lease will be renewed automatically unless the tenant indicates his intention to terminate. Such statutes were enacted as a protection for tenants during a period when vacancy rates were high and a tenant might find better accommodations at the expiration of his lease. Today a tenant is more concerned about his ability to renew than he is about the possibility of an automatic renewal.

Holding Over

2.30   At the expiration of a tenancy the tenant is obliged to surrender possession of the premises without any further notice from the landlord. If the tenant fails to vacate (holds over) the landlord will have the right to evict him. If the landlord elects not to evict, the right of a tenant holding over is determined by common law principles, statutory provisions and lease provisions.

2.31   *Common laws.* The general rule established by the courts is that, in the absence of statute or lease provision, if a tenant holds over after the expiration of a lease term, and the landlord continues to accept the payment of rent, the tenancy is renewed or extended on the same terms and conditions as in the original agreement. The courts have not, however, adopted a uniform rule to determine the duration of the new term of a holdover tenant. In most states, if the original term is for a year or more, holding over creates a tenancy for one year. If the original term is for a period of less than a year, the holdover term will be the same as the original term. In a few states, holding over creates a tenancy at will.

2.32   The courts are also divided on the question of the effect of a notice from the landlord that a higher rent will be charged if the tenant holds over after the expiration of the lease term. In some states the holdover tenant will be liable for the increased rent. In other states, the tenant will not be bound by a landlord's notice of increased rent.

2.33   *Statutory provisions.* Some states[10] have statutory provisions that determine the duration of a holdover tenancy. Some statutes prescribe a month-to-month tenancy; some create a tenancy at will; others codify the common law rule. Some states have statutory provisions to protect the landlord against tenant holdover. Such provisions make a holdover tenant liable for double or triple damages.

2.34   *Lease provisions.* A carefully drawn lease will provide for the contingency of a holdover tenant. Such provisions may prescribe:

> If the tenant remains in possession after the end of said term, the landlord shall have the option of extending the term from month to month, or for one additional year or may consider the tenant as forcibly and unlawfully detaining the premises and subject to all the remedies therefor.

TENANCY FROM MONTH TO MONTH

2.35   A tenancy from month-to-month is most commonly used in substandard housing accommodations in urban areas. Such a tenancy recurs continuously for an indefinite period until terminated by notice of either party. It is different from a tenancy by the month, which terminates without any further notice at the expiration of that month. A tenancy from month-to-month may be created by express or implied agreement between the parties, or by implication of law.

Express or Implied Agreement of the Parties

2.36   A landlord and tenant may create a month-to-month tenancy by an express agreement that the term shall be a period of one month and shall continue from month to month until notice is given by either party of its termination. The parties may also agree that, at the expiration of a lease for a definite period, the tenant may remain on a month-to-month basis. The parties' agreement to create a month-to-month tenancy may be implied from a monthly payment of rent and failure to specify the terms of the tenancy.

Implication of Law

2.37   A month-to-month tenancy may be created by implication of law under circumstances where the parties have not indicated any intention of designating such a term, but where the courts or legislature have determined that a month-to-month tenancy would be reasonable and appropriate. For example, if the parties enter into an oral agreement of lease for a period over one year in a state where such agreement is void under the Statute of Frauds, then a tenancy from month-to-month is created. Paradoxically, the month-to-month tenancy is valid even though it eventually continues for a period in excess of one year. Some states have statutory provisions that create a month-to-month tenancy when a tenant remains after the expiration of a definite term.[11] Most courts will find that a month-to-month tenancy is created when the parties do not have a lease or any agreement other than the monthly payment of rent.

TENANCY AT WILL

2.38   A tenancy at will is a tenancy of an indefinite term that may be terminated at any time by either party. The tenant holds possession with the permission and consent of the landlord, but that permission may be withdrawn by the landlord whenever he wishes to do so. A tenancy at will may be created by express agreement of the parties, but usually arises by implication. For example, a tenancy at will is created when the tenant is authorized to occupy the premises for an indefinite period, until a specific event occurs, such as until the premises are sold or rented to a third person. In some states, a tenancy at will (rather than a month-to-month tenancy) is created if the lease is void or the tenant holds over.

TENANCY AT SUFFERANCE

2.39   A tenancy at sufferance is not a tenancy in the strict legal sense. The tenant at sufferance has no legal right to continue in possession. Even though he originally entered into possession with permission of the landlord, the tenant at sufferance remains only because of the neglect or failure of the landlord to remove him. A tenancy at sufferance differs from a tenancy at will in that a tenant at will has a legal right to continued possession, subject to termination, whereas a tenant at sufferance does not have the legal right to possession. A tenant at sufferance differs from a trespasser in that he entered possession with permission of the landlord whereas a trespasser enters the premises unlawfully. In some states a tenant who holds over without the consent of the landlord is considered a tenant at sufferance.

INDEFINITE TERM UNDER RENT CONTROL

2.40   During World War II, emergency rent-control legislation was enacted to prevent widespread evictions during an acute housing shortage. The purpose of the legislation was to control the amount of rent and also to permit landlords to receive a fair return on their investment. As part of the system of control, tenants were permitted to retain possession for an indefinite period as long as they continued to pay the prescribed maximum rent. Rent control has been discontinued in all areas except New York City and a few cities in Massachusetts.

TERMINATION OF THE TENANCY

2.41   The legal right to terminate a tenancy is important to both landlords and tenants. The landlord is interested in his rights of termination as a device to get rid of an undesirable tenant, to use the premises for another purpose or to raise the rent. The tenant is interested in his rights of termination as a way of escaping his obligation to pay rent for the remainder of the term. In urban areas where there is an acute shortage of apartments, however, tenants are more interested in their rights to *avoid* or prevent termination of their tenancy by the landlord. The rights of the parties on termination depend upon the reason for the termination. A tenancy may be ended for any one of many reasons: expiration of a definite term; notice to terminate an indefinite term; mutual agreement; violation of the terms of the lease; surrender or abandonment of the property; destruction of the premises; and taking of the property by eminent domain. The rights of the parties under each of these circumstances will be discussed below.

EXPIRATION OF A DEFINITE TERM

2.42   A tenancy usually terminates automatically upon the expiration of the prescribed period. In the absence of statutory or lease provision, no notice of termination is required. A few states have a statu-

23

tory requirement that a landlord give notice of termination of a tenancy before it actually takes effect.

2.43   Legal problems arise when, at the expiration of a definite term, the tenant holds over. In such cases the rights of the tenant depend upon the response of the landlord. If the landlord continues to accept the rent, or otherwise indicates his consent to the continuation of the tenancy, the tenant becomes a holdover tenant for a period which varies from state to state: the new period may be a renewal of the original term, a tenancy from year to year, month to month or at will (see 2.8). On the other hand, if the landlord does not continue to accept the rent or otherwise indicate his consent to a continuation of the tenancy, the tenant becomes a tenant at sufferance and is subject to eviction.

2.44   At common law, a landlord was not entitled to recover rent from a tenant at sufferance. Today, however, a landlord may recover the fair rental value of the premises for the period between the end of the term and the date of eviction. In some states, a tenant who holds over without the consent of the landlord may be liable for double or triple the rent.[12] The *Model Code* (Sec. 2-309)) provides that if a tenant continues in possession upon the expiration of a rental period, he will be liable for double the previous monthly rental, prorated daily, for the first month, and the prorated previous rental for any period over one month. This section of the *Model Code* also provides that the landlord may start summary proceedings to recover possession at any time during the first 60 days of holdover unless he accepts the rent (see 5.1). In the absence of a different agreement, the acceptance of the rent by the landlord will create a month-to-month tenancy.

NOTICE TO TERMINATE AN INDEFINITE TERM

2.45   A tenancy for an indefinite term, such as a tenancy from year to year, month to month or at will, may be terminated by a timely and appropriate notice, called a "notice to quit," by either party.

Requirements of a Valid Notice To Quit.
2.46   The words used in a notice to quit must express an unequivocal and unconditional intention to terminate as of a certain date. Unless required by statute to be in writing, an oral notice is sufficient, but it might create an unnecessary and avoidable problem of proof at trial. A written notice may be delivered by mail, handed to the party personally or left with a member of the family or other person of apparent authority on the premises. The tenancy may not be terminated in the middle of a period, and the notice to quit must specify the last day of the period as the termination date. Where that date is in doubt, the notice may terminate the tenancy "at the end of the rental period commencing next after the date upon which you receive this notice." In some jurisdictions,[13] however, the notice to quit must designate the

first day and not the last day of the period as the day of termination. The amount of time of notice required for termination depends upon the period of tenancy.

Month-to-Month Tenancy.

2.47 A notice to terminate a month-to-month tenancy must be given at least one month before the expiration of the term; in most states the notice must call for the termination at the end of the monthly period. Thus, a notice to terminate a monthly tenancy ending January 31 must be served before the beginning of January, and must provide for termination on January 31. A notice to terminate such a tenancy on any previous date, for example, January 21 will be ineffective to terminate the tenancy even if served a month before that date. The *Model Code* (Sec. 2-310) provides that a tenancy from month to month may be terminated by either the landlord or tenant notifying the other at least one month in advance of the anticipated termination.

Tenancy at Will

2.48 At common law a tenancy at will was terminable without notice. Today, however, in the absence of statutes, the courts have imposed a requirement of a reasonable period of notice to terminate. In most states the length of notice required to terminate a tenancy at will is prescribed by statute. The usual statutory period is 30 days or one month. Some statutes, however, require the period of notice to be the same as the interval between the periodic payments of rent. Thus, if rent is paid weekly, one weeks notice is required. The *Model Code* (Sec. 2-309) provides that any tenancy for a period less than month to month may be terminated by either the landlord or tenant by notifying the other party at least ten days before the anticipated termination.

Tenancy at Sufferance

2.49 In the absence of statute, a tenancy at sufferance may be terminated without notice. Statutes in some states, however, require a landlord to serve a notice to quit on a tenant at sufferance. Such statutes usually prescribe a notice of 30 days or one month.

MUTUAL AGREEMENT OF THE PARTIES

2.50 A landlord and tenant may agree to terminate a tenancy at any time before the date of expiration of the term provided in the lease. Such an agreement may be part of the initial understanding of the parties, or may be reached at any time during the tenancy.

Options To Terminate

2.51 At the time of the creation of the tenancy, the parties may agree to give either or both parties the option to terminate under prescribed conditions. For example, a lease for a definite period may contain a provision that the landlord may terminate upon notice of his sale of the property, or his intention to use the premises himself. When an

25

option to terminate is provided in the lease it must be exercised within the prescribed time, and sufficient notice must be given to the other party.

Subsequent Agreement To Terminate

2.52   In spite of any previous agreement of the parties to create a tenancy for a definite period, the parties may agree at any time to terminate the tenancy. The agreement of the tenant to relinquish possession of the premises is sufficient for a binding and enforceable termination. Such an agreement does not need to be in writing, but the party alleging the existence of an oral (or written) agreement to terminate sustains the burden of proof.

VIOLATION OF THE TERMS OF THE LEASE

2.53   The lease may provide for the termination of the tenancy if certain terms and conditions are violated. This is known as the right of "forfeiture."

Common Law and Statutory Limitations on Forfeiture

2.54   To limit the potentially harsh consequences of the exercise of the right of forfeiture, the courts at common law created a number of judicial principles that make it very difficult for a landlord to terminate a tenancy because of a tenant's violation of lease provision or other alleged wrongful act. These principles specify that: the right to terminate must be expressed in clear and unambiguous language; the tenant's act must be willful; the violation must be substantial. The landlord must give clear and specific notice of the tenant's default; ask that the violation be rectified; give notice of intent to terminate if the tenant fails to comply with this request; and act without unreasonable delay at the risk of "waiving" the right to terminate. In some states[14] the procedure for forfeiture is prescribed by statute. The *Model Code* provisions (Sec. 2-312, 2-313) require the landlord to notify the tenant of his violation and give the tenant five days to correct or remove the condition. If the breach continues or recurs after the five-day period, the landlord may bring summary proceedings to evict. If the landlord accepts rent thereafter, he waives his right to terminate for the violation.

2.55   Other than violation of the agreement to pay rent (see 4.44-4.76) the types of lease violation that are most frequently used by landlords to terminate tenancies are unauthorized subletting, unauthorized or unlawful use of the premises, and damages to the premises or failure to repair.

Unauthorized Subletting

2.56   When the lease prohibits subletting and a tenant has breached this prohibition, the courts have, although reluctantly, enforced the landlord's right of forfeiture. The courts tend to discourage the enforcement of forfeiture, however, by limiting its application to situations where a sublease has been executed and a new tenant has taken possession of the premises. The *Model Code* (Sec. 2-403) provides that a tenant shall have the right to sublet subject to the landlord's consent, which may be withheld only for specified reasons. Under the *Model Code*, if the landlord withholds his consent to sublease without reasonable grounds, the tenant may terminate the lease upon 90 days notice to the landlord. (see 4.32).

Unauthorized or Unlawful Use of the Premises

2.57   When the lease so provides, a landlord may terminate a tenancy if a tenant uses the premises for an unlawful purpose or in an unauthorized manner. The use of the premises for the sale of narcotics or the illegal sale of liquor would constitute such a breach. Keeping pets in the apartment may also constitute sufficient grounds for termination. One New York case, however, has held that keeping a dog in an apartment, in and of itself, is not a sufficient violation to permit the landlord to terminate, without showing that the conduct of the dog interfered with other tenants' use and enjoyment of the property so as to constitute a nuisance.[15] This principle has not, however, been universally adopted by the courts of other states.

Damage To the Premises or Failure To Repair

2.58   If the lease so provides, a landlord may terminate the tenancy if the tenant causes damage to the premises or fails to fulfill his obligation to keep the premises in repair. The courts will not enforce this provision unless the damage is substantial. The *Model Code* (Sec. 2-304) prescribes a procedure which gives a tenant the opportunity to remedy his default, and gives the landlord the right to terminate if the tenant's continuing breach constitutes a violation of a duty imposed by statute.

Tenant's Right To Terminate

2.59   Because of the landlord's superior bargaining position, the tenant is generally unable to obtain a lease provision giving him the right to terminate upon the landlord's violation of the lease. To overcome this inequity the *Model Code* (Sec. 2-207) proposes that a tenant be given the right to terminate if the landlord fails to supply heat, water or hot water.

SURRENDER OR ABANDONMENT

2.60   Abandonment of apartments by tenants is a common method by which tenancies are terminated in low-income and deteriorated sections of cities. The tenant's relinquishment of possession becomes a termination in law when the landlord, by express agreement or by implication, accepts possession of the premises.

Tenant's Intention To Relinquish Possession

2.61   A tenant's surrender of the premises is equivalent to an offer to terminate the tenancy. For termination to be effective, the tenant

27

must deliver or relinquish possession with the intention of ending his tenancy. If the tenant leaves the premises temporarily and delivers the key to the landlord for this temporary period, it will not constitute an abandonment, because the tenant did not intend to relinquish his rights to possession. On the other hand, if the tenant by words or action indicates his intention to give up his rights of dominion, the landlord may treat this action as an offer to terminate the tenancy.

Landlord's Intention To Accept Possession

2.62   The surrender of the premises by the tenant terminates the tenancy only if the landlord accepts the abandonment. The landlord may indicate his acceptance by express agreement or by implication. Accepting the keys to the apartment does not, by itself, indicate the landlord's intention to accept surrender of the apartment, for he may take the keys for the limited purpose of protecting the apartment. A landlord is not required to notify a tenant that he rejects his offer to terminate, although such notice would eliminate doubt about the landlord's intentions. Nor does an attempt by the landlord to relet the apartment by itself indicate his acceptance of the surrender. In most states, reletting the apartment will not constitute acceptance of the surrender if the landlord indicates that he will continue to hold the tenant responsible for the rent. In some states, however, reletting the apartment automatically releases the tenant from liability for rent.

Consequences of Abandonment

2.63   When the landlord accepts the tenant's surrender, the tenancy terminates, and all further rights and liabilities of the parties are precluded. The parties remain liable, however, for all obligations that accrued during the period predating the termination. When the parties are represented by attorneys, the matter may be resolved definitively by having the parties execute a general release of their rights against each other.

Effect of Lease Provisions

2.64   The standard form of apartment lease generally contains a clause providing that if the tenant abandons the premises, he will remain liable for the rent until the expiration of the term. Such a clause may also provide that the landlord is not obliged to relet the premises, but that any reletting will not relieve the tenant of his obligation to pay rent. Under such a provision the tenant is liable for the difference between the amount of rent the landlord would have received under the lease and the amount of rent actually received (less cost of reletting). In some states the landlord is required to minimize the tenant's liability by making a reasonable attempt to relet the premises.

Model Code Provisions

2.65   The *Model Code* provision on abandonment (Sec. 2-308) does not impose a duty on the landlord to relet, but instead limits the tenant's liability to the amount of loss the landlord would sustain if he did relet the premises. Under this provision a tenant who quits a dwelling unit intending to terminate his tenancy is liable for the lower of two amounts: the entire rent for the remainder of the term, or all rent not paid during the period reasonably required to rerent the premises at a fair value, plus the difference between the fair rent and the rent originally agreed upon, plus a reasonable commission for renting the premises.

DESTRUCTION OF THE PREMISES

2.66 The right of landlords and tenants to terminate the tenancy because of destruction of the premises depends upon the extent of the damage and also upon the relevant statutory and lease provisions.

Total Destruction

2.67 At common law a tenant was not relieved of his obligation to pay rent nor was his tenancy terminated by the total destruction of the premises. This rule originated because the primary function of the lease was the conveyance of an interest in land for agricultural use. The tenant became the owner of an estate in land. This proprietary interest in land continued even if the buildings were destroyed, and so it was not unreasonable to require the tenant to continue to fulfill his obligation to pay rent. Many states[16] have changed the common law by statutory provisions that relieve the tenant from his obligation to pay rent or give him an option to terminate. In most states the common law rule has been held to be inapplicable to apartment rental.

2.68 The possibility of total destruction of the premises is usually covered by the lease. A typical provision will give the landlord the option to rebuild or terminate, and give the tenant the option to terminate if the landlord does not rebuild within a specified period. This type of clause is of little value to a tenant who requires immediate housing accommodations.

Partial Destruction

2.69 At common law, partial destruction of the premises did not give the tenant the right to terminate the tenancy even though the premises became temporarily unfit for occupancy. Some lease provisions deal with the problem of partial destruction, but usually they allow the tenant to terminate only "if the damage is so extensive as to amount to the total destruction of the leased premises." The *Model Code* (Sec. 2-208) provides that when the dwelling unit is rendered partially or wholly unusable by fire or other casualty, the tenant may vacate the premises or any part of them, and upon notice to the landlord must pay rent only for whatever part of the premises he continues to occupy.

Constructive Eviction

2.70 At common law it was clearly established that the physical ouster or eviction of a tenant was grounds for a tenant's election to terminate the tenancy. The courts reached this decision because the eviction would constitute a violation of the implied warrant of quiet enjoyment of possession by the tenant. The ruling was extended when the courts began to realize that other factors could disturb the tenant's quiet enjoyment as effectively as an actual eviction.[17] The landmark decision involved a tenant who quit the premises because the landlord permitted several women of questionable moral character to use another apartment in the building. The court held that the landlord's action deprived the tenant of quiet enjoyment and was the equivalent of an eviction.[18] This principle developed into the doctrine of "constructive eviction," by which a tenant could end his tenancy by vacating the premises within a reasonable time after he had been substantially deprived of his enjoyment of the premises in violation of an express or implied obligation. Thus, when a landlord fails to keep the premises in repair, in violation of his agreement or other legal obligation to do so, the tenant may treat this condition as equivalent to eviction and terminate the tenancy. The *Model Code* (Sec. 2-205) extends this doctrine even further and provides that a tenant may terminate if the landlord, after notice, fails to remedy any condition that deprives the tenant of substantial benefit and enjoyment of the tenancy (see 6.30, 8.7-8.9).

TAKING THE PROPERTY BY CONDEMNATION

2.71   The tenancy is terminated when the landlord's property is taken by governmental action, through the exercise of the power of eminent domain. The tenant is not entitled to any portion of the eminent domain award. However, statutory provisions for relocation of tenants are provided by the Uniform Relocation Assistance Act.[19]

THE EMERGENCE OF THE QUASI - PUBLIC LANDLORD

2.72   This chapter describes the legal rights of tenants and *private* landlords relating to the creation, duration and termination of the landlord-tenant relationship. Chapter 8 discusses the legal rights of tenants of a *public* landlord. Recent judicial decisions have begun to outline circumstances in which private landlords may be treated as though they were public landlords. The legal basis for this transition is the application of federal constitutional principles to the economic fact that government subsidy is necessary to build housing that can be rented by low- and moderate-income tenants.

THE APPLICABLE CONSTITUTIONAL PRINCIPLES

2.73   The First Amendment to the United States Constitution protects the freedoms of speech, assembly, religion and redress of grievances from interference by the federal government. The Fifth Amendment prohibits the federal government from depriving any person of life, liberty or property without due process of law. The Fourteenth Amendment protects these freedoms from infringement by state governments. Early in constitutional history it was clearly established that these provisions only protect against interference with civil rights by *governmental* action. The First, Fifth and Fourteenth Amendments do not apply to the interference, by one private individual, with the rights of another private individual. Thus, under the traditional interpretation of the Constitution, the rights of a tenant dealing with a public landlord are subject to constitutional protections, while the rights of a tenant in his relationship with a private landlord are not.

WHAT CONSTITUTES GOVERNMENT ACTION

2.74 Ever since the Civil Rights Cases[20] in which the Supreme Court held that the Fourteenth Amendment only restricts "state action" and does not cover discriminatory acts by individuals, the primary legal issue in all actions involving the Fifth and Fourteenth Amendments has been: Has there been sufficient "governmental action" to fall within the meaning of those amendments? As recently as 1949, the highest appellate court of New York held that a private housing company was not subject to the provisions of the Fourteenth Amendment because its action was not "state action," even though the land was acquired through the state's condemnation power, the company received exemptions from real estate taxes, and there was a continuing contract between the company and the state relating to the regulation of rent.[21]

2.75 Then, in the 1960s, the judicial definition of "governmental action" began to be expanded to include the action of private persons where there is a sufficient direct relationship between the private person and the government. In *Burton* v. *Wilmington Parking Authority,*[22] the United States Supreme Court held that the action of a private operator of a public parking authority violated the Equal Protection Clause of the Fourteenth Amendment when he refused to serve a customer because of his race. The court said:

> By its inaction, the Authority, and through it the State, has not only made itself a party to the refusal of service, but has been elected to place its power, property and prestige behind the admitted discrimination. The State has so far insinuated itself into a position of interdependence with (the private operator) that it must be recognized as a joint participant in the challenged activity, which, on that account, cannot be considered to have been so "purely private" as to fall outside the scope of the Fourteenth Amendment.[23]

The principle of the *Burton* decision has been applied in subsequent cases involving various degrees of governmental relationship to the private person.[24] In each case the court has held that the action of the private individual constituted governmental action within the meaning of the Fifth or Fourteenth Amendment. When this principle is applied to a situation involving a private landlord, it results in the creation of a quasi-public landlord.

WHO IS A QUASI-PUBLIC LANDLORD?

2.76   The *Burton* decision has become the basis for the proposition that when federal and state governments place their power, property and privilege behind a private landlord, the landlord loses much of his freedom of action as a private individual, and is subject to many of the restrictions of a public landlord. Two recent decisions in the federal courts have begun to define the forms of governmental "power, property and privilege" that will transform a private landlord into a quasi-public landlord. The first case, *Colon v. Tompkins Square Neighbors,*[25] decided in 1968, involved a landlord who owned a housing project that was constructed on an urban renewal site, financed by an FHA mortgage, aided by city real estate tax exemption, the recipient of rent supplements, and subject to supervision in its daily operation by the City Housing and Development Administration and the Federal Housing Administration. The court held that there was sufficient government participation and involvement with the landlord to subject him to constitutional requirements relating to the admission of tenants. The second case, *McQueen v. Drucker,*[26] decided in 1970, involved a landlord who owned a housing project that was built on an urban renewal site, financed by an FHA mortgage and aided by a real estate tax exemption. The court held that the landlord, by virtue of this arrangement, relinquished the unrestricted right of a private landlord to terminate tenancies upon lease expiration.

CREATION OF THE TENANCY

2.77   The *Colon* case involved a landlord who refused to accept tenants solely because they were recipients of welfare funds. The court held that the Equal Protection Clause of the Fourteenth Amendment prohibits discrimination against welfare recipients, because they are not necessarily, by virtue of that designation, "uncooperative tenants, indifferent occupants or inconsiderate neighbors." The court held that the private landlord was subject to the provision of the Fourteenth Amendment because of his participation in government programs of financial aid. The court also indicated that the landlord would be subject to the Due Process Clause of the Fourteenth Amendment, and would have to adopt "ascertainable standards" for the selection of tenants as well as a fair and orderly procedure for allocating the limited supply of apartments. Thus, the principle seems to have been established that a private landlord who receives certain government financial assistance relinquishes his sole and exclusive right to select tenants, and must adopt standards and procedures of selection that are consistent with the Due Process requirements of the Fourteenth Amendment.

TERMINATION OF THE TENANCY

2.78   The *McQueen* case involved a landlord who terminated a tenancy at the expiration of the term of the lease. The landlord's notice to quit ordered the tenant to vacate, and gave no reason other than the expiration of the term of the lease. Under the prevailing law of that state (Massachusetts), a tenant who holds over after the expiration of a lease may be evicted without cause. During the trial it was established that the tenant was a prominent leader of a tenant's group, that he was an organizer of demonstrations against the landlord, that he had been convicted of assault against the superintendent of the building, and that he caused the landlord to bring several unsuccessful suits for eviction for nonpayment of rent and for use of a washing machine in violation of the lease. Testimony was introduced to indicate that the landlord refused to renew the lease because "he could not stand any further confrontations" with the tenant. From this evidence the court concluded that the primary reason for the landlord's notice to quit at the expiration of the term was the landlord's desire to get rid of the tenant in retaliation for his prior conduct.

2.79 The court compared this situation to a public housing project where the government must base its notice of evicton on "something beyond the mere expiration of the term." In public housing, the recent tendency of the courts has been to require the government to have a sufficient cause to evict, and to give the tenant notice of that cause. The question before the court in *McQueen* was whether the judicial restrictions on termination of a tenancy by a governmental landlord should be extended to a landlord receiving assistance under state and federal programs. The court held that a private landlord receiving such government assistance (i.e., a quasi-public landlord) must give his tenant notice and prove that a good cause exists, and that any provisions of the lease which state that the landlord has power to terminate without cause at the expiration of a fixed term are invalid.

SIGNIFICANCE OF THE "QUASI-PUBLIC LANDLORD" PRINCIPAL
2.80 In 1969, 160,000 housing and apartment units for low-income families were built with direct federal assistance. In 1970 this figure increased to 450,000 units.[27] (The 450,000 total consists of 400,000 units assisted by HUD and 50,000 units assisted by the Farmers Home Administration.) In fiscal 1970, 58 percent of all mortgage loans made had federal involvement.[28] The President's Committee on Urban Housing has recommended that 2.6 million units of housing be added to the nation's housing supply each year, including 600,000 to 800,000 units each year for low-income families.[29] Because of rising costs of construction and land, building officials have predicted that by 1980 more apartment units will be built than single-family houses.[30] The significance of these projections is that, even if the principle of the quasi-public landlord is limited to the facts of the *Colon* and *McQueen* cases (i.e., federal interest subsidy, land cost write-down and property tax abatement), a progressive-

ly increasing proportion of the nation's landlords will be included in this category.

2.81   The language in the *Colon* and *McQueen* cases indicates that the reasons for treating a private landlord as a public landlord are not limited to the facts of those cases. The basis of both decisions is that government placed its power, property and prestige behind the landlord's authority. The *McQueen* decision referred to such a landord as a "Sec. 221(d) (3) landlord" because the costs of construction of the building were financed under a program of interest subsidy and FHA insurance provided under section 221(d) (3) of the National Housing Act. There is every reason to believe that the same principle would apply to a "Sec. 236 landlord," whose costs of construction are financed under the successor program of interest subsidy and FHA insurance provided under section 236 of the National Housing Act. In time this principle could be applied to a "Sec. 202 landlord" (direct loans for rental housing for the elderly and handicapped in the Housing Act of 1959), a "Sec. 231 landlord" (mortgage insurance for new or rehabilitated rental housing for the elderly and handicapped, in the National Housing Act), and eventually to a "Sec. 207 landlord," whose costs of construction of rental housing are financed under the regular FHA program.

2.82   Furthermore, nothing in the *Colon* and *McQueen* decisions limits their applicability to landlords who receive aid under federal programs of assistance. State and local governments may, in many ways, place their power, property and privilege behind the landlord's authority. Tax abatement is only one means. It may even be argued that the power, property and privilege of the state is placed behind the landlord by providing for streets, water, sewer and electric utilities and by administering zoning, building and housing codes, and even by providing police, fire and sanitation personnel and facilities. If the courts are persuaded by this argument, the *Colon* and *McQueen* decisions may transform the landlord-tenant relationship from a private agreement between private parties to a quasi-public relationship subject to the principles of fair play incorporated in the Constitution.

NOTES

1. *E.g.,* Alabama, California and Nevada.

2. *E.g.,* Alabama, Nebraska, New Hampshire, Ohio and Maryland.

3. *The Report of the President's Committee on Urban Housing* (1968).

4. *See* Smith v. Holiday Inns of America, 336 F.2d 630 (6th Cir. 1964); Reitman v. Mulkey 387 U.S. 369 (1967), and recent decisions involving Sec. 236 housing.

5. Act of April 9, 1866, Ch. 31, Sec. 1, 14 Stat. 27; reenacted in Act of May 31, 1870, Ch. 114, Sec. 18, 16 Stat. 144, 42 U.S.C. Sec. 1982 (1958).

6. 392 U.S. 409 (1968).

7. *Pub. L. No.* 90-284, 82 Stat. 73 (1968).

8. *See Organization for Social Science and Technical Innovation, Housing Action* 105 (1969); *Housing and Home Finance Agency, Fair Housing Laws: Summaries and Text of State and Municipal Laws* (1964).

9. *See* M. Brooks, *Exclusionary Zoning* (ASPO Planning Advisory Service Report No. 254, 1970).

10. *E.g.,* New York and California.

11. *E.g.,* Connecticut, Louisiana, New Jersey and Washington.

12. *N.J. Stat. Ann.* Sec. 2A:42-6 (1952).

13. *E.g.,* District of Columbia and Rhode Island.

14. *E.g.,* California, Michigan, New Mexico and North Carolina.

15. Mutual Redevelopment Houses, Inc. v. Hanft, 249 N.Y.S. 2d 988, 42 Misc. 2d 1044 (1964).

16. Ariz., Conn., Ky., Md., Mich., Miss., N.J., N.Y., N. Carl., Ohio, Va., W. Va., Wisc.

17. *See* note. *Partial Constructive Eviction: The Common Law Answer in the Tenant's Struggle for Habitability,* 21 *Hastings L.J.* 417 (1970).

18. Dyett v. Pendelton, 8 Cow. 727 (N.Y. Sup. Ct. 1827).

19. See Uniform Relocation Assistance and Real Property Acquisition Policies Act of 1970.

20. 109 U.S. 3 (1883); See also United States v. Wheeler, 254 U.S. 281 (1920); Corrigan v. Buckley, 271 U.S. 323 (1926).

21. Dorsey v. Stuyvesant Town Corp. 299 N.Y. 512, 87 N.E. 2d 541 (1949); See Wechsler, *Toward Neutral Principles of Constitutional Law,* 73, *Harv. L. Rev.* 1, 30 (1959-60).

22. 365 U.S. 715 (1960).

23. *Id.* at 725.

24. Smith v. Holiday Inns of America, Inc., 336 F.2d 630 (6th Cir. 1964); Hawkins v. North Carolina Dental Soc'y, 335 F.2d 718 (4th Cir. 1966); Ethridge v. Rhodes, 268 F. Supp. 83 (S.D. Ohio 1967).

25. 292 F. Supp. 134 (S.D. N.Y. 1968).

26. 317 F. Supp. 1122 (d. Mass. 1970).

27. HUD Newsletter, Jan. 15, 1971, pg. 2.

28. HUD Newsletter, Feb. 1, 1971, pg. 2.

29. *President's Committee on Urban Housing, A Decent Home* 40 (1968).

30. *U.S. News and World Report,* Nov. 23, 1970, at 72.

3 Conditions of Habitability

3.1   Landlords of sub-standard housing units tend to try to maximize the amount of their "profit" or personal return out of current rental receipts. This form of cash flow profit-taking results in reduced expenditures for repair and improvements and helps to realize the landlord's prophecy that the rate of decrease in value of the property does not warrant his further investment in it. Because of this diminishing economic incentive for landlords to make expenditures for repair, the legal sanctions that may require them to maintain a minimum standard of habitability become important. A landlord's legal obligations to provide and maintain decent conditions of habitability are derived from common law principles, lease provisions and statutory prescriptions of minimum standards.

RESPONSIBILITY FOR HABITABILITY UNDER COMMON LAW

CONDITIONS AT THE BEGINNING OF THE TERM

Limits of the Landlord's Obligations

3.2   At common law the landlord has no obligation to deliver the premises in habitable condition.[1] The common law lease was considered to convey an interest in the real estate for a limited term. The tenant purchased and was entitled to receive peaceful and quiet enjoyment, exclusive control and reasonable use of the property. The lease did not guarantee that the premises were safe, structurally sound or fit for habitation. The primary obligation of the landlord was to give undisturbed possession. When the lease did not contain an express covenant, the courts held that a covenant of quiet enjoyment was implied from the use of such words as "lease," "demise," "let" and "grant."

3.3   After establishing the existence of an implied covenant of quiet enjoyment in leases, the courts faced the question of what constitutes a breach of this covenant. In the beginning, the courts held that this covenant was violated only by an actual eviction, in which the tenant was physically removed. Later, the courts began to recognize that a covenant of quiet enjoyment could be violated by the landlord's interference with the tenant's use of the property without actually expelling him. This principle came to be known as "constructive eviction."[2] Thus, it has been held that a tenant was justified in abandoning the premises when clogged sewer pipes caused noxious odors and a danger to health,[3] when lack of heat made the premises unlivable on cold days,[4] and even when the landlord knowingly allowed occupants of other parts of the building to carry on lewd activities, thereby rendering the premises unfit for respectable people.[5] In all cases the courts confirmed that a substantial interference in enjoyment of the premises constitutes a constructive eviction and justifies abandonment by the tenant. In recent years it has been argued that the doctrine of constructive eviction should be further extended to permit an abatement of rent, even if the tenant does not abandon the premises.[6] The courts have not, however, generally accepted this extension.

Caveat Emptor and No Implied Warranty of Fitness

3.4   The general rule adopted by most states is that in the absence of an express provision in the lease, there is no implied warranty in the landlord-tenant relationship that the premises are in a habitable condition.[7] The tenant has the obligation to inspect the premises before accepting them or to obtain an express warranty of fitness from the landlord. The tenant is considered a purchaser of an estate in land and, as a purchaser, is subject to the doctrine of *caveat emptor* (let the buyer beware). As one court stated:

It is a general principle of law that in the absence of an express agreement

38

on the part of the landlord, and in the absence of fraud, the tenant, under the principle of *caveat emptor,* takes the property for better or worse.[8]

3.5   In some states the general rule of no implied warranty of habitability has been relaxed in respect to a furnished house. In *Pines v. Perssion,*[9] involving a written lease containing no express warranty that a furnished house rented to a group of students was to be in habitable condition, the court held that there was an implied warranty in the lease. There was testimony in *Pines* that the landlord had promised to clean and fix up the house, but this oral testimony was held to be inadmissible to vary the terms of a written lease that was complete and unambiguous on its face. The court held, however, that an exception to the general rule is justified in the case of a furnished house because the tenant does not have adequate opportunity to inspect the premises at the time he accepts the lease.

Recent Judicial Modifications

3.6   In recent years the courts have begun to reconsider the wisdom of applying feudal principles of real property to modern conditions of urban life. For example, in *Pines* the court specifically rejected both the rule of no implied warranty of habitability and the principle of *caveat emptor* when it said:

> To follow the old rule of no implied warranty of habitability in leases would, in our opinion, be inconsistent with the current legislative policy concerning housing standards. The need and social desirability of adequate housing for people in the era of rapid population increases is too important to be rebuffed by that obnoxious legal cliche, *caveat emptor.* Permitting landlords to rent "tumbledown" houses is at least a contributing cause of such problems as urban blight, juvenile delinquency and high property taxes for conscientious landowners.[10]

3.7   This new and enlightened attitude has been adopted by the New Jersey Supreme Court in *Reste Realty Corporation v. Cooper*[11] and *Marini v. Ireland.*[12] In *Reste* the court recognized the realities of the unequal bargaining position of a tenant and said:

> Moreover, an awareness by legislatures of the inequality of bargaining power between landlord and tenant in many cases, and the need for tenant protection, has produced remedial tenement houses and multiple dwelling statutes. . . . It has come to be recognized that ordinarily the lessee does not have as much knowledge of the condition of the premises as the lessor. Building code requirements and violations are known or made known to the lessor, not the lessee. He is in a better position to know of latent defects, structural and otherwise, in a building which might go unnoticed by a lessee who rarely has sufficient knowledge or expertise to see or to discover them. A prospective lessee, such as a small businessman, cannot be expected to know if the plumbing or wiring systems are adequate or conform to local codes. Nor should he be expected to hire experts to advise him. Ordinarily all this information should be considered readily available to the lessor who in turn can inform the prospective lessee. These factors

have produced persuasive arguments for reevaluation of an implied warranty that the premises are suitable for the leased purposes and conform to local codes and zoning laws.[13]

3.8 In *Marini*, the court carried this reasoning one step further and held that in modern urban society a landlord not only implicitly represents that a dwelling unit is fit for habitation, but that he also agrees to maintain the premises in a livable condition. The court held that where there is no express agreement in the lease:

> ... the effect which the parties, as fair and reasonable men, presumably would have agreed on, was that the premises were habitable and fit for living. The very object of the letting was to furnish the defendant with quarters suitable for living purposes. This is what the landlord at least impliedly (if not expressly) represented he had available and what the tenant was seeking. In a modern setting, the landlord should, in residential letting, be held to an implied covenant against latent defects, which is another manner of saying, habitability and livability fitness. . . . It is a mere matter of semantics whether we designate this covenant one "to repair" or "of habitability and livability fitness." Actually it is a covenant that at the inception of the lease, there are no latent defects in facilities vital to the use of the premises for residential purposes because of faulty original construction or deterioration from age or normal usage. And further it is a covenant that these facilities will remain in usable condition during the entire term of the lease. In performance of this covenant the landlord is required to maintain these facilities in a condition which renders the property livable.[14]

CONDITIONS ARISING DURING THE TERM

The Common Law Rule

3.9 At common law, the obligation to repair and maintain the premises was imposed upon the person who had control over the property. Thus, when a landlord conveyed possession and control of the premises to a tenant, the tenant assumed responsibility for maintaining the property and returning it at the end of the lease in substantially the same condition in which he received it. This principle was well adapted to an agrarian society where the tenant took possession of all buildings and farm land, and where the produce and income from the land was dependent upon the tenant's husbandry and efficient use of the estate. Under such conditions the landlord was obliged not to interfere with the tenant's exclusive possession and the tenant was obliged to pay rent and not commit waste. Thus, at common law the tenant, not the landlord, had the duty to maintain and keep the property in repair. His obligation was limited, however, to repair and maintenance necessary to prevent waste and did not include repairs required as a result of ordinary wear and tear or involving substantial or structural replacement.

The Duty To Repair Under Current Law

3.10 In spite of the unsuitability of the common law rule to urban conditions where a tenant of a multiple dwelling has no control over and even less ability to maintain the building, the courts have, as a general rule, continued to impose the duty of repair upon the tenant. In the absence of lease or statutory provision, the tenant must repair and maintain that part of the leased premises under his control. On the other hand, the landlord is responsible for the repair of those prtions of the building within his control, such as common entrances, stairways and hallways. Most courts have held, however, that the landlord need only maintain the premises in the condition at the time of the creation of the tenancy. The landlord does not have to improve the premises to a condition better than that which existed at the beginning of the lease.

Recent Trends in the Law
3.11   In recent years some courts have begun to take the position that in an urban society a residential tenant can expect that the landlord will maintain the premises in a livable condition. In *Marini,* the court said that even in the absence of an express covenant to repair, there is an implied understanding that the landlord will repair damage to vital facilities caused by ordinary wear and tear. Other courts have held that such an obligation arises from municipal housing codes.[15] In spite of the apparent persuasiveness of these decisions, most courts have not yet adopted this position.

Tenant's Right To Repair and Deduct
3.12   At common law the tenant was obliged to absorb the costs of any repairs he made and could not deduct the costs of repairs from the rent. The courts were led to this conclusion by two persuasive common law principles: the landlord had no obligation to maintain the premises in the first place and therefore could not be charged with the costs of repair; and even if the landlord agreed to repair, such an agreement was held to be independent of the covenant to pay rent. This principle was known as the "doctrine of independent covenants." In recent years some states, by statutory provision or judicial decision, have given the tenant a limited right to repair and deduct.

Destruction of the Premises
3.13   A tenant is liable for any damage to the premises caused by his negligence. For example, a tenant is liable for damage caused by fire, if the fire results from his negligence. He is not liable, however, for damage to or destruction of the premises if he is not negligent. If the premises are destroyed by fire or other casualty, the landlord is not obliged to rebuild. At common law the lease was not terminated by the destruction of the premises and the tenant continued to pay rent. This rule has been changed, however, in most states, by statute or lease provision.

Remedy for Tenant's Waste: The Model Code Provisions
3.14   At common law a tenant was required to return the premi-

ses to the landlord in substantially the same condition in which he received them, except for damage resulting from reasonable wear and tear.[16] A landlord's remedy for a tenant's damage to the premises was limited to an action for waste, usually brought at the expiration of the term when he recovered possession. The common law rule worked reasonably well in an agrarian setting where the tenant had exclusive control of the premises. It is inadequate, however, to protect and preserve a multiple dwelling shared by many tenants. The *Model Code* (Sec. 2-303) addresses itself to this problem by specifying the obligations imposed upon tenants. These include the duty to: comply with all applicable laws; keep the premises clean; dispose of garbage properly; not permit anyone to damage or deface the property; and comply with all landlord's rules reasonably necessary to protect the property. If the tenant fails to fulfill these obligations, the *Model Code* (Sec. 2-304) gives the landlord the right, after giving notice to the tenant, to bill him for the cost of remedying the default, and to treat this as a part of his rent.

RESPONSIBILITY FOR HABITABILITY UNDER LEASE PROVISIONS

LANDLORD'S COVENANT TO REPAIR AND MAINTAIN

A Model Lease Provision

3.15   The acute shortage of housing accommodations has given the landlord a superior bargaining position that permits him to rent his dwelling units without any agreement to repair and maintain the premises. The typical printed form lease does not contain a covenant to repair and maintain the premises. Very rarely is a tenant able to negotiate the inclusion of such a provision in the lease. Consequently the following discussion of a "model lease" provision is more academic than real.

3.16   The Council on Community Affairs has drafted a *Proposed Model Rental Agreement*[17] that contains several provisions by which the landlord agrees to repair and maintain:

> The landlord covenants and warrants that at the time of the signing of this agreement or at the time of delivery of possession the premises are in compliance with the Housing regulations of [jurisdiction] in a clean, safe and sanitary condition, in repair and free from rodents and vermin, and as well in compliance with all other applicable laws and regulations of [jurisdiction] relating to the health and safety.
>
> The Landlord covenants and agrees to maintain said premises in such condition for the duration of this agreement and in accordance therewith; provided, however, that the creation other than through normal wear and tear, of unclean, unsafe, and unsanitary or rodent or vermin infested conditions by the negligence of the tenant shall be the responsibility of the tenant and not the landlord to correct. . . .
>
> The landlord agrees specifically among his other warranties to the following: [There follows a listing of specific obligations relating to heat, electricity, water, fixtures, roof and walls].

3.17   The primary contribution of the model lease provisions is to direct attention to the kind of obligations that landlords would reasonably be expected to assume if tenants were in a stronger bargaining position. In view of the economic realities of the housing market, it is unlikely that a landlord would voluntarily incorporate these provisions into a lease. A model lease might become, however, part of a governmental program of licensing and regulation of housing accommodations to protect public health, safety and welfare.

Consideration for Landlord's Covenant.
3.18   If the lease contains a landlord's covenant to repair, it is enforceable against the landlord, since it is supported by the fact that the tenant has also made covenants in the lease. An agreement by a landlord made *after* the execution of the lease and during the tenancy, however, is not enforceable unless the tenant gives the landlord some form of consideration for his promise. For example, when the tenant is bound by the lease to pay an agreed rent for a specified term, his continuation of the tenancy is insufficient consideration for a mid-term promise by the landlord to repair. On the other hand, if the tenant has no lease, his agreement to remain in possession may be sufficient consideration for the landlord to promise to repair.

Provisions for Landlord's Right of Entry to Inspect
3.19   When the lease contains a landlord's covenant to repair, the courts have generally held that the tenant implicitly authorizes the land courts have generally held that the tenant implicitly authorizes the landlord to enter the premises, under reasonable conditions, to make the required repairs. The lease may contain a provision that specifically authorizes the landlord to enter the premises to inspect and repair, but by itself, it is insufficient to constitute a covenant to repair. Without a landlord's covenant to repair or a provision authorizing entry for the purpose of repair, a landlord is not authorized to enter the leased premises to make repairs.

Notice of the Need to Repair
3.20   Even if the lease contains a landlord's covenant to repair, the landlord is not in default of this obligation unless he receives notice or otherwise has actual knowledge of the condition requiring repair. After receiving notice the landlord has a reasonable period of time within which to make the repairs.

Tenant's Remedies for Landlord's Breach
3.21   If the landlord fails to fulfill his obligations to repair, the tenant has a choice of remedies. He may sue the landlord for damages, measured by the reduction in value of the premises resulting from the landlord's failure to repair, or he may make the repairs himself and deduct their costs from the rent. If the costs of repair are not substantial, the tenant will usually choose the latter option. It must be emphasized, however,

43

that with a few minor exceptions,[18] the courts have generally held that a tenant has no right to repair and deuct unless the landlord has expressly agreed to keep the premises in repair. Such an agreemtn is unusual in tenancies based upon the typical printed form lease.

TENANT'S COVENANT TO REPAIR AND MAINTAIN

The Usual Lease Provision

3.22 In the typical printed form lease, it is the tenant, rather than the landlord, who promises to keep the premises in repair. One or all of the following lease provisions are usually found in the printed form of lease:

> That the tenant shall take good care of the premises and shall at the tenant's own cost and expenses make all repairs . . . and at the end or other expiration of the term, shall deliver up the demised premises in good order or condition, damages by the elements excepted.
> That the tenant shall promptly execute and comply with all statutes, ordinances, rules, orders, regulations and requirements of the Federal, State and City Government and of any and all their Departments and Bureaus applicable to said premises, for the correction, prevention and abatement of nuisances, violations or other grievances, in, upon or connected with said premises during the said term; and shall also promptly comply with and execute all rules, orders, and regulations of the Board of Fire Underwriters, or any other similar body, for the prevention of fire, at the tenant's own cost and expense.
>
> That in case the tenant shall fail or neglect to comply with the aforesaid statutes . . . or any of them, or in case the tenant shall fail or neglect to make any necessary repairs, then the Landlord or the Landlord's Agents may enter said premises and make said repairs and comply with any and all of the said statutes . . . at the cost and expense of the Tenant and in case of the Tenant's failure to pay therefor, the said cost and expense shall be added to the next month's rent and be due and payable as such, or the landlord may deduct the same from the balance of any sum remaining in the Landlord's hands. This provision is in addition of the right of the Landlord to terminate this lease by reason of any default on the part of the tenant.[19]

Significance of a Tenant's Covenant

3.23 A tenant's covenant to repair shifts the responsibility for repair from the landlord, whom fair and reasonable men would expect to assume such responsibility, to the tenant, who lacks the knowledge or ability to perform this obligation. The tenant's covenant is sanctioned and made enforceable by the legal system because of the judicial myth that the contract has been determined after an arm's length bargaining of equals. This determination is further confounded by the principle that the courts cannot properly rewrite the terms of a contract voluntarily accepted by the parties, except if it is contrary to public policy.[20] As long as the courts treat a lease as though it were an ordinary business contract, they must respect and enforce the tenant's agreement to assume the responsibility for repairs and maintenance.

RESPONSIBILITY FOR HABITABILITY UNDER HOUSING CODES

3.24   The primary objectives of housing codes are to protect the health, safety and welfare of the occupants of dwellings and to prevent or delay the deterioration of housing accommodations to substandard or slum conditions. Housing codes prescribe minimum standards of occupancy and maintenance, and for the most part impose the responsibility for maintaining those standards upon the landlord. The enforcement of these standards by governmental action has had only limited effectiveness, however, and has led to the development of tenant remedies to obtain more effective enforcement, which are discussed in Chapter 7. The effect of housing codes on the legal relationship between landlord and tenants is examined here.

MINIMUM STANDARDS

Model Housing Codes

3.25   The housing ordinances in most cities, towns and other jurisdictions are based upon one of four different model housing codes.[21] The first model code, *A Proposed Housing Ordinance,*[22] prepared by the American Public Health Association (APHA), is concerned with the health and safety of tenants. This code prescribes minimum standards designed to prevent disease and injury of the tenants. The second model code, the *BOCA Basic Housing Code,*[23] prepared by the Building Officials Conference of America, is concerned with construction and maintenance of the building. This code prescribes minimum standards of the materials, methods of construction and performance of equipment and facilities. The third model code, the *NIMLO Model Minimum Housing Standards Ordinance,*[24] prepared by the National Institute of Municipal Law Officers, is concerned with the legal and administrative aspects of housing code enforcement. This code allows the local governing body to prescribe the minimum standards relating to health, safety, construction and equipment and prescribes only legal and administrative standards. Finally, the APHA joined with the Public Health Service (PHS) in 1967 and prepared a model housing code designed to combine the essential elements of the other three codes. Their effort resulted in the *APHA-PHS Recommended Housing and Maintenance and Occupancy Ordinance*, in which the purposes are set forth as follows:

> *Purposes.* It is hereby declared that the purpose of this ordinance is to protect, preserve, and promote the physical and mental health and social well-being of the people, to present and control incidence of communicable diseases, to regulate privately and publicly owned dwellings for the purpose of maintaining adequate sanitation and public health, and to protect the safety of the people and to promote the general welfare by legislation which shall be applicable to all dwellings now in existence or hereafter constructed. It is hereby further declared that the purpose of this ordinance is to insure that the quality of housing is adequate for protection of public health, safety and general welfare, including: establishment of minimum

45

standards for basic equipment and facilities for light, ventilation, and thermal conditions, for safety from fire and accidents, for the use and location and amount of space for human occupancy, and for an adequate level of maintenance; determination of the responsibilities of owners, operators and occupants of dwellings; and provision for the administration and enforcement thereof.[25]

3.26   Although the housing codes of most local governments are derived from one or a combination of the above codes, local governments have usually been slow to update or modernize their codes once they have adopted them. Most municipal housing codes, based upon the early models, may be separated into four parts: standards of facilities and equipment; standards of maintenance; standards of occupancy; and methods of enforcement.

Standards of Facilities
3.27   The facilities generally covered by housing codes include the bathroom, kitchen, heating and electrical facilities. The sections dealing with bathroom facilities usually require a private flush toilet, a lavatory sink and a bathtub or shower. Some of the older codes do not require these facilities to be part of *each* dwelling unit, but permit the use of common facilities by more than one unit. The sections dealing with kitchen facilities are usually inadequate, for they require a kitchen sink, but fail to require a stove, refrigerator and other facilities to cook and store food. Most codes require heating facilities capable of heating the unit to a specified temperature. The section on electrical standards generally provides for a specified number of electrical fixtures and outlets per room.

Standards of Maintenance
3.28   The housing code provisions relating to the safe and sanitary maintenance of dwelling units prescribe the maintenance required for foundations, walls, ceilings, floors, windows, doors, stairways, and also the facilities and equipment required in other sections. The more recent codes have extensive provisions designed to maintain the unit in rat-free and rat-proof condition.[26] The APHA-PHS Code also prohibits the landlord from shutting off vital services and utilities except during temporary emergencies or when actual repairs or maintenance are in process.[27] This provision may be used to prevent a landlord from turning off utility services as a technique of self-help eviction or as a weapon against rent strikes.

Standards of Occupancy
3.29   Housing code standards of occupancy deal primarily with minimum floor space requirements per occupant of the unit and minimum floor space for sleeping room occupancy. The minimum floor space per occupant varies among the different codes, with most codes prescribing 150 square feet of habitable space for the first occupant and 100 additional square feet for each additional occupant. A study by the

APHA indicates that these space requirements are not sufficient to protect the health and safety of the occupants.[28] Sleeping room occupancy standards usually require 70 feet of habitable floor space for the first person and from 30 to 50 additional feet for each additional occupant.

ENFORCEMENT OF HOUSING CODES

3.30 The prescription of minimum standards for housing accommodations by governmental authorities does not by itself insure tenants of acceptable housing conditions. Housing code standards become meaningful only if the landlord is induced, by persuasion or compulsion, to repair and maintain the premises. The procedures and techniques of housing code enforcement are designed to achieve this objective.

Inspection of the Premises

3.31 Housing code enforcement is dependent, initially, upon the ability of the appropriate municipal enforcement agency to enter and inspect the premises. Most housing codes authorize entry and inspection, and many require the landlord to permit the housing code officer to enter and inspect. Such ordinances have been held invalid as a violation of the Fourth Amendment, which forbids unreasonable search and seizure.

3.32 In *Camara v Municipal Court of San Francisco*[29] the Supreme Court invalidated an ordinance that imposed criminal penalties for refusal to admit an inspector, and held that the Fourth Amendment gives the occupant the right to refuse entry to a housing code inspector without a search warrant. In the vast majority of inspections, where consent is given, a search warrant is not necessary. If entry is denied, however, the inspector must apply to a court for a search warrant. The *Camara* decision indicated that the requirements of "probable cause" for the issuance of a housing inspection search warrant are not as strict as the requirements for a warrant for a criminal investigation. "Probable cause" for a code inspection may be shown by: passage of time since the last inspection; the nature of the building, e.g., apartment house or factory; or the condition of the entire area. In a dissenting opinion in the *Camara* case, Mr. Justice Clark argued that the majority decision created a "newfangled warrant" system based upon a meaningless ceremony of filling out a form application that would destroy the integrity of search warrants and degrade the judicial process that issues them.

3.33 The *Camara* decision made it clear that a search warrant is not necessary where consent is given by the landlord or the tenant. The tenant's consent is required for an inspection of his apartment, but a landlord's consent is insufficient to justify entry into an apartment by the inspector.[30] If the tenant consents to the inspection of his apartment, evidence of code violation may be used against the landlord.[31] It is still not clear, however, whether a tenant's consent is sufficient to permit an inspector to examine the public areas of the building.

Notice of Violation

3.34   After inspection of the premises, the housing code officer prepares a report in which he describes each of the conditions which are in violation of the code. This notice of violation report, also describes the necessary repairs and orders the owner or other responsible person to remove or correct the violations within a specified period of time, generally from 30 to 90 days. It is sometimes difficult to serve the notice of violation because of absentee ownership, dummy corporations and the use of fictitious names. Most ordinances consider the notice served if it is posted on the premises. Proof of service is important because in most jurisdictions a violation may not be prosecuted unless there is evidence that the owner had notice of violation.

Administrative and Formal Hearings

3.35   A person served with a violation notice may challenge the inspector's judgment of the existence of the violation or the method of compliance. Most codes provide for a method of review and appeal of violation notices by a housing board of appeals. Such boards have authority to excuse noncompliance or to modify standards in unusual cases, where a literal enforcement will result in unnecessary hardship. Housing boards of appeals are very rarely used, however, since they have no power to impose sanctions.[32] On the contrary, the violator usually tries to avoid any confrontation with the administrative agency. To encourage voluntary compliance, many enforcement agencies "invite" the violator to an informal administrative hearing. The invitation is sometimes presented in an official-looking "order to show cause", but is ignored by sophisticated violators, who know they will incur no additional penalties for failure to appear. In some jurisdictions the informal administrative hearing is not used because enforcement agencies have found that this procedure produces greater delay than compliance.

Sanctions for Noncompliance

3.36   *Fines and imprisonment.* Under most codes, the landlord's failure to comply with the order to remove or correct the conditions described in the notice of violation constitutes a misdemeanor, and is punishable by fine or imprisonment. The codes generally give the judge wide discretion in determining the amount of the fine, including the power to consider each day the violation remains uncorrected as a separate offense. In practice, judges rarely impose large fines. In New York City, for example, the average fine in housing code violation prosecutions decreased from $26.67 per case in 1960 to $11.47 per case in 1968.[33] Judges, who are reluctant to impose large fines, are even more unwilling to impose jail sentences, even though imprisonment is authorized under most codes. The mere threat of fine and imprisonment is insufficient to induce an unwilling landlord to comply with housing code standards. Many consider the occasional small fine as a cost of doing business.

3.37 *Order to vacate.* Most codes authorize the enforcement agency to declare a building "unfit for human habitation" and to order all tenants to vacate. The rationale is that the threat of income loss will persuade an otherwise unwilling landlord to make the necessary repairs, but if he fails to do so, the health and safety of the tenants must be protected by removing them from the dangerous premises. The order to vacate is rarely used because of the obvious hardship on tenants, and the irreparable damage often inflicted on a vacant building by vandals.

3.38 *Order to demolish.* Most codes authorize the enforcement agency to order the landlord to demolish a building that falls into such disrepair that it endangers the public health, safety and welfare. If the owner fails to comply, the agency may arrange for the demolition and charge the costs to the owner. This remedy is rarely used for many reasons: a demolition dislocates tenants and aggravates an already limited supply of housing; the vacant lot frequently becomes a garbage dump; the power of demolition is an extreme exercise of police power and is authorized only in "emergency" circumstances; and the procedure is costly to the municipality, because by the time a building reaches such a state of disrepair, the owner has generally already abandoned it, and the value of the vacant land often does not cover the cost of demolition, because of prior tax and mortgage liens.[34]

The Housing Court
3.39 Dissatisfaction with the attitude of judges in criminal courts, who tend to treat housing code violation cases as an annoying interruption of their more important duties, has led to the development of special housing courts in some jurisdictions (Baltimore, Chicago, Atlanta and New York City). A housing court is frequently little more than a part or term of the regular municipal criminal court. It is designed to train a number of judges to appreciate the importance of housing code enforcement—to give them the expertise to develop a consistent policy based upon knowledge of the housing code and its more frequent violators.[35] This combination of judicial commitment and knowledge tends to deter violations, because specialized housing judges are more likely to act quickly and decisively against inveterate housing code violators. The system tends to work less effectively when judges are rotated rather than permanently assigned to the housing court.

Emergency Repairs
3.40 Although most housing codes give the enforcement agency power to make emergency repairs where necessary to protect the public health and safety, this power is rarely exercised.[36] When funds are appropriated for this purpose, they are usually insufficient. In addition, once such funds are expended upon repairs, it is virtually impossible to recoup them from the landlord. Even though he may be liable personally and the property and rents made subject to a lien for the costs of repair,

49

the value of the buildings is usually insufficient to recoup the repair costs after payment of prior mortgages and recorded liens. Experience with the program has also demonstrated that repairs administered by an agency of government invariably cost more than repairs made privately.[37] Furthermore, many enforcement agencies have found that emergency repairs involve them in the management of the worst slum properties and make them vulnerable to criticism and political attack.[38]

Licensing

3.41   A few states authorize municipalities to use licensing to maintain minimum standards of habitability.[39] By the use of licensing power a city may impose standards of eligibility for a license, prohibit unlicensed operations and charge a license fee to help finance the cost of inspections. Licensing may also overcome the legal problem of entry for inspection,[40] by requiring the applicant's consent to periodic inspections as a condition of eligibility. In spite of the apparent advantages of licensing, this system has not had widespread acceptance because its effective enforcement would only result in increased abandonment of marginal substandard tenements. Until the present supply of low-rent housing is increased to accommodate the tenants who now live in substandard dwellings, there is little advantage in vacating them.

Receivership

3.42   The objective of housing code enforcement is not to punish the landlord for violations, but to protect the public safety, preserve the property and prevent injury and damage. When the threat of sanctions fails to induce the landlord to repair and maintain the building, more direct and affirmative action may be necessary. The receivership program provides a mechanism by which seriously deteriorated buildings may be taken over by a court-appointed receiver, who will supervise the necessary repairs and manage the building until the costs of repairs are recovered.[41]

THE FAILURE OF HOUSING CODE ENFORCEMENT

3.43   In spite of the detailed and extensive prescriptions of minimum standards of habitability set forth in housing codes, the governmental agencies charged with enforcing them have not achieved the objectives of such legislation. There are many reasons for this failure.

Insufficient Financial Support

3.44   The municipal department responsible for code enforcement is notoriously unable to obtain an adequate share of the limited municipal financial resources. When funds are allocated in the budget, the competing claims of other departments leave the housing agency with the fiscal leftovers. The influence of the enforcement agency is easily outweighed by such formidable competitors as the departments of fire, police and sanitation, the law department, the department of investigation, the personnel department and the bureau of the budget.[42]

Overlapping Municipal Authority
3.45   The responsibility for housing code enforcement is often fragmented among numerous agencies. Some standards of habitability are enforced by the housing agency, while others are within the jurisdiction of the fire or health departments. The inspecting officers are trained to look for, and are responsible for, reporting only those violations within the jurisdiction of their own department. Duplication of effort and inefficient use of personnel dilute the already meager and inadequate funds available for inspection.

Opposition of Influential Political Forces
3.46   The police, fire and sanitation departments can usually rely upon the combined political support of its membership and the general public, who directly benefit from their services. Housing agencies, on the other hand, must overcome the political opposition of groups subject to housing code regulations. These groups include such powerful forces as the owners and managers of real estate, builders and investors in housing construction.

Lax Judicial Enforcement
3.47   In most cities prosecution of housing code violations is administered by criminal courts. Criminal court judges often consider more serious crimes to be their primary concern and treat housing code violations as something of a bother to be disposed of as quickly as possible. Consequently, the courts tend to ease the crowded court calendar by imposing minimal fines in return for guilty pleas. The landlords, in turn, treat the minimal fine as a license to do business.[43]

Economic Impediments
3.48   Even when the landlord wants to maintain his property within legal standards, he is confronted with numerous obstacles.

3.49   *Increased rent to tenants.* A landlord who invests additional money in his building expects to recoup his investment through income from increased rent. When the rent is raised, low-income tenants can no longer afford the apartment.

3.50   *Inadequate supply of relocation facilities.* It is difficult to perform substantial repairs and alterations while the tenants remain in their apartments. A strict enforcement of the housing code would require temporary relocation facilities during the period of repair. Such facilities are rarely available.

3.51   *Difficulty in obtaining financing.* Lending institutions have been notoriously reluctant to finance repairs of substandard housing. It is considered unsound banking practice to accept slum tenements as security for loans for several reasons: First, the rental income is limited by tenants' ability to pay. Second, the resale value after repair is usually less than the sum of the existing value plus cost of repair. And third, association with slum properties, and the possibility of becoming their owners upon foreclosure, is detrimental to the "clean, honest and wholesome" image that lending institutions require in order to attract depositors.

3.52 *Tax assessment increase.* To the extent that repairs and alterations increase the assessed value of the property, landlords will be required to pay higher property taxes. Even though the tax increase may turn out to be inconsequential, fear of reassessment often deters a landlord from making repairs.[44]

EFFECT OF HOUSING CODES ON LANDLORD-TENANT OBLIGATIONS

Private Rights Based on Public Wrongs

3.53 The primary purpose of housing codes is to protect tenants from substandard and unhabitable housing conditions. Housing codes seek to impose upon the landlord a legal obligation to maintain prescribed minimum standards. The landlord's failure to comply with these minimum standards subjects him to governmental sanctions. In spite of the fact that the codes are designed to protect tenants, the courts have held that the landlord's obligation is to the municipality and not to the tenant. The statutory duty to repair does not create a contractual duty that may be enforced by the tenant. In *Davar Holdings, Inc. v. Cohen*[45] a tenant sought to recover from his landlord the cost of painting his apartment, performed at his own expense, when the landlord failed to paint after being so ordered by the enforcement agency pursuant to the New York Multiple Dwelling Law. The court held that the landlord was not liable to the tenant for these costs. Even though the landlord had violated a statutory obligation to repair, the court said:

> . . . the controversy is between the landlord and the public authorities. It is the landlord and not the tenant who must satisfy the Department that the work has been performed properly. This statute providing, as it does, its own penalties, should not, as between landlord and tenant, be further extended in scope. Moreover, it is to be noted that outside of the penalties fixed by the statute itself, the liability of the landlord has been enlarged only to the extent of subjecting him to additional liabilities, not in contract, but in tort, with respect to the tenant and others.[46]

The holding in the *Davar* case is the rule in most states but is nevertheless inconsistent with other decisions in which the courts have held that if a statute is intended to protect a certain class of people from specified harm, an injured member of the protected class may recover damages from the violator of the proscribed acts.[47] The United States Supreme Court, for example, recognized this principle when it permitted a stockholder to bring suit for violations of the Security Exchange Act even though the Act made no provision for such private action. The Court determined that an injured party should be permitted to protect his statutory rights even though an administrative agency was supposed to do so.[48]

3.54   In spite of these judicial precedents, most courts have denied the tenant the right to recover damages resulting from the landlord's failure to comply with housing codes. In the absence of special statutory provisions, the only remedy the tenant has is to complain to the housing agency and wait for administrative enforcement.[49]

Landlord's Liability in Tort

3.55   The courts' failure to hold that the landlord's *statutory* duty creates a *contractual* duty to repair has been countered by the proposal that the landlord is still liable. It has been argued that serious violations of housing codes constitute wrongful acts for which a tenant is entitled to redress in a civil suit against the landlord.[50] The general principles upon which this proposal is based have long been recognized and have been formulated in the *Restatement of Torts*:

> The violation of a legislative enactment by doing a prohibited act, or by failing to do a required act, makes the actor liable for an invasion of another if:
> (a) the intent of the enactment is exclusively or in part to protect an interest of the other as an individual; and
> (b) the interest invaded is one which the enactment is intended to protect; and
> (c) where the enactment is intended to protect an interest from a particular hazard, the invasion of the interests results from that hazard; and
> (d) the violation is a legal cause of the invasion, and the other has not so conducted himself as to disable himself from maintaining an action.[51]

3.56   Serious violations of the housing code, such as the failure to provide hot water or to maintain the stairways in safe condition would be included in the *Restatement* formulation of tort liability. The problem with relying upon tort law to impose liability on the landlord is the difficulty of determining the measure of damages. If a tenant is injured as a result of a fall caused by a defective stairway, tort liability will enable the tenant to bring action for damages for his personal injuries. The traditional damages principles for tort liability would not, however, enable the tenant to prevent the injury by repairing the stairway and charging the costs to the landlord. Even if a tenant is injured as a result of a defective condition in violation of the housing code, the landlord may not be liable for the injuries. In most states, evidence that the condition causing the injury is in violation of the housing code has been held irrelevant to the landlord's liability. A few states, including New York[52] and New Jersey[53] have held that violation of the housing code is negligence *per se,* so that a landlord is liable if he had notice of the defective condition. Other states have taken a compromise position, permitting the jury to consider the fact that the condition causing the injury was in violation of the housing code as evidence of the landlord's negligence.[54]

Tenant's Liability for Rent: Illegality of Contract

3.57   A well-established principle of contract law is that a contract is illegal and unenforceable if it violates statutory declarations of public policy.[55] Many legal scholars have suggested that the principle of illegal contract is applicable to the landlord-tenant relationship.[56] The District of Columbia Court of Appeals has adopted this position in *Brown v. Southall Realty Company*,[57] where it denied a landlord's action for rent on the grounds that the lease, entered into while housing violations existed, was an illegal contract.

3.58   If adopted by other courts, this decision might have far-reaching effects upon the landlord-tenant relationship, in that it would legalize withholding rent as a method of enforcing housing codes. The tenant's bonanza would be short-lived, however, without additional modification of property law, since a tenant under a void lease becomes a tenant at will.[58] In most jurisdictions, he could then be evicted upon 30 days notice. The ability to avoid payment of rent and even the right to recover rent previously paid may be of little consequence to the tenant who cannot find other accommodations. For this reason it has been suggested that *Brown* would have had greater impact on the landlord-tenant relationship if the court had based its decision on the theory of an implied covenant of habitability rather than illegality of contract.[59]

Effect of Exculpatory Lease Provisions On Housing Code Obligations

3.59   Housing codes impose the responsibility for repairs and maintenance of multiple dwellings upon the landlord.[60] The typical lease transfers that responsibility back to the tenant. Exculpatory lease provisions do not, however, release the landlord from legal responsibility to the municipality. They affect only the legal responsibilities between the landlord and tenant and limit the tenant's remedies when the landlord fails to fulfill his statutory obligations. This distinction would be inconsequential if housing codes were effectively enforced. The codes' failure to insure minimum standards of habitability, however, has focused attention upon lease provisions that deprive tenants of legal remedies to support code enforcement.

3.60   A few states have statutory provisions that declare exculpatory clauses invalid as contrary to public policy.[61] Even where there are no statutory prohibitions, it has been argued that such provisions should be declared invalid by the courts as "unconscionable contracts of adhesion."[62] A contract of adhesion is an agreement "in which one party's participation consists in his mere 'adherence,' unwilling and often unknowing, to a document drafted unilaterally and insisted upon by what is usually a powerful enterprise."[63] The landlord falls within the description of a "powerful enterprise" that imposes a standardized form contract upon the tenant on a take-it-or-leave-it basis. The bargaining position of the tenant is so inferior that he does not bargain at all but merely adheres to the terms of the lease. In this respect a lease is similar to an insurance policy, a contract with a public utility and other one-sided agreements, where the courts closely scrutinize the relationship and refuse to enforce provisions that are unconscionable.[64]

TENANT'S RESPONSIBILITIES UNDER HOUSING CODES

3.61   In many instances, deteriorated conditions of multiple dwellings are exacerbated by housing code violations committed by the tenants themselves.[65] Poor housekeeping habits and careless disposal of garbage attract and sustain rats, roaches and vermin. Careless use of plumbing and electrical facilities causes damage and creates hazards and inconvenience to all tenants. Wanton destruction and vandalism to facilities and theft of equipment discourage the most diligent and law-abiding landlord from making expenditures for maintenance and repair. Illegal overcrowding of apartments by tenants imposes additional strains upon facilities and quickens the rate of deterioration.

Housing Code Standards

3.62   Modern housing codes prescribe the responsibilities of tenants in detail.[66] The *Model Code* (Sec. 2-303) makes the tenant responsible for the maintenance of his dwelling unit in general and specifies the following obligations in particular:

1. Keep the apartment clean and sanitary.
2. Dispose of garbage in a clean and sanitary manner.
3. Keep plumbing fixtures clean and sanitary.
4. Use and operate plumbing and electrical fixtures properly.
5. Not permit any person on the premises with his permission to damage, deface and remove any part of the structure or equipment.

3.63   Other sections of housing codes establish minimum space and density requirements and impose these provisions on both landlord and tenants.[67] Overcrowding is common in slum areas, where the combined income of more than one family is frequently necessary to pay the rent, and where it is often difficult to determine the actual number of persons residing in an apartment.

Failure of Enforcement

3.64   Violations of housing codes by tenants are rarely prosecuted for a number of reasons.[68] First, most inspections result from a tenant's telephoned complaint, for the landlord is not likely to register a complaint that will invite inspection by the enforcement agency. Furthermore, it is difficult to prove that a given tenant is responsible for a violation. Rapid turnover of tenants provides a ready defense that the condition existed prior to occupancy or was caused by another tenant. Third, code enforcement depends upon tenant cooperation. If tenants are prosecuted for code violations they will hesitate to complain and provide evidence of the landlord's violations. Finally, prosecution of tenants often results in strong political opposition, particularly from some vocal minority groups.[69]

Housing Clinics

3.65   The preceding obstacles to enforcing tenant obligations through criminal sanctions emphasize the need to encourage voluntary tenant compliance. Many tenants in urban slums can be persuaded to improve their housekeeping habits through education, and by programs that provide an outlet for their frustration with being tenants and under-privileged citizens. Experimental programs of housing clinics have been tried in Baltimore[70] and Chicago[71] with some success. Since housing clinics can contribute to the improvement of tenants' attitude and conduct only if tenants attend and participate in the program, it has been suggested that the program be used by the housing court as an alternative to criminal sanctions, and that inveterate tenant violators be given a choice of paying a fine or attending housing clinic sessions.[72]

Duty to Inform

3.66   One of the manifestations of lack of understanding between landlords and tenants is the landlord's complaint that a tenant who needs repairs does not inform him, but calls the housing inspector.[73] Where there is no resident landlord or janitor, it is reasonable to expect tenants to inform the landlord of any defective condition which the landlord may be unaware of. (Model Code Sec. 2-305). The attitude of tenants in deteriorated buildings, however, is that informing the landlord is a meaningless requirement of a legal system that is blind to the realities of a slum tenancy.

NOTES

1. *Powell, The Law of Real Property,* Sec. 233 (1967).

2. *See* Note, *Partial Constructive Eviction: The Common Law Answer in the Tenant's Struggle for Habitability,* 21 *Hastings L.J.* 417 (1970).

3. McCurdy v. Wyckoff, 73 N.J.L. 368, 63 A. 992 (Sup. Ct. 1906).

4. Higgins v. Whiting, 102 N.J.L. 279, 131 A. 879 (Sup. Ct. 1926).

5. Weiler v. Pancoast, 71 N.J.L. 414, 58 A. 1084 (Sup. Ct. 1904).

6. Schoskinski, *Remedies of the Indigent Tenant: Proposal for Change,* 54 *Geo. L.J.* 519, 530 (1966).

7. 1 *American Law of Property,* Sec. 3.45, (A.J. Casner ed. 1952); *Powell, on Real Property,* Sec. 221 (2), at 185 (1967).

8. Cole v. Lord, 160 Me. 223, 202 A. 2d 560 (1964).

9. 14 Wis. 2d 590, 111 N.W. 2d 409 (1961).

10. *Id.* at 596, 111 N.W. 2d at 412-13.

11. 53 N.J. 444, 251 A. 2d 268 (1969).

12. 56 N.J. 130, 265 A. 2d 526 (1970).

13. 53 N.J. at 452, 251 A. 2d at 272.

14. 56 N.J. at 144, 265 A. 2d at 533.

15. Brown v. Southall Realty Co., 237 A. 2d 834 (D.C. 1968).

16. 1 *American Law of Property,* Sec. 3.78 (A.J. Casner ed. 1952).

17. *See* Murphy, *A Proposal for Reshaping the Urban Rental Agreement,* 57 *Geo. L.J.* 464 (1969)

18. *E.g.,* Marini v. Ireland, 56 N.J. 130, 265 A. 2d 526 (1970). See discussion *supra* 3.8.

19. *Blumberg's Improved Gilsey Form Lease.*

20. *E.g.,* Kessler, *Contracts of Adhesion—Some Thoughts About Freedom of Contract,* 43 *Colum. L. Rev.* 629 (1943).

21. *See* Mood, *The Development, Objective and Adequacy of Current Housing Code Standards,* in *Housing Code Standards* (The National Commission on Urban Problems, Research Report No. 19, 1969).

22. *American Public Health Association, A Proposed Housing Ordinance* (1952).

23. *Building Officials Conference of America, Inc. BOCA Basic Housing Code* (1964).

24. *National Institute of Municipal Law Officers; NIMLO Model Minimum Housing Standards Ordinance* (1964).

25. *U.S. Public Health Service, APHA-PHS Recommended Housing Maintenance and Occupancy Ordinance* (1967).

26. *Id.* Sec. 7-03.

27. *Id.* Sec. 7-10.

28. *American Public Health Association, Standards for Healthful Housing, Planning the Home for Occupancy* (1950).

29. 387 U.S. 523 (1967).

30. Stoner v. California, 376 U.S. 483 (1964).

31. Connecticut v. Schaeffel, 4 Conn. Cir. 234, 229 A.2d 552 (1966).

32. *See,* Note, *Enforcement of Municipal Housing Codes,* 78 *Harv. L. Rev.* 801, 814 (1965).

33. N.Y. Times, April 12, 1970, at 29, Col. 1.

34. *Supra* note 34, at 833.

35. *See* B. Levy, *The Housing Court, Mayor and Manager* (Nov. 1960).

36. *Supra* note 34, at 835.

37. *Id.* at 835.

38. For a discussion of some of the problems of emergency repair, see Note, *A Program for Housing Maintenance and Emergency Repair,* 42 *St. John's L. Rev.* 165 (1967).

39. *E.g., N.J. Stat. Ann.* Sec. 55; 13A-12(1970); *N.Y. Mult. Dwell Sec. 300 Pa. Stat. Ann.* tit.53, Sec. 15097 (1957).

40. For discussion of problem of entry for inspection, see text accompanying note 31 *supra.*

41. The problems of housing receivership are discussed in Chapter 7.

42. *See* Sayre & Kaufman, *Governing New York City,* at 270 (1965).

43. *See* B. Levy, *The Housing Court, Mayor and Manager* (Nov. 1960); also N.Y. Post, April 8, 1970, at 50, Col. 1; N.Y. Post, July 7, 1966, at 19.

44. G. Sternlieb, *The Tenement Landlord,* at 216 (1966).

45. 255 App. Div. 445, 7 N.Y.S. 2d 911 (1st Dept. 1938), *aff'd* 280 N.Y. 828, 21 N.E. 2d 882 (1939).

46. *Id.* at 448, 7 N.Y.S. 2d at 914.

47. *See* Levine, *The Warranty of Habitability,* 2 *Conn. L. Rev.* 61, 86 (1969)

and the citations contained therein; Thayer, *Public Wrongs and Private Action,* 27 *Harv. L. Rev.* 317 (1914).

48. J.I. Case Co. v. Borak, 377 U.S. 426 (1964).

49. For a further discussion of other tenant remedies, see Chapter 7.

50. *E.g.* Sax & Hiestand, *Slumlordism as a Tort,* 65 *Mich. L. Rev.* 869 (1967).

51. *Restatement of Torts* Sec. 286 (1963).

52. Alty v. Lieberson, 233 N.Y. 16, 134 N.E. 703 (1922).

53. Michaels v. Brookchester, Inc. 26 N.J. 379, 140 A.2d 199 (1958).

54. *E.g.,* Whetzel v. Jess Fisher Management, 282 F.2d 943 (1960).

55. 6 *Williston, Contracts* Sec. 1787 (rev. ed. 1938); *Restatement of Contracts* Sec. 598, Comment C (1932).

56. *E.g.,* 1 *American Law of Property* Sec. 3.11 (A.J. Casner ed. 1952); Schoshinski, *Remedies of the Indigent Tenant: Proposal for Change,* 54 *Geo. L.J.* 519, 537 (1966).

57. 237 A.2d 834 (D.C. Ct. App. 1968).

58. 3 *Thompson, Real Property* Sec. 1018 (1959).

59. Note, *Landlord and Tenant: Lease Agreement Void as an Illegal Contract When Dwelling Is in Violation of Local Housing Code at Time of Letting: Brown v. Southall Realty Company,* 30 *U. Pitt. L. Rev.* 134 (1968); *see also* Levine, Note 49 *supra.*

60. *Note, Enforcement of Municipal Housing Codes,* 78 *Harv. L. Rev.* 801, 802 (1965).

61. *E.g., N.Y. Real Prop. Law* Sec. 234; *Ill. Ann. Stat.* ch. 80, Sec. 15a (Smith-Hurd 1966).

62. Levine, note 49 *supra,* at 77; *see also* Kessler, *Contracts of Adhesion—Some Thoughts About Freedom of Contract,* 43 *Colum. L. Rev.* 629 (1943).

63. Ehrenzweig, *Adhesion Contracts in the Conflict of Laws,* 53 *Colum. L. Rev.* 1072, 1075 (1953).

64. *See Corbin, Contracts* Sec. 128 (1950); Henningsen v. Bloomfield Motors, Inc. 32 N.J. 358, 161 A.2d 69 (1960).

65. Sternlieb, note 46 *supra,* at 73-75.

66. *E.g., APHS-PHS Code,* note 27 *supra.*

67. *Id.*

68. *See, F. Grad, Legal Remedies for Housing Code Violations,* (The National Commission on Urban Problems, Research Report No. 14 1968) at 88.

69. Note 62 *supra,* at 811.

70. See Bateman & Stern, *Baltimore's Housing Court, Social Work,* Oct. 1961, p.43.

71. *U.S. Dept. of Health, Education and Welfare, Public Health Service, Health Education Aides—A Method for Improving the Urban Environment Tested in Chicago, Illinois* (National Center for Urban and Industrial Health, 1968).

72. Note 62 *supra,* at 825.

73. Statement of H. Nichols, in *Tenant-Landlord Relations.* (Workshop Proceedings, Sponsored by the National Association of Housing and Redevelopment Officials, April 9, 1970.)

4 Rent

NATURE OF THE RENTAL AGREEMENT

DEFINITION AND ORIGIN OF RENT

Definition

4.1   Rent is the consideration that a tenant pays to a landlord for the use of the premises. It is usually payable in money, but may be paid in services, property or produce of the land. The obligation to pay rent is based upon an agreement, either expressed or implied, by which the landlord "lets" the premises and the tenant agrees to compensate the landlord for its use and possession. When there is no express agreement to pay rent, the courts will usually hold that an agreement is implied by the tenant's possession of the premises, unless the tenant can show that the parties intended that no rent was payable. In some states, this implied obligation to pay rent for possession of property is codified by statutory provision. Once the rent is due and payable, the right to recover the accrued rent becomes a form of intangible personal property belonging to the landlord. Until it is due and payable, the unaccrued rent remains a form of real property; that is, the right to future rent constitutes an interest in the land.

Origin

4.2   Because the obligation to pay rent is based upon an express or implied agreement, it would seem reasonable that other obligations of the parties to each other would be based upon the law of contracts. Unfortunately for modern tenants of residential units, the obligation to pay rent originated in feudal property law and the courts have continued to apply archaic property law principles rather than modern contract law principles in determining the liability of tenants for rent.

4.3 Under the feudal system, a lord made a grant of land to his vassal-tenant in return for rent in the form of various services and produce of the land. The tenant's obligation to provide services and produce continued as long as he remained in possession. The primary obligation of the lord was his covenant of quiet enjoyment, by which he guaranteed that the tenant would enjoy physical possession of the premises without interference by the lord or his agent or by assertion of a superior title. Under feudal property law the lord was entitled to rent as long as the tenant remained in possession, even if the landlord failed to fulfill other covenants in the lease.

Feudal Classification of Rent

4.4 At early common law the right to rent was classified into three categories. "Rent service" was the right of a landlord to receive rent. It gave him the right to enforce payment of rent by distraint, i.e., seizing the tenant's property as security for the payment of rent. (For a discussion of distraint see 4.60). "Rent charge" was the right of an assignee to receive the rent during the limited period of the lease. This right included the power of distraint. "Rent seck" was the right of the landlord's assignee to rent, but without the power of distraint. Today the right to enforce the payment of rent by distraint is governed by statute in most states and the classification of rent into these categories is no longer significant.

Other Charges

4.5 In the absence of an express agreement in the lease, rent does not oblige the tenant to make other payments to the landlord or other persons. For example, the tenant's agreement to pay for insurance, taxes, utilities or repairs is ordinarily not part of his obligation to pay rent. However, a carefully drawn landlord's lease will define "rent" to include the tenant's other obligations and will describe a default in these obligations as a default in the payment of rent.

TIME OF PAYMENT

Common Law Versus Current Practice

4.6 At common law, in the absence of other agreements, rent was not payable until the end of the term or at the expiration of specified intervals. This rule was based upon the needs of an agrarian society, in which rent was payable out of the produce of the land. Today, landlords make rent payable in advance by a provision in the lease. The lease customarily provides for an annual rent payable "in advance in equal monthly installments on the first day of each and every month during the term." The *Model Code* (Sec. 2-301) codifies current business practice by providing that rent is payable at the time and place agreed to by the parties and in the absence of such agreement rent is payable in advance at the beginning of every month.

Nonapportionability of Rent

4.7   At common law rent was not apportionable. It was due and payable in full on the date of expiration of the term or other specified date. Because rent did not accrue daily, when a tenant abandoned the premises a landlord was not entitled to a money judgment for any period that had not expired at the time of judgment. The landlord was thus required to wait until the expiration of the term to sue for the full amount of rent or to bring successive suits periodically as the rent became due. On the other hand, if the tenant made a payment in advance and then abandoned the premises, the landlord was entitled to retain the advance payment even though he subsequently rented the premises and suffered no loss. The *Model Code* (Sec. 2-301) changes the common law rule and makes rent uniformly apportionable from day to day.

Acceleration of Rent

4.8   To avoid the necessity of waiting for the expiration of the term before the landlord may recover both the rent accrued to date and the rent anticipated in the future, a landlord's lease commonly contains an "acceleration clause." Such a clause provides that upon the tenant's default in the payment of any one installment of rent, the rent for the remainder of the unexpired term becomes due and payable upon demand and without further notice to the tenant. Acceleration clauses based upon the tenant's default in rent or other serious violation of the lease have been upheld,[1] but clauses based upon the tenant's failure to perform "any" covenant in the lease have been held unenforceable as a penalty.[2] The courts have distinguished the two clauses on the grounds that acceleration because of "any" default might include those of an inconsequential and trivial nature and would impose too harsh a penalty upon the tenant.[3]

4.9   If the lease contains an acceleration clause, the landlord is not bound to enforce it. He may choose to accept late payment of an installment even though the rent for the entire term has become due under the provision. A landlord's failure to enforce the acceleration clause on one occasion does not, however, preclude his right to enforce it subsequently.

PLACE AND METHOD OF PAYMENT

Place of Payment

4.10   A well-drawn lease will fix the place where rent should be paid. If it does not, the rent is usually payable at the leased premises. The parties may by agreement or custom determine another place of payment. The tenant may continue to make payment at that place until notified by the landlord of a different place of payment. In low-income urban rental units it is not unusual for the landlord or his agent to call for rent at the premises.

Method of Payment

4.11 When payment is made by check and delivered or mailed to the landlord, it is not effective until the check has cleared the tenant's bank. The tenant's cancelled check provides evidence of payment. When payment is made in cash, problems often arise about the amounts and dates of payment. Under ideal circumstances the landlord should agree:

> to provide receipts in writing for all money paid as rent by the tenant and to state on each receipt the amount received, the date the money is received by him and the period for which the money pays the rent on these premises. In the event the landlord fails to provide receipts in accordance with the agreement, and a dispute over rent arises, the landlord shall be obligated to refer to and pay the cost of an accountant for an accounting.[4]

4.12 To avoid problems of rent collection and disputes that arise from payment by cash, many landlords refuse to accept cash payments and insist upon payment by check or money order. In low-income areas this requirement may inconvenience tenants who do not maintain checking accounts because of insufficient funds or business experience, or because of literacy handicaps. The *Model Lease*[5] addresses this problem with a provision that:

> where a landlord's refusal of cash payments for rent requires the tenant to purchase a money order or other cash equivalent, any service charge or other expense incurred in securing said money orders or other cash equivalent may be deducted, along with any postage, from succeeding rental payments.

Payment into Court

4.13 Upon a tenant's default in rent payment, the landlord will institute a court action for eviction and recovery of rent. (For a discussion of summary proceedings see Chapter 5.) Under most state statutes this proceeding will be dismissed if the tenant pays the rent and court costs at any time during the proceeding. Even after a judgment is rendered, it is common practice to stay execution for a limited period of time (usually five days) so that the tenant may pay the rent and costs. If the landlord refuses to accept payment, most statutes permit the tenant to pay the rent plus costs to the court and in that way terminate the proceedings.

Rent Escrow and Abatement

4.14 In most states, the payment of rent to a trustee or escrow fund or otherwise withholding rent from the landlord does not constitute payment and subjects the tenant to landlord remedies for nonpayment of rent. In a few states tenants may withhold or pay rent into escrow under certain prescribed circumstances.[6] It has been proposed that the law be changed in all jurisdictions to permit a tenant to "rightfully withhold rent."[7] The proposed Model Tenants' Remedies Act[8] seeks to accomplish that objective with the following provision:

> For a period of time that a tenant is rightfully withholding rent from the landlord or paying such rent to a court or receiver pursuant to this act, the landlord shall have no right to evict the tenant for such rents during that period of time . . . the landlord shall have no right to raise the rent of such tenant.[9]

AMOUNT OF RENT

Determined by the Parties

4.15   In the absence of rent control legislation[10] the amount of rent is determined by bargaining between the parties. The landlord seeks to obtain the highest rent possible, limited only by the competition of comparable units within the area. Tenants seek to find the best possible units within their ability to pay. In the absence of rent control the supply and demand for housing determines the amount of rent agreed to by the parties. The legal system enforces the agreement of the parties without considering the adequacy of the accommodations, the relative bargaining power of the parties, the amount of profit, if any, of the landlord, the ability of the tenant to pay or the comparative need for housing among various classes of tenants.

Modifications of Rental Agreement

4.16   Having agreed to the amount of rent, both landlord and tenant are bound by that agreement for the duration of the term. The parties may, by mutual agreement, increase or reduce the amount of rent. The validity of a subsequent agreement to modify the rent usually depends upon the principles of contract law. The agreement must be supported by a valid consideration; unilateral action by either party is insufficient. Accepting a sum less than the agreed rent does not, by itself, constitute an agreement to reduce the amount of rent, but if continued over a period of time it would be evidence of the landlord's intention.

4.17   The lease may expressly provide for a change in the amount of rent during the term. For example, the tenant may agree to pay a proportionate share of an increase in taxes, insurance or other operating expenses. A written lease may be modified subsequently by an oral agreement, except in a few states where statutes make oral modification of a written lease unenforceable.

4.18   The parties are bound by their agreement on the amount of rent only for the term of the lease. When the term expires, if the tenant has no option to renew the lease, the landlord may demand any increase in rent he chooses. In low-income areas tenants often occupy their apartment on a month-to-month basis, without benefit of a lease; under such circumstances the landlord may terminate the tenancy at will (see 2.41-2.71) or may require the tenant to pay an increase in rent as a condition of continuing the tenancy. Similarly, if a tenant stays after the expiration of his lease, the landlord may increase the rent during the holdover period.

Double Rent

4.19   The lease may contain a provision that doubles the rent for any period during which a tenant remains in possession after the term expires. Even in the absence of a lease provision a holdover tenant may be liable for double rent in some states.[11] Such lease and statutory provisions are designed to protect a landlord from loss that may result if a tenant holds over during a peak rental period and then vacates when it is more difficult to rent the premises. Such statutory provisions may be indefensible in areas with extremely low vacancy rates.

Additional Rent

4.20   Some leases define "rent" to include other charges or obligations of the tenant such as payments of utilities, insurance, taxes or repair of damages he causes. By defining such charges as "additional rent" the landlord may summarily dispossess the tenant if they are not paid.[12] Otherwise the landlord's only remedy for nonpayment would be an action for a money judgment, which with low-income tenants, is of little value.

Rent Concessions

4.21   Landlords sometimes find it advantageous to offer rent concessions, or periods of free rent, as part of the rental agreement. Rent concessions were in common use during the 1930s when vacancy rates were high and responsible tenants were hard to find. Rent concessions are used today as an inducement to tenants of luxury apartments. They may also be used to encourage tenants to maintain the premises or to continue prompt rent payments.

LIMITATIONS OF TENANTS' OBLIGATION TO PAY RENT

DEFECTIVE CONDITION OF THE PREMISES

Common Law Principles

4.22   At common law, the tenant was obliged to continue paying his rent at the risk of eviction, regardless of the condition of the premises. This inequity was the consequence of a number of well-established common law principles.

4.23   *No implied warranty of fitness.* In the absence of an express agreement, the common law courts determined that there is no implied warranty that the premises are fit or habitable.[13] The tenant was obliged to inspect the premises and either take them "as is" or obtain an express agreement (covenant) from the landlord to repair. If the landlord did not repair the premises, or agree to do so, the tenant was considered to have accepted the defective conditions.

4.24   *No duty of landlord to repair and maintain.* At common law, the party in possession of the property had to repair and maintain it. Consequently, defective conditions arising during the term of the tenancy were the tenant's responsibility.

4.25   *Independence of covenants.* At common law a lease was considered a conveyance of an interest in real estate rather than a contract of continuing mutual promises. Once having conveyed the property to the tenant, the landlord's right to rent was unconditional. Thus, even if the landlord made a covenant to repair or maintain the property, his right to rent was independent of his obligation to repair. The tenant had to pay rent or risk eviction even if the landlord breached his covenant to repair. The tenant's only remedy was a separate action for damages resulting from the landlord's breach.

Lease Provisions
4.26   The tenant's obligation to pay rent in spite of defective conditions of the premises may be established by agreement of the parties. The lease will usually not express this agreement so blatantly, but will achieve the same result by providing that the tenant repairs and maintains the premises (see 2.36). Having agreed to repair the premises himself, the tenant relinquishes his right to withhold rent as a means of requiring the landlord to assume this obligation.

Statutory Provisions
4.27   In some states the tenant's obligation to pay rent in spite of defective conditions is limited by special statutory provisions or by judicial interpretation of the housing code.

4.28   *Repair and deduct statutes.* A few states have statutory provisions authorizing tenants to deduct the costs of repair from their rent under prescribed circumstances (see 6.40). The effectiveness of these statutes is limited however by restrictions on the amount of the maximum deduction (usually from $50 to $100) and by provisions which permit the tenant to waive his right to repair and deduct.

4.29   *Housing codes.* Some judicial precedent relieves a tenant of his obligation to pay rent when the defective condition of the premises substantially violates the housing code.[14] Such judgments consider that a lease entered into in violation of housing codes is void and unenforceable (see 2.57).

Constructive eviction
4.30   If a landlord seriously and permanently interferes with the tenant's enjoyment of the property, the courts will treat this interference as though the landlord had actually evicted the tenant. If the tenant abandons the premises for this reason he has no obligation to pay rent. It has been argued that this doctrine of constructive eviction should be expanded to relieve a tenant from liability for rent when the premises are

rendered unhabitable by the landlord's neglect even if the tenant does not abandon the premises (see 6.7-6.9).

Recent Judicial Trends

4.31   A number of courts have recently begun to reconsider the wisdom of applying feudal concepts of property law to the landlord-tenant relationship in an urban society. The underlying assumption of recent decisions is that it is unfair to require the tenant to continue to pay rent when the landlord fails to maintain a minimum standard of habitability. Although these decisions have attracted the interest and attention of many legal scholars it is too early to determine their impact upon the development of landlord-tenant law.

4.32   In most cases the sublease or assignment of a tenant's right to possession under a lease does not relieve the tenant of his obligation to pay rent.[15] However, the nature and extent of his liability depends upon the particular circumstances and the provisions of the lease.

SUBLEASE AND ASSIGNMENT

Sublease and Assignment Distinguished

4.33   The technical distinction between a sublease and an assignment is that a sublease involves the transfer of the tenant's interest for a period less than his entire lease term whereas an assignment involves the transfer of the tenant's interest for the entire remaining period of his term. In a sublease, the tenant may return to the property for a limited period but an assignment conveys all of the tenant's interest. In spite of this technical distinction the two terms are commonly used interchangeably, and they will be here.

Consent of the Landlord

4.34   In the absence of a lease or a statutory provision restricting his right to assign,[16] the landlord's consent is not necessary. As a practical matter the landlord's consent is required because almost all printed form leases contain a provision by which the tenant agrees not to assign without the landlord's consent.[17]

4.35   *Consent required with landlord's complete discretion.* A frequently used assignment clause provides: "The tenant agress not to assign without first obtaining the landlord's written consent."[18] The landlord may refuse to consent to an assignment for any reason, including those that are arbitrary and unreasonable.

4.36   *Consent dependent upon satisfactory new tenant.* A second type of assignment clause frequently used provides: "The tenant agrees not to assign without first obtaining the landlord's written consent, but such consent will not be withheld if a satisfactory substitute tenant is proposed." The courts are divided on the question whether the landlord must act reasonably when rejecting a proposed new tenant[19] or whether an arbitrary refusal to accept a proposed tenant will be sustained. The Model Code (Sec. 2-403) permits the landlord to withhold his consent only if the proposed tenancy would be less favorable to the landlord than the existing tenancy for such reasons as: insufficient financial responsibility; number of persons in the proposed household; number of persons under 18; proposed maintenance of pets; unwillingness of the proposed tenant to assume the obligations under the existing lease. The *Model Code* places the burden of proving a rejection is reasonable upon the landlord.

4.37   *Consent not to be unreasonably withheld.* A third type of assignment clause in common use provides: "The tenant agrees not to assign without first obtaining the landlord's written consent, such consent not to be unreasonably withheld." The courts have interpreted this provision to require that the landlord behave reasonably, but in an action against the landlord for an alleged violation of this provision, the burden of proof is on the tenant.

Continuing Liability After Assignment
4.38   The landlord's consent to assignment does not, of itself, release the original tenant from his obligation under the lease. The tenant remains liable for the rent unless the landlord expressly consents to a release or unless the tenant can show that the parties intended to terminate the tenancy and substitute the new tenancy in its place. Some courts have held that the original tenant guarantees the payment of the rent by the new tenant and is liable if the new tenant defaults in his obligations.[20] A well-drawn assignment of lease will require the new tenant to assume all the obligations of the tenant under the original lease, including, of course, payment of rent.

ABANDONMENT OF THE PREMISES

4.39   An agreement or act that terminates the tenancy also terminates the tenant's obligation to pay rent. Upon termination, the tenant remains liable for unpaid rent to date but is relieved from all other obligations. The methods by which a tenancy is terminated are discussed in Chapter 2 (2.41-2.71). Here we are concerned with the tenant's liability for rent when he leaves without the landlord's consent to a termination of tenancy.

Surrender Distinguished From Abandonments
4.40   A surrender of the premises terminates the tenancy and the obligations of both parties. Surrender requires a mutual agreement in which the landlord accepts delivery of possession by express agreement or by implication. Abandonment, on the other hand, is a unilateral act by which a tenant quits the premises without the consent of the landlord.

An abandonment does not terminate the tenancy and the tenant remains liable for the rent. The legal questions that arise after abandonment are whether the landlord has a duty to re-rent the premises to lessen the tenant's liability and under what conditions the reletting constitutes an acceptance of possession and terminates the tenant's liability.

Landlord's Duty To Mitigate Damages

4.41   The lease may require the landlord to lessen the tenant's liability by reletting the premises. If it does not, the courts are divided on whether the landlord must mitigate the tenant's damages.[21] Most courts hold that the landlord does not have to relet the premises. Under the majority view a landlord may permit the premises to remain vacant and try to recover the full amount of the rent from the abandoning tenant. The minority view, that a landlord is under a duty to lessen the tenant's liability by reletting the premises, is based upon a general principle of contract law that requires a plaintiff to make a reasonable effort to minimize his loss.[22]

Effect of Reletting

4.42   The majority view is, in part, based upon the premise that reletting constitutes an acceptance of the tenant's surrender. As one New York Court stated:

> The [landlord] was under no duty to relet the premises for the benefit of the [tenant] . . . and if it had done so . . . its action would have amounted to an acceptance of the proferred surrender, and the [tenant] would have been released from further liability.

4.43   In states where this reasoning is adopted a landlord is faced with the following dilemma: If he does not relet the premises, the amount of his loss will depend upon how much he recovers from the abandoning tenant at the expiration of the term; if he does relet the premises the abandoning tenant is relieved of liability. To avoid this dilemma some courts have held that reletting does not constitute acceptance of a surrender if the landlord notifies the tenant that he refuses to accept surrender but he intends to relet for the tenant's account. Other courts have held that the effect of reletting depends upon whether the landlord intends the reletting to be an acceptance of a surrender or a reasonable effort to lessen the tenant's damages. A Connecticut court summarized the state of the law as follows:

> In some states, a reletting terminates the lease as a matter of law. A second line of authorities hold that this result follows unless there is notice to the tenant of the landlord's refusal to accept the surrender and of his intention to relet. The third school does not set up any arbitrary standard, but holds the question of acceptance to be one of intention and a question of fact.[24]

LANDLORD'S REMEDIES FOR RECOVERY OF RENT
ACTIONS FOR RENT[25]
Distinguished From Summary Proceedings
4.44 An action for rent is a legal proceeding in which a landlord seeks to recover rent owed him. Summary proceedings are designed to expedite the landlord's recovery of the premises upon the tenant's default in the payment of rent or any other lease obligation (see 6.3-6.15). Under some statutes the landlord may obtain a judgment for rent as well as possession of the premises. In other states he must bring a separate action to recover rent.

Prerequisites of Action
4.45 In most states an action for rent may be brought only if a landlord-tenant relationship exists by expressed or implied agreement. When such an agreement exists the action may be brought even if the tenant has never taken possession of the premises. In most states a landlord need not make a formal demand for rent before starting suit. In some states he must first comply with special conditions. For example, in New York a landlord of a multiple dwelling must allege the existence of a valid certificate of occupancy to maintain an action for rent.[26]

Election of Remedies
4.46 If a tenant fails to pay his rent and remains in possession, the landlord has a number of remedies. He may choose to evict the tenant and sue for all rent due until that date. He may bring suit for each installment of rent as it becomes due. Or, he can wait until the expiration of the term and then bring one suit for all rent owed under the lease. The risk involved in the latter two alternatives leaves little choice in most cases, and landlords of residential property usually start eviction proceeding promptly to prevent rent owed but not paid from accumulating.

4.47 Similarly, when a tenant abandons the property, the landlord must either bring suit for each installment of rent as it becomes due or bring one suit for all rent due at the expiration of the term. To avoid this dilemma landlords commonly include an acceleration clause in the lease that makes the rent for the entire term due and payable upon default in the payment of any one installment of rent (see 4.8, 4.9).

Tenant's Defenses
4.48 A tenant has only a limited number of defenses to an action for rent. He may claim he made prior payment, that the contract was illegal, that the landlord perpetrated fraud and misrepresentation, or that the tenancy was terminated. The landlord's failure to fulfill an agreement to repair is not a defense to an action for rent.[27] But in recent years some courts have begun to reevaluate the entire question of mutuality of obligations under a lease, and some decisions have favored the creation of a tenant's defense when the landlord fails to provide habitable conditions.[28]

Amount of Recovery

4.49　　　　If the landlord wins an action for rent, the damages will depend upon the particular facts of the case. If the tenant remains in possession, the landlord will recieve all rent in default at the time that the action is instituted. In a few states, the law requires that the judgment include all rent accrued until the date of judgment. If the tenant has abandoned the premises and the landlord has relet, then the amount he recovers will be the difference between the agreed rent and the amount received from reletting. If the tenant has abandoned and the landlord has not relet, the amount will depend upon whether the law requires the landlord to make a reasonable effort to relet the premises (see 4.41).

Attorney Fees

4.50　　　　If the lease contains a provision that the tenant is liable for the landlord's attorney's fees incurred in a suit to recover rent, such fees may be included in the judgment. The legal fee is determined by the trial judge based upon the legal services actually rendered, but they can be no greater than the amount reasonably necessary under the circumstances. Lease provisions for the payment of attorney fees are usually upheld, except when they are shown to be merely a device for exacting a penalty.[29] Sec. 3-402, of the *Model Code* makes a lease provision shifting attorney fees to another party unenforceable because it invites oppression by landlords.

Confession of Judgment

4.51　　　　In some jurisdictions a provision in the lease authorizes the landlord or his agent to "confess judgment" against the tenant in an action for recovery of rent. Such a provision deprives the tenant of any opportunity to defend himself against the landlord and expedites a judgment against him. In most states, confession of judgment provisions have been held invalid and unenforceable.[30] *Model Code* (Sec. 3-404) not only makes such provisions void and unenforceable, but also makes it a misdemeanor to include such a provision in a lease. The purpose of this criminal penalty is to prevent tenants from giving up their legitimate rights because they fear the consequences from the landlord

Compared to Distress and Attachment

4.52　　　　When the tenant fails to pay rent the landlord is not limited to legal action to recover the rent in default. Common law precedent and statutory lease provisions provide a number of techniques by which a landlord may lay claim to the tenant's household goods and other property as security for the unpaid rent. The landlord's legal remedies against a defaulting tenant include *liens,* a legal claim upon the tenant's property as security for the payment of an obligation; *distraint,* a common law self-help right to seize the tenant's property; *attachment,* a procedure established by statute to seize the tenant's property to pay the rent. In some states all three techniques are available. In other states, distraint and liens have been superseded by a statutory procedure of attachment.

4.53   A lien is a commonly used legal device by which a creditor is given the right to satisfy a debt out of the proceeds of the sale of the debtor's possessions. A landlord's lien is only one of a large variety of creditors' liens including judgment liens, mechanics' liens, tax liens and others. The effectiveness of a landlord's lien, the scope of property included and the method of enforcement depend upon the manner in which the lien was created.

Creation of a Landlord's Lien

4.54   A landlord's lien on a tenant's property is not an automatic or inherent right. The lien exists only if it is created by statute, by lease or by another agreement between the landlord and the tenant. Consequently, the scope of the agreement—the property involved and its effectiveness—depends upon its terms or statutory provisions.

Extent of Tenant's Property Subject to the Lien

4.55   If the lien is created by lease provision, the agreement will describe the property of the tenant that is subject to the lien. A typical provision will include all property of the tenant on the premises. Whether this includes property acquired after the execution of the lease or during the term of the tenancy depends upon the intention of the parties. Once the tenant's property is made subject to a landlord's lien, the lien continues to be attached to that property even though the tenant removes it from the premises. Ordinarily the property of third persons is not subject to the landlord's lien even if it is on the premises.

4.56   When the lien is created by statute, the provisions must be examined to determine which property is subject to the lien. Some statutes are broad and include all property of the tenant on the premises, while other statutes specify the kinds of property covered, such as household goods and furniture. Certain property, such as clothing, is sometimes exempted. Under some statutes the lien attaches as soon as the property is brought on to the premises, while under others it does not attach until legal proceedings begin.

Enforcement

4.57   When the lien is created by the lease, the method of enforcement may also be provided. The landlord may be authorized to enter the premises and take possession of the tenant's property,[31] which he may then sell; the proceeds may be used to pay the amount of rent in default. By paying the rent the tenant may prevent the sale and be entitled to recover the property.

4.58   If the lease fails to provide a method of enforcing the lien, the landlord may take possession of the tenant's property only by appropriate judicial proceedings. The tenant may interpose any defense relating to the validity and interpretation of the lease and the landlord's performance of his obligations.

73

4.59   When the lien is created by statute, it will prescribe the method of enforcement. Under statutory provisions the landlord is usually not permitted to seize the tenant's property, but must enforce the lien by an authorized form of judicial proceeding. After obtaining a judgment, the landlord must sell the tenant's property in accordance with the rules and procedures provided by law and must account to the tenant and other lien holders for the proper distribution of the proceeds of sale.

DISTRAINT (DISTRESS)

4.60   Distraint, also called distress, is a common law right of a landlord to seize a tenant's property as security for the payment of rent. At early common law the landlord could not sell the distrained property but could hold it as ransom for the payment of rent in default. In England the power to sell property without a judgment was given to landlords in 1689.[32] Most states have retained the common law remedy together with the right of sale, while some have modified the common law remedy. States abolishing the remedy did so either expressly or by a judicial finding that the statutes providing for attachment proceedings were intended to limit distraint.[33]

Limitations on the Availability of the Remedy

4.61   Distraint may be used only where: a valid landlord-tenant relationship has existed; rent is due; and the tenant's property is (or was) on the premises. Distraint is an extraordinary creditor's remedy in that it not only permits self-help, but also gives legal sanction to the action without a judgment or prior judicial determination of the merits of the claim. the common law justification for giving this special advantage to landlords was the fact that landlords provide tenants with land, which was then the primary measure of wealth and source of income. Unless landlords were given a sufficient and satisfactory means of protecting their most valuable asset, they would have been unwilling to relinquish possession to tenants without adequate credit or other security.[34] Consequently, landlords were given this special advantage over other creditors, but only to the tenant's property on their land and for claims arising out of default in rent.

Property Subject to Seizure

4.62   At common law the landlord could seize any personal property on the premises, including property belonging to strangers. Today most states allow only property belonging to the tenant, subtenant or assignee to be seized. Ordinarily property belonging to the tenant but not on the premises is not subject to distraint. However, if after rent is in default, the tenant removes his property from the premises to prevent the landlord from seizing it, then the landlord may, within a time prescribed by statute, seize the property wherever it is found.

4.63   At common law property, such as tools of the tenant's trade,

74

perishable articles and intangible assets, was exempt from distraint. Today most states have provided statutory exemptions. For example, New Jersey exempts the tenant's clothing and other property selected by the tenant up to a value of $500.[35] The protection afforded the tenant by such statutory exemption may be more apparent than real if it applies only to the sale of his property.[36] If it does, the tenant may be deprived of the use of his property until the sale, at which time he may claim exempted property.

Enforcement

4.64   Under common law and by statute in most states the landlord. must obtain a warrant of distress before seizing the tenant's property. In some states the landlord is authorized to issue the warrant himself. In other states the warrant is issued by a court. However, even when a court warrant is required, it is issued without notice to the tenant, in an *ex parte* proceeding before a justice of the peace or other lower court judge. The only proceeding required is an application and an affidavit from the landlord. In some states the landlord must file a bond to indemnify the tenant for damages if the distraint turns out to be wrongful. After obtaining the warrant, the landlord may seize the tenant's property himself or may request a sheriff, marshal or other public officer to perform the seizure. However, the public officer is under no obligation to perform the service and may refuse to execute the warrant. Whether executed by a public officer or by the landlord, the seizure must be performed peacefully and without a forcible entry. The landlord or public officer may not break the door, pick the lock, or even use a pass key. Consequently, landlords usually simply change the lock or padlock the door rather than enter and remove the tenant's property.

4.65   Landlords are discouraged from actually removing the tenant's property by numerous technical requirements: The tenant must be given proper and timely notice of the sale, and the notice must contain both an inventory of the property and a statement of the amount of rent due. The property's value must be certified by one or more appraisers. The landlord must, in some states, furnish a bond to indemnify all participants against liability for damages if, for any reason, the sale is subsequently held to be illegal. He must also account for the excess of the proceeds of sale over the amount of rent due, and may be held liable if a third person's property is wrongfully sold.

Tenant's Remedies

4.66   A tenant may forestall a landlord's distraint at any time by paying the rent due. However, once the distraint is effected, the tenant may have to pay the costs of the proceeding. If he wants to recover his property and to contest the landlord's right to receive rent, he must institute "replevy" proceedings in which a surety bond is substituted for distrained property. Except in unusual circumstances this is not a practical alternative because of cost of the surety bond frequently exceeds the amount of the rent due. If the tenant's property is wrongfully distrained—for example if the rent has been paid or is not due—the landlord and the sheriff or other executing officer are liable to the tenant for any damages which arise. In some states the landlord is liable for double or triple damages.

The Model Code Provisions
4.67   Because of the danger of oppressive use of distraint by a landlord, the *Model Code* (Sec. 3-403) abolishes it. If the landlord padlocks the premises or otherwise excludes the tenant, he is liable for three months rent or triple damages plus attorneys' fees (Sec. 2-400)

ATTACHMENT
4.68   The risks of physical harm and breach of the peace inherent in any self-help recovery of unpaid rent has led to the enactment of landlord's attachment proceedings in many states. Their purpose is to substitute an orderly and fair judicial process for the often inequitable and oppressive methods of landlord's self-help. In many states landlord's attachment proceedings are the only landlord remedy.

4.69   A landlord attachment is designed to aid the landlord in collecting his rent by a judicially supervised sale of the tenant's property. The ordinary attachment is available to any creditor against any of his debtor's property where there is reason to believe that the debtor may dispose of it while a lawsuit is pending. The ordinary attachment is ancillary to the creditor's action on the debt. A landlord's attachment, however, enables him to use the tenant's property as security while the merits of the landlord's claims are determined.

The Landlord's Allegations
4.70   The proceeding starts by a landlord's petition based on an affidavit containing allegations required by the law. The landlord will usually be required to allege the existence of a landlord-tenant relationship and the amount of the rent due and owing, and in some states, his prior demand for payment. The petition will request an attachment of the tenant's property on the premises.

The Bond
4.71   In some states the landlord must file a bond, similar to the one required in ordinary attachment, to indemnify the tenant for any loss he may sustain if it is subsequently determined that the landlord is not entitled to the attachment.

The Release Bond
4.72   In most jurisdictions the tenant may obtain release of the attached property while the proceeding is pending by posting his own bond, sometimes called a *replevy* bond or bail bond, that guarantees the payment of any judgment obtained by the landlord.

Tenant's Defense
4.73   The tenant's defense may include the tender or payment of rent or any technical failure of the landlord to comply with the requirements of the attachment statute.

The Trial
4.74   The trial of a landlord's attachment proceeding is conducted according to the usual rules of civil actions. Either party may demand a jury, to which disputed issues of fact will be submitted. Issues of law are decided by the court.

The Judgment
4.75   If the landlord succeeds in proving his cause of action, he is entitled to have the judgment rendered to him. In some states the judgment is rendered only against the named property of the tenant. In other states, if the court obtained personal jurisdiction over the tenant, a personal judgment against the tenant may be rendered.

The Writ of Attachment
4.76   The ultimate objective of a landlord's attachment proceeding is a writ, or judicial order to the marshal, sheriff or other executing officer to arrange for the sale of the tenant's property and to use the proceeds to satisfy the landlord's judgment.

SECURITY DEPOSITS

THE PURPOSE OF SECURITY DEPOSITS

4.77   At common law the landlord relied upon his right of distraint as a means of enforcing the payment of rent. The tenant's goods and chattels on the rented premises constituted a form of security if the tenant failed to pay the rent when due.[37] Although most states have enacted a form of statutory lien or distraint, the inconvenience, delay and cost of enforcing the law resulted in the practice of requiring the tenant to deposit money with the landlord to secure the payment of rent.[38] Security deposits are intended to protect a landlord from various forms of loss that may result from a tenant's default.

The Period of Vacancy
4.78   A common method of terminating a tenancy in low-rent housing is for the tenant to abandon the premises without notice to the landlord. Even when the landlord is diligent in his demand for prompt payment of rent it is not unusual for a month to go by before he discovers and confirms the fact of the tenant's abandonment. During the period of vacancy the premises are nonproductive except that a legal cause of action is created; but it is of limited value against a missing tenant of questionable financial responsibility.

Value of the Bargain
4.79   The purpose of a lease or any other enforceable contract is

to bind both parties to agreed terms for a specified period. The landlord may not raise the rent above the agreed amount, but he is entitled to receive the agreed amount during the term. If economic conditions change during that period the landlord may not be able to find another tenant who will pay rent as high as stipulated in the defaulted lease.

Costs of Reletting
4.80   Even when the tenant provides sufficient notice, the landlord may incur costs of reletting. Advertising costs, real estate broker commissions and administrative expenses incurred in finding a replacement tenant contribute to the loss caused by a tenant's default.

Cost of Repair
4.81   Security deposits are also used to protect the landlord from having to pay for damages to the premises caused by the tenant. Although tenants are not responsible for damages resulting from ordinary wear and tear, a landlord often finds damages resulting from negligence or willful destruction after a tenant has left. Further, the premises may be vandalized or robbed by third persons when the tenant abandons without giving notice.

THE LEGAL CHARACTERIZATION OF DEPOSITS
4.82   The respective rights of the landlord, tenant and third persons to the security deposit depends in part upon the legal characterization of the funds by the courts. Under varying conditions, courts have held a security deposit to be: an advance payment; a bonus or consideration for letting: liquidated damages; or security for the tenant's performance.

Advance Payment
4.83   It is in the landlord's interest to describe the security deposit as an advance payment of rent. This may be achieved by a lease provision describing the deposit as a payment of rent for the last few months of the term. In a Connecticut case involving such a clause, where there was no other provision relating to security or forfeiture upon tenant's default, the court held that the landlord did not have to return the money after the tenant's default.[39] This decision has been criticized because the court based its conclusion upon a legal fiction that even in the absence of a specific clause in the lease, a tenant's default accelerates the termination of the lease making the advance payment due and payable.[40]

Bonus or Consideration for Letting
4.84   The characterization of a security deposit most advantageous to the landlord is that the deposit is a bonus or consideration for letting. However, other clauses may belie that description by providing for the deposit's return upon full performance of the tenant's obligations under the lease. The most successful device for accomplishing the landlord's objective is a rental schedule in which the tenant is required to pay a large sum in the first few months and a smaller amount thereafter. This

device provides the landlord with a security deposit and also deprives the tenant of the right to recover the excess payment.

Liquidated Damages

4.85   A liquidated damages clause provides that the landlord may retain the entire deposit, even if it is above actual damages, if the tenancy is terminated by the tenant. Such a provision is a direct and explicit statement of the parties' intention. Nevertheless it may be ineffective because the courts have often held liquidated damages clauses to be a penalty and therefore invalid. On the other hand, if the court upholds the provision as a valid agreement of the amount of liquidated damages, the landlord will be limited to this amount, even if the actual damages exceed it.

Security for Tenant's Performance

4.86   In the typical residential tenancy the most accurate and equitable characterization of a security deposit is a fund to secure the faithful performance of the tenant's obligations under the lease. Under this interpretation the tenant is entitled to the return of any amount deposited less the amount of any loss incurred by the landlord resulting from the tenant's breach of obligation. If the landlord's damages exceed the amount of the deposit, the tenant is liable for the full amount of the damages.

4.87   If the security deposit constitutes a fund for the faithful performance of the tenant's obligations, there still exists the difficult question concerning the relationship of the landlord and tenant to that fund. The courts have construed that relationship in three different ways: debtor and creditor; pledgor-pledgee; and trustee-beneficiary.[41]

4.88   *Debtor-creditor.* If the relationship of landlord and tenant to the fund is one of debtor-creditor, the title to the fund passes to the landlord, and the landlord may use the funds as his own and does not have to keep them segregated from his other assets. This provides the least protection to the tenant, who must rely on the landlord's personal resources for the return of any part of the fund.

4.89   *Pledgor-pledgee.* If the relationship is one of pledgor-pledgee then title to the fund remains with the tenant even though possession is given to the landlord. The pledgee (landlord) is required to keep the fund segregated in some form, such as a bank account, and may not use the fund for his private purposes. This relationship provides the tenant with some form of protection particularly if the landlord is in financial difficulty because of liability to other creditors.

4.90   *Trustee-beneficiary.* If the relationship is one of trustee-beneficiary, then the landlord receives title to the fund subject to a fiduciary duty to maintain it for the benefit of the tenant and to account for misuse of those funds. This relationship provides the greatest amount of protection to the tenant, but most courts have been unwilling to impose a trust relationship without an express lease provision. New Jersey[42] and New York[43] have laws that protect a tenant's security deposit by creating a trust relationship.

RESPONSIBILITIES OF THE LANDLORD

Payment of Interest
4.91   In the absence of an agreement the landlord is not required to pay interest on the security deposit he holds.[44] Experience has indicated that the cost of accounting for interest on relatively small security deposits would exceed the interest earned. For this reason most states do not impose this requirement on the landlord. The *Model Code* (Sec. 2-401) has adopted a similar position.

Segregation of the Fund
4.92   The duty of the landlord to segregate the security deposit from his own funds depends upon the characterization of the deposit by the courts. If the deposit is considered an advance payment, bonus or consideration, the landlord is not required to keep the deposited monies segregated. If, however, the deposit is considered a pledge or trust, the landlord may not mingle the deposit with his own monies.[45] If the landlord uses funds received in trust or pledge as his own, such action constitutes a conversion and entitles the tenant to their immediate return.[46]

Preservation of the Funds
4.93   The landlord must exercise prudence and due care in protecting the security deposit, but he is not liable for its loss or reduction in value as long as he exercises such care.[47] Under most circumstances, a landlord holding a security deposit in trust or pledge would fulfill this standard of care by depositing the funds in a bank account. If the funds are lost or destroyed because of the landlord's failure to exercise due care, he remains liable for its return. A more difficult problem arises if the landlord becomes insolvent during the term of the lease. The preservation of the fund for the benefit of the tenant will depend upon whether the tenant is held to be just another creditor with a right to share the limited assets or a pledgor or beneficiary with prior claim to the fund.[48]

REPAYMENT TO THE TENANT

4.94   One cause of tenant hostility towards landlords is that some landlords withhold security deposits and unilaterally determine the amount of the deposit to be applied to the repair of alleged damages.[49] This hostility is aggravated by the lack of clear and definite standards to determine the extent or validity of the landlord's claim and by the inadequacy of remedies to secure repayment from an obstinate or unreasonable landlord.

Tenant's Default: Liquidated or Actual Damages
4.95   When a tenant vacates the premises before the term expires, the landlord sometimes may retain the security deposit. His right to the

security deposit is clear when the premises remain unoccupied and he suffers a loss of rental income. However, if the premises are re-rented, there is question whether he must return the excess after applying the deposit to satisfy actual damages for unpaid rent. If the deposit is characterized as advance payment, consideration, bonus or liquidated damages the landlord is not obligated to return it.[50] Yet it would seem that only that portion of the security deposit that compensates the landlord for his actual damages should be withheld.[51] This is the position advanced by the *Model Code* (Sec. 2-401), which limits the landlord's claim to only that part of the security deposit necessary to repair the premises.

Damage to the Premises

4.96   The landlord may apply the security deposit to the cost of repair of damage over the normal wear and tear to the premises. There is little criticism of the equity of this principle, except for the great potential for abuse. The problem is particularly acute in deteriorated residential accommodations, where high tenant turnover and cumulative uncorrected damages make it difficult, if not impossible, to determine responsibility for damages. It has been suggested that in a tenant's suit for the return of a security deposit, the landlord should be required to prove: "(1) that damage exists; (2) that the damage was caused during the tenant's period of possession; (3) that the damage is beyond normal wear and tear; and (4) the cost of repair of the excess damages."[52]

Sanctions for Failure to Repay

4.97   The problem of securing repayment of security deposits is more economic than legal because the cost of bringing a legal action frequently exceeds the amount of a tenant's recovery. A number of reforms have been suggested to assist tenants to recover security deposits from a recalcitrant landlord.[53]

4.98   *Double damages.* If the landlord fails to repay the deposit remaining after damages have been repaired, he may be liable in a civil action for double that amount. This remedy has been adopted in Pennsylvania,[54] where the statute also imposes the burden of proving actual damages upon the landlord.

4.99   *Criminal penalties.* The wrongful retention of a tenant's deposit may be a criminal act. This remedy has been adopted in New Jersey, where violation of the law subjects the landlord to a fine of $200 or a 30-day jail sentence.[55]

4.100   *Small claims jurisdiction.* The money and time spent in legal actions are reduced substantially when the action may be brought in a small claims court without an attorney. Because the amounts that can be recovered in small claims courts are often limited, this remedy is sometimes not effective. In New Jersey the usual limit of recovery of $200 is extended to $500 when the claim involves the return of all or part of a security deposit.[56]

4.101   *Application to last month's rent.* A tenant can most effectively secure the return of the security deposit by refusing to pay rent for the last rental period. The landlord may object to applying the security deposit to the payment of rent because it is also intended to secure payment for damages caused by the tenant. Nevertheless, this technique presents the landlord with a *fait accompli* under circumstances where his threat of summary eviction is of little consequence. Where the landlord suffers actual loss resulting from damage to the premises, the costs of bringing a legal action and the burden of proof are shifted to him.

4.102   Controversies between landlords and tenants relating to security deposits often arise when the parties fail to anticipate the problems that may result from the transfer of the interest of either the landlord or the tenant during the term of the lease.

Transfer of the Landlord's Interest
4.103   In the absence of a lease provision the courts are divided on the question of whether the original landlord must return the security deposit after the sale of the building and all its assets. Most states hold the landlord responsible for the return of the security deposit even though the deposit is transferred to the purchaser of the building.[57] A few states have shifted the responsibility for the return of the deposit from the original landlord to the purchaser.[58] A New York law gives the landlord the option to transfer the deposit to the purchaser and notify the tenant, return the deposit to the tenant, or retain the deposit and notify the tenant that the building has been sold and that he will continue to hold the deposit.[59] In states where the obligation to return the security deposit is held to be personal and not attached to the land, the purchaser of the building does not have to return the deposit if the funds are not transferred to him;[60] nor can the purchaser force the seller to transfer the security deposit to him.

Transfer of the Tenant's Interest
4.104   In the absence of a specific agreement a tenant who assigns or subleases his apartment remains liable for the payment of rent and other conditions of the lease. The landlord's consent to the assignment and acceptance of rent from the new tenant does not release the original tenant from his obligations under the lease. Consequently, assignment or sublease does not entitle the tenant to the return of the security deposit. The landlord may retain the deposit until the lease ends. After assignment the new tenant assumes the principal liability for the rent and the old tenant becomes a guarantor or surety.[61] Because of this principal-guarantor relationship, the courts have applied suretyship principles to determine when the liability of the original tenant is discharged. Thus, he may be discharged of liability under the lease if the landlord deals directly with the new tenant and changes the terms of the lease.[62] Once discharged of liability, he is entitled to the return of the security deposit.[63]

NOTES

1. Engleberg v. Morris, 202 N.Y.S. 2d 670, 25 Misc. 2d 409(1960).

2. 884 West End Ave. Corp. v. Pearlman, 201 App. Div. 12, 193 N.Y.S. 670 (1922), Att'd. 234 N.Y. 589, 138 N.E. 458 (1922).

3. Engleberg v. Morris, *supra* note 4, at 673.

4. Murphy, *A Proposal for Reshaping the Urban Renewal Agreement,* 57 *Geo. L.J.* 464, 482, hereafter referred to as *Model Lease.*

5. *Id.,* Sec. 14.

6. *E.g.,* New York, Massachusetts, Pennsylvania. For discussion see 6.17.

7. Dooley & Goldberg, *A Model Tenants Remedies Act,* 7 *Harv. J. Leg.* 357 (1970).

8. *Id.* This proposed legislation is not to be confused with the *Model Code.*

9. *Id.*at 395, Sec. 14, *Model Tenant's Remedies Act.*

10. On December 30, 1971 residential rentals became subject to Phase Two rent regulations under the Federal temporary economic stabilization program.

11. *E.g.,* Florida, Illinois, New Jersey.

12. Chicago Housing Authority v. Bild, 346 Ill. App. 272, 104 N.E. 2d 666 (1952).

13. 1 *American Law of Property* (A.J. Casner ed. 1952) sec. p. 267.

14. Brown v. Southall Realty Co., 237 A.2d 834 (1968).

15. 51 *C.J.S. Landlord and Tenant,* Sec. 30-53 (1968); 49 *Am. Jur.* 2d, *Landlord and Tenant,* Sec. 391-479 (1969).

16. *Kan. Gen. Stat. Ann.* Sec. 67-511 (1965); *Ky. Rev. Stat. Ann.* Sec. 383, 180 (1948); *Mo. Rev. Stat. Ann.* Sec. 441, 030 (1949); *Tex. Rev. Civ. Stat.* art. 5237 (1948).

17. *Effect of Household Provisions Requiring the Leasor's Consent to Assignment,* 21 *Hastings L.J.* 516 (1970).

18. See *Appendix* #4 Blumberg & Gilsey Leases.

19. Kendis v. Cohn, 90 Cal. App. 41, 265 P. 844 (1928).

20. *E.g.,* Silver v. Friedman, 18 N.J. Super, 367, 87 A.2d 336 (1952).

21. *See,* Groll, *Landlord-Tenant: The Duty to Mitigate Damages,* 17 *De Paul L.R.* 311 (1968).

22. *E.g.,* McCormick, *Damages* Sec. 127 (1935).

23. M.L. Improvement Corp. v. State, 118 Misc. 605, 194 N.Y.S. 165 (1922), *aff'd.* 204 App. Div. 733, 199 N.Y.S. 263 (1923).

24. McGrath v. Shalett, 144 Conn. 622, 159 A.633 (1932).

25. For a general discussion of this area see 52 *C.J.S. Landlord and Tenant,* Sec. 552-571 (1968); 49 *Am. Jur.* 2d, *Landlord and Tenant,* Sec. 626-650 (1969).

26. Guarino v. Timares, 196 Misc. 414, 94 N.Y.S. 2d 262 (1949), appeal denied 276 App. Div. 847, 93 N.Y.S. 2d 734 (1949).

27. Peters v. Kelly, 98 N.J. Super 441, 237 A.2d 635 (1968). This case has been specifically overruled however by Marini v. Ireland, 56 N.J. 130, 140, 265 A.2d 526, 531 (1970), but only as to the question whether a denial of a motion by a tenant for a failure to make factual allegations, or a failure to supply proof that rent in default is appealable.

28. Marini v. Ireland, 56 N.J. 130, 265 A.2d 526 (1970); Reste Realty Corp. v. Cooper, 53 N.J. 444, 251 A.2d 268 (1969); Pines v. Perssion, 14 Wis. 2d 590, 111 N.W. 2d 409 (1961); Brown v. Southall Realty Co., 237 A.2d 834 (1968); See discussion in 3.6-3.8, 3.57-3.58 and 5.23.

29. Midwest Properties Co. v. Renkel, 38 Ohio App. 503, 176 N.E. 665 (1930).

30. *See Confession of Judgment,* 102 *U. Pa. L. Rev.* 524 (1954); *The Form 50 Lease: Judicial Treatment of an Adhesion Contract,* 111 *U. Pa. L. Rev.* 1197 (1963).

31. Cohen v. Korol, 9 N.J. Super. 182, 75 A.2d 629 (1950).

32. 2 W. & M. c. 5 sec. 1689.

33. *See Landlord and Tenant: Distress for Rent,* 6 *U. Chi. L. Rev.* 505 (1939).

34. *See* 1 *L. Jones, Liens* Sec. 540 (3d ed. 1914).

35. *N.J. Stat.* 2A: 33-3 (1952); Other states have acted similarly: e.g. *Cal. Civ. Proc.* sec. 690.

36. Gibbons, *Residential Landlord-Tenant Law: A Study of Modern Problems with Reference to the Proposed Model Code* 1, 21 *Hastings L.J.* 369, 409.

37. *See Seewritz Deposits and Guarantees Under Leases,* 1966. *Real Property Probate and Trust Journal* 405.

38. *See* Wilson, *Lease Security Deposits,* 34 *Colum. L. Rev.* 426 (1934).

39. Schoen v. The New Britain Trust Co., 111 Comm. 466, 150 A.696 (1930).

40. *Landlord and Tenant—Lessee's Recovery of an Advanced Payment of Rent,* 25 *Ill. L. Rev.* 440 (1931).

41. *See Correlative Rights of Landlord and Tenant to Security Deposit,* 43 *Yale L.S.* 307 (1933); Harris, *A Reveille to Lessees,* 15 *So. Calif. L.R.* 412 (1942).

42. *N.J. Stat. Ann.* Sec. 46:8-19 (1970).

43. *N.Y. Real Prop.* Sec. 233 (1970).

44. *In re* Cromwell's Estate, 102 Misc. Rep. 503, 169 N.Y.S. 204 (1918).

45. *E.g., N.Y. Real Prop.* Sec. 233 creates a trust that prohibits the co-mingling of funds.

46. Mallory Assoc. v. Barring Realty Co., 300 N.Y. 297, 90 N.E. 2d 468 (1949).

47. Savage Oil Co. v. Johnson, 141 S.W. 2d 994 (1940).

48. *See* Gleick, *Rent Claims and Security Deposits in Bankruptcy,* 18 *Mo. L. Rev.* 1 (1953).

49. *N.J. Landlord-Tenant Relationships Study Commission Interim Report,* at 17 (1970).

50. Note 38 *supra.*

51. Heyman v. Linwood Park, 41 N.J. 437, 125 A.2d 345 (1956); *See Legal Representation of the Poor,* (E. Jarmel ed. at 325, 1968).

52. *Legal Representation of the Poor, supra,* Note 38, at 326.

53. *Supra* note 48, at 17.

54. *Pa. Stat.* title 68 Sec. 250.512 (1957).

55. *N.J. Stat. Ann.* 46:8-25 (1968).

56. *N.J. Stat. Ann.* 2A:6-43 (1968).

57. Karfma v. Williams, 92 N.J.L. 182, 104A. 202 (1918).

58. See *Correlative Rights of Landlord and Tenant to Security Deposit,* 43 *Yale L.J.* 307 (1933).

59. *N.Y. Penal Law* Sec. 1302A.

60. Four-G Corp. v. Puta, 25 N.J. 503, 138 A.2d 18 (1958).

61. 1 *American Law of Property,* Sec. 3.11 (A.J. Casner ed. 1952).

62. Gerber v. Pecht, 15 N.J. 29, 104 A.2d 41 (1954).

63. See 43 *Yale L.J.* 307 (1933); *but see* Partnoff v. Medinkowitz, 99 A.2d (1953).

5 Actions for Eviction

SUMMARY PROCEEDINGS

5.1   At common law, the landlord's legal remedies for eviction and recovery of rent were expensive and time consuming and tended to encourage him to take the law into his own hands. To discourage the hazardous and sometimes violent consequences of landlords' self-help evictions, all states have enacted some form of summary eviction proceeding to provide a speedy, inexpensive and equitable way to recover possession of property. Such proceedings are known by different names in different states, including summary proceedings, summary eject-ment proceedings, dispossessory warrant proceedings, forcible entry proceedings, and landlord and tenant proceedings, among others. Although the details of the statutes vary widely among states, most provide for grounds for eviction, a procedure for instituting and conducting the proceedings, defenses and counterclaims, scope of the judgment and methods of enforcement, and appeals from the judgment.

GROUNDS FOR SUMMARY PROCEEDINGS

5.2 Summary proceedings for eviction may be instituted only on the grounds specifically set forth in the law. Although the statutory provisions vary among the states, the following are usually included as grounds for summary proceedings.

Holding Over After the Term Expires

5.3 Most laws permit the proceeding to be started when the tenant fails to vacate when the term expires. In some states, this is interpreted to apply only when the lease has expired in time, and not when it has been terminated by the landlord because of the tenant's violation of the lease. Other states[1] authorize summary proceedings after the expiration of the lease in time, and also after expiration caused by an event described in the lease or at the option of the landlord.

Nonpayment of Rent

5.4 Most summary proceedings are brought because the tenant fails to pay the rent when due. In most leases, rent is due and payable in advance at the beginning of each month. If the lease so provides, rent may include additional charges such as the cost of excess electricity.[2]

Breach of Agreement

5.5 Statutory provisions for breach of agreement as grounds for summary proceedings vary greatly. Some states only provide for specified violations of the lease, or violations of major conditions or agreements that would have been grounds for forfeiture at common law. In other states a breach of any of the rules in the lease, such as keeping pets,[3] is sufficient grounds for summary proceedings. Where there is doubt as to whether a breach of agreement exists in fact, the courts will usually favor the tenant.[4] Consequently, landlords rarely use this reason as grounds for eviction. They can evict tenants more effectively by giving notice to terminate a short-term tenancy.

Other Statutory Grounds

5.6 Some statutes provide other grounds for summary eviction, such as unlawful use of the premises or unauthorized subletting. The *Model Code* (Sec. 3-202) provides that in the absence of lease agreement, summary eviction proceedings may be brought for expiration of the lease, nonpayment of rent, breach or violation, dismissal as a landlord's employee (e.g., in-residence janitor), mortgage foreclosure of a tenant-purchaser, wrongful ouster by the tenant in possession, and refusal of the tenant to vacate to permit repairs caused by fire or other casualty.

PRIOR NOTICE OF DEFAULT

5.7 Some statutes require the landlord to give the tenant notice before starting eviction proceedings. Whether such prior notice is necessary generally depends upon the grounds for eviction.

Notice of Grounds for Eviction

5.8   The statutory provisions regarding prior notice vary widely. When the law requires that a specified reason for eviction be given, the courts have usually held that notice of default for one reason is insufficient to bring summary proceedings for a different reason. In some states, the requirements of prior notice may be waived by lease provision, while in other states it may not. In some states a landlord must make a demand for rent before starting eviction proceedings for nonpayment. Most states require the landlord to give prior notice of a lease violation. In most states prior notice is not necessary for summary proceedings against a tenant whose lease runs through a definite period, but is necessary for summary proceedings against a tenant for an indefinite term, such as from month to month or at will.

Form and Content of the Notice

5.9   In some states (e.g. New Jersey) oral notice is sufficient, but in other states (e.g. New York) the prior notice must be in writing. In either case, the notice must be sufficiently clear and definite to inform the tenant of the landlord's intentions to terminate and the grounds upon which his claim is based. When written notice is required, the statute will usually prescribe how it must be served. Some laws require that notice be personally served on the tenant while others permit a copy to be left on the premises, posted on the door or sent through the mail.

SERVICE OF PROCESS

5.10   A proceeding for summary eviction is initiated by a legal document designated in different states as a summons, a warrant, a precept or a notice. Its contents and the way it is served are prescribed by law. The service informs the tenant that a legal proceeding has been started against him and notifies him where and when he must appear to defend himself. There are three different methods of service, one or more of which may be authorized by law.[5]

Personal Service

5.11   Personal service provides the most assurance that the tenant receives notice of the proceeding, since the process must be personally handed to the tenant. It is frequently difficult and expensive, however, to find the tenant at home or at work, and process servers are usually inclined to avoid the confrontation whenever possible, particularly in deteriorated and high-crime areas.

Substituted Service

5.12   Under some statutes, when the process server finds an adult person other than the tenant in the apartment, he may serve the process on that person. In some states, the process server may also be required to mail another copy of the summons to the named tenant.

Conspicuous Service

5.13   Under some laws, when the process server has been unable to find the tenant or any other suitable person at home, he may complete the service by posting the papers on the tenant's door.[6] In New York, under the so-called "nail and mail" provisions, the process server must mail another copy to the tenant.

5.14   Unfortunately, there is a fourth method of service, unauthorized but notorious, called "sewer service."[7] The process server may make no attempt to serve the tenant but fraudulently provide an affidavit stating that the tenant was served by one of the authorized methods. When this occurs, the tenant does not learn about the proceedings until the sheriff or marshal arrives with an order to evict.

THE LANDLORD'S ALLEGATIONS

5.15   In most states, the summons or notice is attached to another legal document called a complaint, petition or affidavit. The two are usually printed together on one legal form called a "summons and complaint" or a "notice and petition." The purpose of the second document is to set forth the landlord's allegations, or statement of the facts on which his action is based. Under most laws, the landlord's petition must contain allegations that satisfy each of the following requirements.[8]

The Right to Sue
5.16   The petition must allege that the petitioner is the landlord or another person with a right to possession. This requirement may be fulfilled by an allegation that the petitioner owns the property, is a duly authorized agent of the owner, or derives his right to sue in some other authorized manner.

The Tenant's Interest in the Dwelling Unit
5.17   The petition must allege the existence of a lease, oral agreement or other circumstances under which the tenant holds possession of the premises. This allegation is important because it will determine the nature of the notice, if any, that is required before the proceedings can be instituted.

Description of the Premises
5.18   The description of the premises must be sufficiently clear to identify the dwelling unit. The premises must be within the jurisdiction of the court in which the suit is brought.

The Grounds for Eviction
5.19   The petition must allege facts that constitute one of the statutory grounds for summary proceedings.[9] If the grounds for eviction are breach of agreement, the petition must allege the specific violation, the landlord's demand for compliance and the tenant's refusal. If the tenant is a holdover, the landlord must allege a timely notice to quit. In some states, the landlord must allege a timely demand for payment of rent.

Statement of the Relief Sought
5.20   The complaint in summary proceedings asks for an order of eviction. In most states, the court is authorized to grant, and the complaint will therefore ask for, a money judgment for rent due. In a few states,[10] a landlord may not join an action for rent in the same proceeding. The *Model Code* (Sec. 3-208) authorizes a money judgment in summary proceedings, but not in the case of a default judgment unless the court is satisfied that the tenant received actual notice of the proceedings.

THE TENANT'S DEFENSE AND COUNTERCLAIMS
5.21   In most jurisdictions, a tenant who has a defense or counterclaim to the landlord's cause of action must file an answer in writing. The tenant may deny the allegations of the landlord's complaint or may allege facts that create an affirmative defense or counterclaim. The *Model Code* (Sec. 3-210) provision permits the tenant to answer orally or in writing at the time of the hearing, and permits the tenant to advance any legal or equitable defense or counterclaim against the landlord.

5.22   One of the most significant issues of the landlord-tenant relationship is the extent to which a tenant may defend, in a proceeding for nonpayment of rent, on the grounds of defective or unhabitable conditions on the premises.

Judicially Created Defense
5.23   The Wisconsin[11] and New Jersey[12] courts have led the trend in the creation of a tenant's defense in summary proceedings on the grounds of the landlord's failure to repair. In *Marini*, the Supreme Court of New Jersey held that when a landlord fails to make repairs of vital facilities necessary to maintain the premises in livable condition, the tenant may, after notice to the landlord, make the repair himself and deduct the costs from future rents.[13] Thus, the court held that the tenant was not in default in his rent, since he had paid the costs of repair. This far-reaching judicial decision is at the frontier of the development of landlord-tenant law, but it still represents a minority judicial position.

Statutory Defenses
5.24   The legislatures of some states (e.g., New York, Massachusetts and Pennsylvania) have created a statutory tenant's defense in dispossess proceedings in cases where serious violations of housing codes have been noted by the code enforcement agency.

Counterclaims
5.25   Under most statutes a tenant may interpose a counterclaim against the landlord in the dispossess proceeding. For example, if the tenant's property is damaged because of the landlord's failure to repair faulty plumbing, the tenant may allege the damage as a counterclaim against the landlord's claim for rent. In some states, the proceeding is

limited to an action for possession only, and counterclaims for money damages are not permitted.[14]

THE TRIAL

5.26　　　The trial of a dispossess proceeding takes place with a minimum of formality. Every effort is made to dispose of the matter with speed. When the facts are not in dispute, the court may direct a verdict for either party. The trial procedure in landlord-tenant cases has been criticized by legal scholars as an inequitable anachronism in a twentieth-century urban society.[15] This criticism stems from the inequities that result from the high rate of uncontested cases, the problems associated with jury trials, the lack of legal representation of indigent tenants and, in some states, the thwarting of the entire process by confessions of judgment.

Uncontested Proceedings

5.27　　　Most landlord-tenant proceedings are uncontested. For example, in New Jersey in a recent court year, 17,013 out of a total of 25,019 eviction proceedings were uncontested by the tenant.[16] The high rate of default reflects the prevailing attitude that tenants have little hope for vindication in the hostile and callous setting of a judicial proceeding.[17] Their attitude is reenforced by the realization that, even when the proceeding is contested, the tenant usually loses. When the tenant prevails, he generally does so because his notice was improperly served, which can be corrected by another action by the landlord.[18]

The Right to a Trial by Jury

5.28　　　In most states a tenant may demand a trial by jury in a dispossess proceeding. Usually such demand requires the payment of a jury fee. In New Jersey, for example, a tenant must pay a fee of $8.50 for a six-man jury of $14.00 for a 12-man jury.[19] Landlords generally do not request a jury trial because the proceeding will have to wait its turn on the crowded jury calendar. Tenants rarely receive a jury trial unless they are represented by an attorney, since they generally do not know that they waive the right to a jury unless they request one within the time prescribed by law. In New Jersey, for example, where a jury trial must be demanded one day before the trial date, only three cases were tried by jury out of a total of 8,006 contested landlord-tenant cases during the 1967-1968 court year.[20]

5.29　　　Even when a jury trial has been requested within the time prescribed, only disputed questions of fact will be submitted to the jury. All questions of law are decided by the court. For example, when the facts are not in dispute, the question of whether the tenancy is from month to month or from year to year is a question of law for the court to decide. It is also possible for the court to render judgment for the landlord, in spite of a jury verdict for the tenant, if the court finds that the evidence is insufficient to support the jury's verdict.

5.30   The tenant's right to a trial by jury may be waived by a provision in the lease. Such a provision is binding upon the tenant unless prohibited by law.[21] Most states have not adopted strong measures to protect the right to a jury trial because of its debatable value. A jury trial is time-consuming and expensive for the landlord, the tenant and the court. It results in the delay of the hearing for a number of months during which the landlord is tempted to use methods of self-help eviction. A jury trial is useful to a tenant to the extent that it postpones the determination of his obligations and reduces the risk of unfair treatment by a hostile judge. Because of these conflicting equities, the *Model Code* (Sec. 3-211) offers the option of court trial or jury trial but strongly urges that a court trial be adopted. (The optional provision for jury trial gives either party the right to demand a jury at the time of the hearing, unless a jury trial is waived in the lease.)

Representation by an Attorney

5.31   An indigent or low-income tenant who cannot afford an attorney is faced with a formidable handicap in dispossess proceedings. The United States Supreme Court has held that an indigent defendant in a *criminal* prosecution must be provided with an attorney.[22] This principle has not been extended, however, to judicial proceedings in which an indigent tenant faces the risk of losing his home. The *Model Code* (Sec. 3-101) requires the court to appoint a private attorney to represent a tenant who is unable to afford his own counsel. Even if this provision were widely adopted, it is unlikely that sufficient funds would be appropriated to pay for the attorney fees of all tenants who would be eligible for this assistance. Such a provision would also require an extensive expansion of court facilities to handle the deluge of cases that were previously disposed of by tenant default.

5.32   The inequity created by the inability of low-income tenants to afford an attorney is aggravated by lease provisions that require the tenant to pay for the landlord's attorney fees as well. Landlords have argued that such provisions are justified because the attorney fees are a direct consequence of the tenant's violation of the lease. The drafters of the *Model Code* have determined that such a lease provision tends to encourage oppression of tenants by landlords. The *Model Code,* therefore, makes the agreement of either the landlord or the tenant to pay for the other's attorney unenforceable.[23]

Confession of Judgment

5.33   The right of a tenant to a trial in summary proceeding may be thwarted completely by a confession of judgment provision in the lease. Such a provision appoints the landlord as the tenant's attorney to confess judgment in the dispossess proceeding. Except in a few states, where it is authorized by statute, a confession of judgment provision in a lease is usually held invalid and unenforceable.[24] The *Model Code* (Sec. 3-404) makes such a provision void and unenforceable and subjects the landlord to prosecution for a misdemeanor if he includes such a clause in the lease.[31]

THE JUDGMENT

5.34   After trial or default by the tenant (if the landlord fails to appear the proceeding is dismissed), the court enters a final judgment determining the rights of the parties.

Possession and Rent

5.35   If the verdict or decision is rendered in favor of the landlord, a judgment will be entered awarding him possession of the premises. In those states where summary proceedings are not limited to eviction, but also include claims for rent, the judgment may include a monetary award for the amount of unpaid rent. When the proceedings are based upon the tenant's nonpayment of rent, payment by the tenant before judgment is entered eliminates the necessity of entering a final judgment in favor of the landlord. In those states where a holdover tenant is liable for double or triple damages the judgment will include an award for that amount.

Costs

5.36   The judgment will include an award for court costs. This amount varies widely in different states, but is generally not very substantial. For example, the court costs in New Jersey are $11.10 and in New York $4.50.[25] These fees are intended to cover the costs of process serving and filing, but do not include attorney's fees. When a money judgment for unpaid rent is rendered, the court costs in some states include a small percentage of the unpaid rent. The *Model Code* (Sec. 3-212) recommends a ceiling of $25.00 on court costs to protect a tenant who withholds rent wrongfully, although in good faith, to prod a landlord into making repairs.

Conditional Stay of Execution

5.37   When the judgment awarding possession to the landlord is based upon the tenant's nonpayment of rent, the judgment commonly includes a stay of execution for a short period of time (usually five days), during which time the tenant may pay the rent and costs. If the tenant fails to pay the rent during that period the landlord may obtain a warrant of eviction.[26] In some states[27] when the proceeding is based upon a termination of the tenancy and the court finds that immediate eviction would cause hardship to the tenant, the court may grant a stay of execution for a longer period of time. In New Jersey, for example, it is not unusual for the judgment to contain a stay of execution for a month or more.[28]

The Warrant of Eviction

5.38   At the expiration of the stay, the landlord is entitled to a warrant of eviction, also known as a warrant or writ of dispossession. The warrant is issued on application to the court or clerk, and authorizes the marshal, sheriff or other executing officer to remove the tenant and other occupants and their personal property, and to put the landlord into full possession of the premises. In some states, the executing officer is required to give the tenant notice of his intention to evict. In New York City, for example, the marshal must give the tenant 72-hours notice, and may conduct the eviction only after the 72-hour period, on weekdays only, and only during the hours from 9 AM to 3 PM .[29] The *Model Code* (Sec. 3-215) requires 24 hours notice and permits execution only between sunrise and sunset. The traditional method of eviction is to remove all of the tenant's personal property from the premises and to place it on the sidewalk in front of the building. The unconscionable hardship inflicted upon the tenant through theft, damage and vandalism has caused some jurisdictions[30] to require the executing officer to place the tenant's property in a municipal warehouse. Nevertheless, this minimum deference to human decency and dignity is not common practice, and the *Model Code* imposes no such duty upon the landlord or the municipality.

APPEAL AND CERTIORARI

5.39   The judgment may be reviewed by an appellate court by either of two procedures: appeal or certiorari. Appeal is provided for by statute; certiorari, a common law proceeding, may be available to review dispossess proceedings for a limited purpose such as whether the lower court has jurisdiction.

Statutory Limitations

5.40   Most states authorize and provide for appeal of a judgment in a dispossess proceeding. All statutory conditions and requirements must be met. These requirements include timely notice and application and filing of a bond. In New Jersey the judgment in a summary eviction proceeding in a county district court may not be appealed.[31] The New Jersey statute, however, permits the court to transfer a landlord-tenant case to the Superior Court if the judge, within his discretion, finds that the case involves an important issue. These judges are reluctant to exercise their discretion in favor of tenants and, consequently, landlord-tenant law is infrequently modified by the judicial process.[32] The New Jersey law has been upheld in a case where it was attacked as an unconstitutional violation of procedural due process.[33]

5.41   Summary proceeding appeal provision vary in the extent of the review by the appellate court. In some states (e.g. Connecticut, New York) the appeal is based upon the prior proceedings and record in the lower court. In other states (e.g. Hawaii, Minnesota, Montana) the case is tried *de novo,* i.e., from the beginning with new testimony and evidence. In either case, the appellate court usually has no greater jurisdiction than the lower court from which the appeal was taken.

Requirement of a Bond

5.42   The statutory provision for appeal in most states requires the appellant (the tenant, in most cases) to provide a bond or other satisfactory assurance that he will pay all costs of appeal and all rent or other damages accruing to the landlord while the proceedings are pending.[34] This requirement has been criticized as a device by which low-income tenants who cannot afford such bonds are effectively denied the right to appeal.[35] The validity of the bond requirement under the Connecticut summary proceeding statute has been upheld by the United States Supreme Court.[36]

Stay of Execution

5.43   Statutory provisions in most states provide a procedure by which the warrant of eviction may be stayed pending the outcome of the appeal. Time may be a critical issue to a tenant who was never served with prior notice and learns that he is about to be evicted. In some states[37] the tenant's one last chance to stay the action of the marshal is to obtain an "order to show cause." A judge will then decide whether there is sufficient reason to stop the execution of the warrant.

SELF-HELP EVICTIONS

FORCIBLE EJECTION AT COMMON LAW

5.44   At common law a landlord was permitted to remove a tenant from the premises upon termination of the tenancy, without the use of legal process, if the eviction could be accomplished peacefully. The legal problems that arose under this rule involved questions of whether the landlord had a right of re-entry and whether the eviction was accomplished "peacefully."

The Landlord's Right of Re-entry

5.45   Under certain circumstances, the landlord's right of re-entry at common law was clear. For example, if the tenant abandoned or surrendered the premises, the landlord had the right to re-enter and take possession. In addition, the landlord had the right of re-entry without legal process when the tenancy terminated. The issue became more complex when landlords began to include a provision in the lease that authorized their re-entry upon the violation of the terms and conditions by the tenant. A lease not uncommonly gave a landlord the right to recover possession upon the tenant's default in the payment of rent. The summary right of self-help eviction became less defensible when the lease provided for termination for other violations of the agreement which sometimes involved disputed questions of fact. When such disputes arose the likelihood of peaceful re-entry diminished and it became necessary to determine the limits of force that a landlord might use to recover possession.

Limitations on the Use of Force

5.46   The landlord's right to use force in self-help evictions was prohibited by law in 1381.[38] Most American states impose criminal penalties on landlords who use force to evict and give tenants the right to recover possession if they are evicted in violation of the law.[39] Thus, the principle is now established in most states that a landlord may not use force to recover possession, but may evict a tenant without legal process if it can be accomplished peacefully.

JUDICIAL AND STATUTORY MODIFICATION OF THE COMMON LAW RULE

Distinguishing "Peaceful" and "Forceful" Evictions

5.47   Although the rule was clearly established that forceful evictions were prohibited and peaceful evictions were permitted, the courts found it very difficult to establish criteria to determine whether a given eviction was forceful or peaceful.[40] A physical expulsion of the tenant involving breaking into the premises, personal violence or breach of the peace clearly constituted a forceful eviction. The definition of "forceful" was expanded by the courts to include evictions effected without physical violence, but through fear or apprehension of danger in the mind of the evicted tenant. Landlords responded to this expanded judicial definition of "forcible entry" by performing the eviction in the tenant's absence, thereby avoiding a confrontation that might cause fear or apprehension of danger in the mind of the tenant. The landlord would wait for the tenant to leave the premises, enter by the use of a pass key, remove the tenant's furniture and belongings and then change the lock on the door. In most states the courts have held that the entry with a key and the subsequent refusal to surrender the premises, unaccompanied by any acts or threats of force, does not constitute a forcible entry.[41] However, in a few states the courts have attempted to eliminate self-help evictions even when performed "peacefully" by creating a judicial myth of "implied force." In *Jordan v. Talbot*[42] the California Supreme Court expanded the definition of forcible entry to include any unauthorized entry and removal of the tenant's property by the landlord even when he enters using a key when the tenant is absent.

5.48   In the Jordan case the court held that there is a "forcible entry" even though the initial entry was peaceable because the tenant was subsequently excluded by threats of violence. The court based its decision on testimony that when the tenant returned to her apartment, found it locked and inquired about her belongings, the landlord's employee told her, "Get the hell out of here. You're out of this place. Don't talk to me about it. Call Mr. Talbot [the landlord]."

Summary Proceedings as Exclusive Remedy

5.49   The courts in some states have held that the statutory provisions for summary proceedings by which a landlord may obtain a quick and expensive eviction through legal process were intended to supercede the landlord's right of self-help eviction. Although there may be some merit to this position, most courts have continued to recognize the landlord's right of peaceful self-help eviction as an alternate remedy to summary eviction proceedings. Most judges feel that it is up to the legislature to determine whether summary proceedings are intended to be the only landlord remedy for eviction.

The Model Code Provisions

5.50   The *Model Code* seeks to protect a tenant against landlord's self-help action that either evicts or excludes him (usually by changing the lock) from the premises. If the landlord removes or excludes a tenant without a valid court order, the *Model Code* (Sec. 2-408) gives the tenant a choice of either recovering possession of the premises or terminating the tenancy. In addition, the landlord is made liable for three months rent or triple damages sustained by the tenant, and the costs of a suit, which includes a reasonable attorney's fee.

NOTES

1. *Ind. Ann. Stat.* Sec. 3-160 (1968).

2. Chicgao Housing Authority v. Bild, 346 Ill. App. 272 104 N.E.2d 666 (1952).

3. 7039 Wentworth Ave. Bldg. Corp. v. Trough, 332 Ill. App. 635 76 N.E.2d 350 (1947).

4. Carteret Properties v. Variety Donuts, Inc., 49 N.J. 116, 228 A.2d 674 (1967).

5. *E.g., N.Y. Real Prop. Actions Law* Sec. 735 (McKinney Supp. 1969-70); *see also Model Code* Secs. 3-204, 205, 206.

6. *E.g., N.J. Rev. Stat.* Sec. 2A:18-54 (1952).

7. *See* note, *Abuse of Process: Sewer Service,* 3 *Colum. J. of L. & Soc. Prob.* 17 (1967).

8. See *Model Code* (Sec. 3-208).

9. See discussion of grounds for summary proceedings, *supra* 5.2.

10. *E.g., Conn. Gen. Stat. Rev.* Sec. 52-532(1958); *N.J. Stat. Ann.* Sec. 2A:18-53(1952).

11. Pines v. Perssion, 14 Wis. 2d 590, 111 N.W.2d 409 (1961).

12. Reste Realty Corp. v. Cooper, 53 N.J. 444, 251 A.2d 268(1969); Marini v. Ireland, 56 N.J. 130, 265 A.2d 526(1970).

13. Marini v. Ireland, note 12 *supra.*

14. *E.g., Conn. Gen. Stat. Rev.* Sec. 52-532 (1958); *N.J. Stat. Ann.* Sec. 2A:18-53 (1952).

15. Bruno, *New Jersey Landlord-Tenant Law: Proposals for Reform,* 1 *Rutgers-Camden L.J.* 299 (1969); *see also* Gibbons, *Residential Landlord-Tenant Law: A Survey of Modern Problems with Reference to the Proposed Model Code,* 21 *Hastings L.J.* 369 (1970).

16. *Annual Report of N.J. Administrative Director of Courts* 1967-1968, table F-1, at 109.

17. Bruno, *supra* note 15, at 300.

18. Gibbons, *supra* note 15, at 373.

19. *N.J. Stat. Ann.* Sec. 2A:2-37(1969).

20. *N.J. Annual Report, supra* note 16.

21. *E.g., Ill. Ann. Stat.* Ch. 57 Sec. 112(Smith-Hurd).

22. Gideon v. Wainwright, 372 U.S.335(1963).

23. *Model Code* (Sec. 3-402); for a discussion of similar restrictions involving small loan agreements, see J. Patrick, Jr., *The Legality of Attorney's Fee and Collection Cost Clauses Under the Alabama Small Loan Act.* 25 *Ala. Law.* 296(1964).

24. *See* note, *Confessions of Judgment,* 102 *U. Pa. L. Rev.* 524(1954); Note, *The F form 50 Lease: Judicial Treatment of an Adhesion Contract,* 111 *U. Pa. L. Rev.* 1197(1963).

25. Gibbons, *supra* note 15, at 375.

26. *E.g. N.Y. Real Prop. Actions Law* Sec. 732(2) & 732(3) (McKinney 1963).

27. *E.g., N.J. Stat. Ann.* Sec. 2A: 42-10.6(Supp. 1969); *N.Y. Real Prop. Actions Law* Sec. 751 (McKinney 1963).

28. *Gibbons, supra* note 15, at 376.

29. For a discussion of the eviction procedure in New York, see *N. Leblanc, A Handbook of Landlord-Tenant Procedures and Law, With Forms,* at 18-20(2nd. ed. 1969).

30. *E.g.,* New York; see *Leblanc, supra* note 37, at 19.

31. *N.J. Stat. Ann.* Sec. 2A: 18-59(1952).

32. Bruno, *supra* note 15, at 301.

33. Randell v. Newark Housing Authority, 384 F.2d 151(3d Cir. 1967).

34. The *Model Code* (Sec. 3-214) adopts the same position.

35. Gibbons, *supra* note 15, at 377.

36. West Haven Housing Authority v. Simmons, 5 Conn. Cir. 282, 250 A.2d 527 (1968), *Appeal dismissed* 399 U.S. 510(1970); *reh denied* 400 U.S. 856(1970). *But see* Lindsey v. Normet, U.S., 40 L.W. 4184 (Feb. 23, 1972) where an Oregon appeal bond requirement of twice the rental value was held invalid by the Supreme Court.

37. *E.g., N.Y. Civil Prac. Law & Rules* Sec. 5704.

38. *See* The Forcible Entry Act of 1381, 5 Ric. 2. For a discussion of the history of self-help evictions in England, *see* Barnett, *When the Landlord Resorts to Self-Help: A Plea for Clarification of the Law of Florida,* 19 *U. Fla. L. Rev.* 238 (1966).

39. *E.g., N.J. Rev. Stat.* Sec. 2A:39-8(1952; *Mich. Comp. Laws Ann.* Sec. 600: 2918(1968).

40. For a collection of New Jersey cases on this issue, *see* Note, *Self-Help in New Jersey,* 1 *Rutgers-Camden L.J.* (1969).

41. Brooks v. Brooks, 84 *N.J.L.* 218, 86 A.2d 537. (Sup. Ct. 1913).

42. 55 Cal. 2d 597, 361 P.2d 20(1961); *see* Note, *Repossession of Realty and Chattels: Jordan v. Talbot—Prelude to Elimination of Self-Help in California* 9 *U.C.L.A. L. Rev.* 453(1962).

6 Tenant Remedies to Correct Unhabitable Conditions

6.1   The many administrative, political and economic impediments to effective enforcement of housing codes have encouraged tenants to create and develop numerous programs and techniques to force landlords to maintain minimum standards of habitability. The development of tenant remedies has been retarded by the feudal principles described in Chapter 4, such as the doctrine of *caveat emptor*; the principle of independence of covenants; the judicial rejection of implied warrant of habitability; and judicial unwillingness to expand the concept of constructive eviction.

6.2   In spite of these conceptual difficulties, the courts and state legislatures have begun to respond to the changes actually taking place in the landlord-tenant relationship by endorsing an array of tenant remedies. Among them are: rent abatement; rent escrow; receivership; tenant right to repair and deduct; tenant unions; and protection against landlords' retaliation.

RENT ABATEMENT

6.3   At common law the tenant's obligation to pay rent was suspended or abated only under certain circumstances. The court considered a lease a conveyance of an interest in real estate and characterized the periodic payment of rent as nothing more than a convenient way of paying the full amount for the entire term. Consequently, the obligation to pay rent was suspended only when the tenant was actually evicted or the landlord's legal title to the property was questioned. Although the courts recognized the tenant's right to stop paying rent if the landlord breached an implied covenant of quiet enjoyment, the courts denied the existence of an implied covenant of habitability in the landlord-tenant relationship. Thus, at common law the tenant had no legal right to refuse to pay rent on the grounds that the premises were unhabitable or below minimum standards of deceny. In recent years, the right of tenants to refuse to pay rent for substandard and unhabitable premises has been expressed by courts and legislatures.

THEORIES OF JUDICIAL RENT ABATEMENT

6.4   The judicial creation of a tenant right of rent abatement has been based upon such diverse legal principles as the implied warrant of habitability created by housing codes; constructive eviction; illegal contract; and partial failure of consideration.

Implied Warranty of Habitability Created by Housing Codes

6.5   In the absence of a statute, the great majority of American courts have adhered to the common law principle that the tenant is not justified in refusing to pay rent because the condition of the premises is substandard. Nevertheless, legal scholars have advanced the theory that the minimum standards prescribed in housing codes oblige the landlord to maintain leased dwelling units in accordance with them.[1] Although most courts have not yet recognized the persuasiveness of this position, a Wisconsin court enthusiastically adopted this principle in *Pines v. Perssion*.[2] In that case the court recognized that the legislature's enactment of housing code standards constituted a policy determination that it was socially and politically desirable to impose the duty of compliance on the landlord. By the imposition of this duty, the legislature had intended to abrogate the common law rule of no implied warrant of habitability.[3]

6.6   In any state where the courts accept this principle, the tenant can successfully maintain that substandard conditions are a breach of an implied warranty of fitness and that his obligation to pay rent is suspended pending fulfillment of the landlord's obligations. The landlord would argue that the proposed change in legal doctrine fails to consider the economic realities of the landlord-tenant relationship. The condition of the premises has already been reflected in the amount of rent charged. That is, in the housing market the condition of the premises is the best that the tenant can obtain for the amount of rent he is able to pay. If the tenant could find better conditions for the same rent elsewhere, he would have done so. Since the parties have, through the free market system of private contract, bargained and determined the amount of rent appropriate to the condition of the premises, to impose a greater obligation than the landlord anticipated would be an improper interference with this relationship. In addition, the landlord would argue that if the objective of legislative policy is to secure safe and sanitary housing facilities, then relieving the tenant of his obligation to pay rent would only frustrate that legislative intent. The only revenue from which a landlord can derive funds for repair and maintenance is rent. Once rent stops the ability of the landlord to pay for needed repairs also stops and the conditions of habitability further deteriorate. The tenant's rejoinder is that fear of losing rental income will induce the landlord to maintain his premises.

Constructive Eviction[4]

6.7　　At common law a tenant's obligation to pay rent ended when the landlord evicted him. Judges reasoned that if the landlord violated his implied covenant of quiet enjoyment, the tenant's obligation ended. In time, the courts expanded this principle to permit termination of rent under conditions that are closely equivalent to eviction. This extension was accomplished through the creation of a judicial fiction called "constructive eviction."

6.8　　Constructive eviction is a judicial concept that holds that when a landlord substantially interferes with his tenant's enjoyment of the premises the courts will treat that situation *as though* the landlord had actually evicted the tenant. To persuade a court to evoke this principle it was necessary for the tenant to show that the landlord's interference was serious and permanent in character, causing the tenant to abandon the premises.

6.9　　In recent years it has been argued that the doctrine should be expanded to include situations where the interference by the landlord is of such magnitude that the premises are rendered unhabitable.[5] The municipal court of the City of New York adopted this doctrine in *Magen Realty Corp. v. Glotzer,*[6] where the landlord failed to repair the tenant's fire-damaged apartment but abated the rent in proportion to the extent of the diminished use. The court said:

> While it is true that in order to sustain the defense of constructive eviction, there must be an abandonment of the premises...that rule rests on the reasoning that if the premises in fact were not fit for occupancy, the tenant would not have retained possession but would have moved elsewhere, and his remaining in the premises belies any claim that they were not fit and habitable. Such a rule would prevail where a market of avail-

able apartments or dwelling accommodations exists. However, where there are no living accommodations available elsewhere or there is such a scarcity of them that impels the legislature to declare a public emergency to exist because of such conditions, the reason upon which the rule exists disappears and the rule should therefore be relaxed.[7]

Illegality of Contract[8]

6.10   The third legal principle upon which judicial rent abatement may be based is the principle that a contract is unenforceable when its terms violate existing law. In a civil suit for damages, such as an action for rent, the tenant has a valid defense if he can prove that the contract on which the action is based is illegal. It may be argued that the rental of dwelling units in violation of the minimum standards prescribed in housing codes makes the lease an illegal contract and provides the tenant with a defense against an action for rent.[9]

Partial Failure of Consideration

6.11   Failure of consideration is a defense in a civil suit for damages arising from breach of contract because the plaintiff (the landlord) must prove that he has fulfilled his part of the bargain in order to recover damages. It can be argued that a landlord should not be entitled to rent unless he proves that he rented the premises in habitable condition. There are, however, a number of formidable legal obstacles. The underlying problem is that a lease is considered a conveyance of an interest in real estate as well as a contract. Because of this characterization, the principles of property law rather than those of contract law were applied by the courts. At common law the consideration for rent was the conveyance of the property and, therefore, covenants in the lease were independent of each other. Even if the landlord agreed to keep the premises in repair, the covenant of the tenant to pay rent had no relationship to the landlord's covenant to repair. Consequently, the landlord's failure to repair did not constitute a failure of consideration. This doctrine of the independence of covenants is still the prevailing rule of law.

6.12   It has been argued that this rule is inconsistent with the realities of the urban landlord-tenant relationship. The principle of the independence of covenants was established in a period of Anglo-American law when the essence of the lease transaction was, in fact, a temporary conveyance of an interest in land for agricultural use. The rule was appropriate for that era and was consistent with the intentions of the contracting parties. In an urban society, the lease of housing accommodations not only conveys possession of the premises but should also include the services and maintenance required for decent and safe habitation. Thus, the reason for the rule is no longer applicable to today's conditions, no longer represents the intentions of the parties and should be nullified by the courts.

STATUTORY RENT ABATEMENT

6.13   Despite recent progress in the judicial development of tenants' rights to rent abatement for unhabitable premises, most courts have chosen to exercise judicial restraint on the grounds that this type of policy judgment is properly within the scope of legislative authority. Statutory control of rent abatement would appear to be more desirable for the additional reason that legislative procedures should be prescribed to enable both landlords and tenants to protect their respective interests. The New York Multiple Dwelling Law (Section 302-a) illustrates the kind of regulations and procedures that statutory rent abatement may provide.

6.14   Under the New York law, a tenant may defend against a landlord's summary dispossess proceedings for nonpayment of rent on the grounds that certain serious violations of the housing code have been noted by the enforcement agency and that those violations have not been corrected for six months prior to the proceeding. The tenant must deposit with the court all of the rent claimed by the landlord. If the tenant is able to prove the allegation the deposited rent is returned to him and he may receive a court order completely abating the rent until the violations are corrected. If the landlord wins the case, the deposited rent is turned over to him. The law prescribes a procedure and a number of conditions that must be fulfilled for this tenant remedy to be effective.

1.   The alleged violation must be one of a prescribed test of serious "rent impairing" violations. Not every violation of the housing code may provide a basis for rent abatement. Only those violations that constitute a serious threat to the life, health or safety of the occupants may be used. In response to this provision, the New York City Department of Buildings has published a list of violations classified as "rent impairing."

2.   The violations must be noted on record by the code enforcement agency. This defense is unavailable until the code enforcement agency officially notes the violation and sends notice of it to the last registered owner of the building.

3.   The violation must have existed uncorrected for six months after notice to the owner.

4.   The landlord may overcome the tenant's defense if he can prove that there is no violation in ᶠact, that the violation has been corrected, that the violation was caused by a tenant, or that the tenant has prevented repair by refusing entry to the premises.

6.15   Rent abatement legislation has also been adopted in Massachusetts[10] and Pennsylvania.[11] The Pennsylvania legislation is similar to the New York provision in that a municipal agency must first certify that a dwelling is unfit for human habitation. After such certification the tenant's obligation to pay rent ends, but he must place his rent payments into an escrow account. If the premises are repaired by the landlord and the dwelling is certified as fit for habitation, the monies are turned over to the landlord. If they are not so certified the court may return the monies to the tenants or may use the funds for the repair of the premises. This last provision makes the Pennsylvania provision a hybrid combination of the rent abatement and the rent escrow type of law.

RENT ESCROW

6.16   The primary difference between the tenant remedies of rent abatement and rent escrow is that rent abatement only suspends the tenant's obligation to pay, whereas the rent escrow remedy provides a procedure by which the rent is paid into a fund to be used for the repair and improvement of the premises. In addition, rent abatement is a defensive remedy that is available only in response to a landlord's summary dispossess proceeding or action for rent. An effective rent escrow remedy, on the other hand, permits the tenant to institute the necessary action to improve the condition of the premises by using the rental monies for the costs of repair. Because of the necessity for a prescribed procedure and for administrative machinery, the rent escrow remedy requires statutory authorization.

THE NEW YORK PROGRAM

6.17   The New York Real Property Actions and Proceedings Law is one illustration of a rent escrow remedy. Under this program one-third of the tenants in a multiple dwelling containing six or more apartments may attempt to obtain a court order directing that all rents be deposited with the court. The monies may be used to pay the costs of remedying certain conditions, such as lack of heat, running water, light, electricity, adequate sewage disposal facilities, or rodent infestation or any other condition dangerous to life, health or safety which has existed for five days or more. The law requires that notice of the proceeding be given to the owner, to all other tenants in the building, and the mortgagee and other lien holders. The law provides the landlord with a number of defenses. He may argue that the alleged conditions do not in fact exist, that they have been corrected, that they were caused by the tenants, or that repair has been prevented by the tenants. If the court finds that the alleged condition does exist and the landlord has no defense to the action, it may be directed that *all* rents be paid into court or that the landlord or lien holder remedy the defects. If the repairs are not made promptly the court may appoint an administrator to collect the rent and use the proceeds for repairs.

ADVANTAGES OF THE RENT ESCROW PROGRAM

Funds for Repairs
6.18   The primary advantage of a rent escrow program such as the

New York program is that it provides for the use of the rental-income to correct the defective conditions. This eliminates the self-defeating aspect of rent abatement, which tends to encourage a landlord to throw up his hands and abandon marginally deteriorated property. When the cost of repair is not excessive, the rental income may be sufficient to alleviate the dangerous condition.

No Dependence Upon Prior Government Action
6.19   Unlike the rent abatement remedy, rent escrow does not require tenants to wait for a code enforcement agency to inspect the premises and file a notice of violation. Tenants may *allege* that conditions are dangerous and may prove the existence of these conditions without reference to any governmental record of violation.

Affirmative Tenant Action
6.20   The escrow program eliminates the psychological and legal disadvantage of having to defend against a landlord's summary eviction proceedings. Instead of placing their right to habitation in jeopardy because of their failure to pay rent, rent escrow enables tenants to take the offensive and be assured that even if they lose, the worst that can happen is that they will have to pay court costs and the amount of the deposited rent to the landlord.

Entire Rent Roll Available for Repairs
6.21   Unlike rent abatement, the escrow program authorizes the court to direct the payment of the entire rent roll, including the rent of nonpetitioning tenants, into the fund. The entire rent roll might provide enough money to correct conditions that would not otherwise be economically feasible.

DISADVANTAGES OF THE PROGRAM

Need for Concerted Tenant Action
6.22   The petition for rent escrow requires the participation of one-third of the tenants in the building. Even this small percentage is an obstacle, particularly in slum neighborhoods, where the residents are unaware of their legal rights, distrustful of the judicial system and fearful of landlord retaliation.

6.23   The program is useful only when the defective condition affects the entire building. An individual tenant whose apartment is defective will be unable to persuade other tenants to join him in the suit and will not be entitled to use his rent money to repair his apartment.

Difficulty in Finding an Administrator
6.24   The payment of the rent into court does not of itself remedy the substandard conditions of the building. The court must find and appoint a person willing and able to use those funds efficiently and productively. This person must have the confidence of the tenants, the requi-

site business and financial expertise, and the personal integrity to justify a court appointment. Candidates with these qualifications are hard to find.

Insufficient Funds for Maintenance and Repairs
6.25   The rent escrow remedy is predicated upon the questionable premise that the landlord's lack of action causes the premises to fall into disrepair and that his removal will permit the use of the rent monies to improve conditions. The tenants may find that the cost of repairs far exceeds the limited rental income. Moreover, a benevolent administrator may have problems collecting the rent and the landlord may be unwilling to pay the costs of maintenance as long as he does not receive the rental income.

6.26   Even if the administrator has the full amount of the rent available for repairs, he will find that contractors are unwilling to finance the cost of major repairs and are unwilling to depend on future rent receipts. Without the ability to borrow, the administrator is limited to low-cost and minor repairs.

HOUSING RECEIVERSHIP

6.27   The need for a legal apparatus by which a court-appointed administrator may finance the long-term repayment of the cost of substantial repairs has led to the creation of a program of housing receivership in six states. The legislatures of New Jersey, New York, Connecticut, Indiana, Massachusetts and Illinois have authorized receivership programs. It is arguable that housing receivership is not a tenant remedy in the strict sense, because a proceeding to appoint a receiver must be instituted by the code enforcement agency in the first four of the above-named states. In Massachusetts, however, there is express statutory authority for tenants to institute receivership proceedings and in Illinois a receiver must be appointed as a result of a class action on behalf of tenants to compel compliance with housing code standards. Some authorities claim that housing receivership is one of the most effective remedies for improving the standards of habitability in deteriorated housing accommodations.[13] On the other hand, its effectiveness has been questioned by a special study prepared for the National Commission on Urban Problems.[14] The experience in New York City illustrates the kinds of legal, economic and administrative problems involved in housing receivership legislation.

THE LEGAL PROBLEMS
6.28   The original New York City receivership law was enacted in 1937[15] and provided for the appointment of a receiver who was authorized to secure payment of the costs of repair by offering a lien that was superior to existing mortgages. This legislation was declared unconstitu-

tional in a suit brought by the bank that held the mortgage that was subordinated by the "prior lien." In the landmark decision of *Central Savings
Bank v. City of New York*[16] the New York Court of Appeals invalidated
the program on the grounds that the plaintiff-mortgagee was deprived
of his constitutional rights in that:

1. The receiver's prior lien deprived the mortgagee of substantive
   due process of law by diminishing the protection of the security of
   the existing mortgage;
2. The receiver's prior lien impaired the obligation of the mortgage contract in violation of the United States Constitution (Art. I,
   sec. 10); and
3. Failure to provide sufficient notice and opportunity to be heard
   deprived the mortgagee of procedural due process of law.

During the two decades after the *Central Savings Bank* decision the first
two grounds for invalidity, substantive due process and contract impairment, were eliminated by numerous decisions that broadened the
scope and the validity of legislative police power regulations. However,
the third problem, of insuring procedural due process to the mortgagee,
remained as a legal obstacle to a valid receivership program. This was
finally overcome in the revised New York City Receivership Law enacted
in 1962.[17]

6.29　　The 1962 legislation authorized the code enforcement agency
to petition the court to appoint a receiver upon evidence that the conditions of the building constitute a serious fire hazard or a serious threat
to the life or safety of the tenants. Notice of the proceeding is to be served
on the owner and all mortgagees and lienors of record. All parties are
given the opportunity to eliminate the defective conditions and to show
cause why the commissioner of the Department of Real Estate should not
be appointed as receiver to remove the violations. If the owner, mortgagee or other lienor does not elect to undertake the improvements,
the Department of Real Estate is authorized to advance the funds,
to pay the costs of repair and to obtain a lien on all future rents and income from the building. The validity of this legislation was upheld in
1964 in *Matter of Department of Buildings of the City of New York*.[18] In
this decision the court distinguished the 1962 legislation from the program invalidated in *Central Savings Bank* on two grounds: first, the
1962 act provides the mortgagee and other lienors with sufficient notice
and opportunity to meet the requirements of procedural due process;
and second, the revised program does not authorize a prior lien on the
property itself but only gives the receiver a prior lien on the rental income
from the property. The court found that the lien on the rental income
does not impose so drastic a limitation upon the mortgagee's right as the
1937 provision that would have permitted foreclosure of the mortgagee's
entire security. The court concluded that there was no violation of substantive due process or contract impairment because the mortgagee's

rights were not substantially limited; therefore the exercise of the police power to meet the critical public need for the preservation of decent housing was not precluded.

6.30　　Within a year after this decision, New York amended the receivership law to give the receiver a prior lien on the title to the property.[19] The present law once again authorizes the receiver to secure the payment of the costs of repair with a lien that has priority over the existing mortgage. In enacting this amendment the New York legislature indicated its confidence that if the court is faced with this issue again it will reject the *Central Savings Bank* decision.

THE ECONOMIC PROBLEM

6.31　　With the legal questions substantially resolved, the success of the receivership program depends upon the receiver's ability to overcome the underlying economic obstacles to the preservation of old and deteriorated housing structures. The mere transfer of control and management from the landlord to a receiver does not in any way solve the problem of insufficient rental income to pay for the high costs of repair. The National Commission on Urban Problems study[20] disclosed that the combination of low rents and high maintenance costs required to maintain buildings taken into receivership made it impossible for the receiver to recover the costs of repair within a reasonable time. Even after adding the proceeds from tax foreclosures in the first two and a half years of operation of the receivership law only 10 percent of the $1.5 million spent in the program has been recovered.

THE POLITICAL PROBLEM

6.32　　It can be argued that the need to preserve the dwindling supply of housing for low-income tenants is sufficiently great to justify expanding the receivership program in spite of the likelihood that the city will never recover the amount of its investment. This argument is made despite the fact that once the building is taken into receivership, the landlord is deprived of all financial incentive to recover his property. Thus, the city becomes the owner-manager of increasing numbers of problem-ridden slum properties while tenants are making their dissatisfactions more vocal and municipal fiscal restraints are becoming more stringent. The potential political consequences of this predicament are evident. New York, for all practical purposes, abandoned the program of housing receivership in 1965.[21]

TENANT RIGHT TO REPAIR AND DEDUCT

THE COMMON LAW RULE

6.33　　At common law the tenant had to keep the premises in repair. This duty included all repair necessary to preserve the property, but did not oblige him to undertake costly construction or to replace any part of the structure that wore out in normal use. The common law rule was developed in an agrarian society when the tenant had control of the landlord's property and was likely to discover the defective condition and to remedy it to prevent waste of the property. Once the tenant took possession the landlord had no right of entry or control of the premises.

6.34   The common law rule imposing the duty of repair on tenants has been nullified or modified by statute in most states. The typical housing code prescribes minimum standards of facilities and maximum occupancy per unit and obliges the landlord to maintain the premises in accordance with those standards. The courts are divided on whether such statutory provisions give the tenant the right to make repairs mentioned by housing codes.

6.35   In some states, if a statute requires the landlord to keep the premises in repair, a tenant may make necessary repairs and deduct the costs from the rent,[22] if the landlord fails to make such repairs after receiving notice of the need. In other states, the statutory obligation of the landlord to repair does not entitle the tenant to make the necessary repairs and deduct the cost from the rent.[23]

LEASE PROVISIONS

6.36   Responsibility for keeping the premises in repair must be negotiated and decided by the landlord and the tenant. Depending upon their respective bargaining positions, this obligation may be imposed upon either party by the terms of the lease.

Effect of Landlord's Agreement To Repair

6.37   When the landlord agrees to keep the premises in repair and fails to do so, the tenant may make the repairs himself and deduct the costs from the rent. Before making the repairs the tenant must notify the landlord of the condition and give him a reasonable time to make the repairs. If the landlord fails to comply with the lease provision, the tenant may deduct all reasonable and necessary expenses incurred in making such repairs.

Effect of Tenant's Agreement To Repair

6.38   The typical apartment lease usually imposes the obligation of repair on the tenant in language such as the following:

2nd. That the tenant shall take good care of the premises and shall at the *tenant's own cost and expense* make all repairs.

3rd. That the tenant shall promptly execute and comply with all statutes, ordinances, rules, orders, regulations and requirements of the Federal, State and City Government and of any and all their Departments and Bureaus applicable to said premises, for the correction, prevention and abate-

111

ment of nuisances, violations or other grievances, in, upon or connected with said premises during said term; and shall also promptly comply with and execute all rules, orders, and regulations of the Board of Fire Underwriters, or any other similar body, for the prevention of fires, at the tenant's own cost and expense.[24]

6.39   If the lease contains an agreement by the tenant to keep the premises in repair at his own cost and expense, he may not deduct the cost of repairs from the rent. Such a provision has been held binding in determining the rights between the landlord and tenant, even though housing codes may impose the duty of repair upon the landlord.[25] The landlord's superior bargaining position, created by the acute shortages of decent dwelling units in urban areas, enables the landlord to shift his obligation to the tenant.

Rent and Deduct Statutes
6.40   A number of states have responded to the need for an explicit law authorizing tenants to deduct the cost of repairs from their rent[26]. The typical "repair and deduct" law provides that if the premises are not fit for human occupancy, and in the absence of an agreement to the contrary, a tenant may deduct from his rent a limited amount of the cost of repairs (usually up to one month's rent) if the landlord fails to make repairs after being given notice and opportunity to repair. In spite of their expressed purpose such statutes fall short of providing an effective tenant remedy for a number of reasons.

Waiver of Rights by Lease Provision
6.41   Most repair and deduct laws are, by express provision, made subject to agreement between the landlord and tenant. In states where repair and deduct statutes have been enacted, the landlord can, and usually does, include a provision in his lease whereby the tenant waives his rights under this law.

Limitations on Deductible Costs
6.42   The expenditures for repair are usually limited to one month's rent or a limited sum of money (e.g., $50 to $100). Such a sum is usually insufficient to make the tenant's apartment habitable and is useful only for the repair of minor defects.

TENANT RIGHT TO CIVIL DAMAGES

6.43   It is arguable that a tenant who, in return for his rent, receives housing accommodations that are unhabitable, may be entitled to damages in a civil suit against the landlord for breach of contract. This legal argument has never developed into an effective tenant remedy for a number of reasons. First, the legal basis for a breach of contract action has been undermined by judicial application of numerous feudal concepts and property law. Second, the measure of damages available in such suit is at best indefinite, and at worst, inadequate. And third, the socioeconomic realities of the landlord-tenant relationship discourage affirmative tenant action against landlords.

THE LEGAL THEORIES FOR CIVIL DAMAGES

6.44   Two possible legal theories upon which a tenant may bring a civil suit for damages against a landlord who provides defective, substandard and unhabitable accommodations are breach of contract and torts (wrongful injury). A breach of contract action rests upon an express or an implied agreement by the landlord to provide and maintain the premises in habitable condition. In the absence of such an agreement, the tenant must prove an implied agreement existed. With few exceptions,[27] the courts have held that there is no implied covenant of habitability in the landlord-tenant agreement, in spite of the criticism by legal scholars that this common law rule is inappropriate and misapplied in an urban society.

6.45   A tenant's action based on tort is equally difficult to sustain. A tort action requires an allegation that the landlord intentionally, negligently or maliciously inflicted harm causing injury to the tenant. This position would be buttressed by an allegation that the landlord's action or inaction is unlawful because it is in violation of the housing codes. The action could be based on any one of several tort theories: negligence, *prima facie* tort or nuisance. All actions would be subject to the defense that the tenant consented to the circumstances that caused the harm and by this consent agreed to assume the risks or waive his right to complain.

THE MEASURE OF DAMAGES

6.46   Even if a court were to accept one of the foregoing theories of a tenant's suit for civil damages, the extent of such damages would be difficult to calculate. Damages for breach of contract are usually measured in terms of the monetary position that the plaintiff would have been in had the contract been fulfilled in accordance with its terms. The tenant's damages, therefore, are calculated as the difference between the fair market value of the premises and the amount of the rent. If it can be shown that in the prevailing market the condition of the premises has been reflected in the amount of the rent, the tenant's damages would be minimal. It is arguable that the tenant's damages for breach of contract should be measured by the costs of repair of the premises. However, the landlord's reply to this argument is that he never agreed to provide such improved conditions for the agreed amount of rent.

SOCIOECONOMIC REALITIES

6.47   Proposals for the expansion of tenant civil suits for damages belie the socioeconomic realities of the landlord-tenant relationship. Tenants who are most in need of a legal remedy to improve unhabitable conditions are least able to engage in the costly and sophisticated legal machinations involved in civil suits for damages. The burden of proof is on the plaintiff; the costs of fees for attorney and expert witnesses are high and every day in court results in the loss of a day's wages. Even if he wins, the amount of the judgment will usually not cover these costs. Whether he wins or not the nature of the controversy will engender strong feelings of hostility and animosity with the landlord. In the absence of an agent strong enough to protect the tenant against retaliatory action by the landlord, tenant civil suits are unlikely to become an effective tenant remedy.

TENANT UNIONS

6.48   The willingness of tenants to submit to substandard housing conditions, onerous lease provisions or no lease at all, is a reflection of the individual tenant's limited bargaining power against a landlord in a housing market characterized by a great demand for, and limited supply of, low-cost housing. The long-term remedy for the inequality in bargaining positions is a substantial increase in the supply of housing. In the meantime, this inequality may be balanced by collective bargaining through tenant unions.[28]

DIFFICULTY IN ORGANIZING TENANTS

6.49   The success of the tenant union movement will depend to a large extent upon the willingness of tenants to join and support a tenant organization to negotiate a collective bargaining agreement with the landlord. In spite of the many potential advantages of a tenant union, organization of tenants has been slow and difficult. Low-income tenants have been particularly reluctant to join. Many distrust and fear such organizations because they have had no previous experience with labor unions; others have been embittered by their labor union experience. Some are fearful of landlord retaliation. The high mobility of low-income tenants caused by uncertain and sporadic employment creates a continuously diminishing membership base. Middle-income tenants are frequently easier to organize when the issues are clear and the grievances acute, but they tend to withdraw and direct their interests elsewhere once their problems are resolved. Both low- and middle-income tenants tend to resent paying union dues, without which the organization cannot function effectively.

UNION BARGAINING TACTICS

6.50   Once organized, a tenant union may exert pressure on a landlord to gain recognition as the tenants' bargaining agent. The most effective weapon at its disposal is the rent strike. The tenant members pay their rent into a union escrow account instead of paying it to the landlord, who then brings a summary eviction proceeding for nonpayment

114

of rent. In the absence of statutory authorization, the union lawyer defends the action by raising the various defenses discussed under Rent Abatement (see 6.13-6.15). Even if the rent must be paid later to avoid execution of an eviction order, the delay in receiving rent, the costs of attorney's fees and the aggravation and frustration of a legal battle with an organized and militant adversary makes the rent strike an effective tactic for gaining recognition as the bargaining agent for all the tenants.

6.51　　At the same time, pressure may be exerted upon the landlord by focusing public and political attention on the tenant grievances by picketing the building and the residence of the landlord. This tactic raised the question whether the picketing may be enjoined on the ground that the purposes of the picketing are unlawful. In a landlord's suit for an injunction, the tenant union will take the position that the picketing is lawful because the purpose is to bring the building up to minimum legal standards prescribed by housing codes and to provide an orderly and lawful procedure for the resolution of tenant grievances. It may be argued further that the lawfulness of these purposes is substantiated by federal legislation calling for "a decent home and a suitable living environment for every American family,"[29] and by the federal legislation providing for community action programs that require "the maximum feasible participation of residents of the areas."[30] One lower court in New York, however, has suggested that picketing to improve housing standards may be unlawful on the grounds that the state legislature had intended that the code enforcement procedures be the *exclusive* tenant remedy to avoid the social disruption associated with picketing.[31]

6.52　　The use of picketing and rent strikes in the battle for recognition of the tenant union frequently intensifies the bitterness and hostility of some tenants. These attitudes often result in unlawful acts. Vandalism and intentional destruction of the landlord's property, even though not sanctioned by the union, may help to persuade the landlord to respond to the tenant union's demand for recognition.

RESPONSE OF THE LANDLORDS

6.53　　The response of the landlord may depend upon the extent of his holding and whether he is a resident owner. However, he will very likely consider the following courses of action in response to tenant unions tactics.

Eviction

6.54　　In the absence of statutory authorization for rent abatement or rent escrow, a tenant who fails to pay rent makes himself liable for eviction. Although the landlord usually cannot afford to bear the loss of wholesale evictions, he may succeed in demoralizing the effort by selective eviction of the strike leadership.

115

Threats and Intimidations

6.55   Many tenants may be induced to withdraw support from the union by threats of retaliation after the strike is over. In tenant union fights for bargaining recognition there is no equivalent of "unfair labor practices" legislation.

Termination of Services

6.56   When the rent is withheld the landlord may cut off the heat, the hot water and elevator service and justify this action on the grounds that he cannot afford to pay for these services without the rental income.

Threats to Abandon the Building

6.57   If the advanced deterioration of the building provides the motive for concerted tenant action, it also lends credence to the landlord's threat to abandon the property. This has become more than an idle threat in some cities where wholesale abandonment by landlords has created even greater hardship on tenants who cannot find substitute accommodations.[32]

Repair of the Premises

6.58   If the property is worth preserving, the landlord may undermine support for a tenant union by improving the maintenance and condition of the building. Once these concessions are made, many tenants lose interest in the union and withdraw their support.

PROVISIONS OF THE UNION CONTRACT

6.59   If the tenant union prevails in its bid for recognition as the collective bargaining agent for the tenants it will seek to negotiate an agreement with the landlord containing the following provisions[33]:

Union Recognition Provisions

6.60   The landlord will agree to recognize the union as exclusive bargaining agent, include union dues in rent and "check-off" payment to union, not discriminate against union members, notify the union of all buildings owned or managed by him, and notify the union of the names of all tenants who move in.

Grievance Procedure Provisions

6.61   The agreement will establish a procedure for the transmission of tenant complaints, arbitration of disputes, and rent withholding upon the landlord's failure to comply.

Substantive Landlord Agreements

6.62   The landlord will agree to make specified repairs and maintenance and maintain a rent scale for the period of the contract.

Substantive Union Agreement

6.63   The union will agree to encourage tenant responsibility and maintenance and to avoid strikes as long as the landlord complies.

116

PROTECTION AGAINST LANDLORD RETALIATION

6.64 A tenant who arouses the antipathy of his landlord places himself in a vulnerable position. Most tenants of substandard apartments occupy them without a lease and without a fixed term (see Chapter 2, discussion of the period of tenancy). Without a lease to limit the rent and insure a continuing term, the landlord is free to raise the rent or terminate the tenancy upon 30 days notice.

6.65 The various tenant remedies have only limited usefulness if the landlord may use his power to raise rent or to evict in retaliation for a tenant's exercise of them. The threat of eviction is an effective deterrent to tenant action for many reasons.[34] Low vacancy rates in most cities make it difficult to find a substitute apartment. Furthermore it is likely that any new apartment within the same rent range will not provide conditions better than the previous one. Third, the tenant fears that he may not be able to get an apartment anywhere if he becomes known as a troublemaker. Finally, the expense of moving can create financial hardships for a low-income tenant. In recent years the courts and the legislatures of some states have responded to the need for some form of tenant protection against a landlord's retaliatory eviction.

JUDICIAL PROTECTION

6.66 In the landmark decision of *Edwards v. Habib*[35] a United States Court of Appeals held that proof of a retaliatory motive is a good defense to an eviction action. The case involved a month-to-month tenant who made complaints concerning code violations to the code enforcement agency. Upon inspection, the enforcement agency found 40 violations and ordered the landlord to make the necessary repairs. The landlord gave the tenant 30 days notice to quit the premises and, thereafter, instituted proceedings to evict. The court held that the tenant had a defense to the eviction action if he could prove that the landlord was evicting him because he reported the housing code violations. The court based its decision on two grounds: *statutory interpretation,* i.e., enforcement of housing codes depends upon tenant's reporting violations, and judicial enforcement of retaliatory eviction would defeat congressional intent; and *public policy,* i.e., the purpose of the housing codes is to protect the health and safety of tenants, and the violations of housing codes are illegal and contrary to this public policy.

6.67 The decision in *Edwards v. Habib* was based upon statutory construction but the opinion contains an extensive discussion of two constitutional issues that were also involved: whether a tenant's right to report housing violation is included under the constitutional right of citizens to petition the government for redress of grievances, and whether there is a constitutional right to inform the government of violations of the law. These constitutional issues have arisen in later cases.

6.68   In *Hosey v. Club van Cordlandt*[36] a United States district court held that evicting a tenant in retaliation for his activities in organizing other tenants to complain of housing code violations is a violation of the Fourteenth Amendment. The case involved a week-to-week tenant in a residential hotel who met with other tenants in his room to consider making complaints to the code enforcement agency. The landlord notified the tenant that his room had been let to another tenant beginning one week from the date of notice. When the landlord threatened to bring eviction proceedings, the tenant brought suit in a federal court to enjoin the landlord from bringing such proceedings. The court held that the tenant's right to organize other tenants to improve the conditions of the building is included within the First Amendment rights of freedom of speech and assembly and is made binding against the states by the Fourteenth Amendment.

6.69   There are limits to which the court will go in protecting a tenant. In *Wheeler Terrace v. Sylvester*[37] a Court of General Sessions for the District of Columbia held that the principle of *Edwards v. Habib* would not protect tenants who organized a tenant council to *take over* the apartment building by bringing economic pressure on the landlord through rent strikes. The court held that the landlord's need to protect his ownership of a building was a legally valid reason for eviction. In its opinion the court stated that the tenants' rights of free speech cannot be exercised to disturb the landlord's right of peaceful enjoyment of his property.

LEGISLATIVE PROTECTION

6.70   The judicial response to retaliatory evictions leaves many questions unanswered. If a landlord may not evict a tenant for a retaliatory motive, how long may the tenant remain in possession? What are the rights of the landlord when the tenant's complaints are unfounded? What are the rights of the landlord if the conditions are caused by the tenant, or if the landlord wants to recover possession for his own use or for a bona fide sale?

6.71   The few states[38] that have enacted legislation have failed to deal with such questions in a comprehensive manner. The New Jersey provisions make a landlord's reprisal against a tenant a criminal offense punishable by fines of up to $250 or six months in jail, or both. If a tenant receives a notice to quit within 90 days after he makes a complaint, he can argue that the landlord's eviction is retaliatory.

6.72   The New Jersey statute and the Illinois and Maryland legislation do not resolve the many subsidiary problems that arise out of an allegation of landlord retaliation. The Model Code's provisions (Sec. 2-407), on the other hand, provide that a tenant may not be evicted, or his rent raised *for six months* after complaining, in good faith, to the code enforcement agency. However, the code provides for various circumstances under which the landlord may recover possession in spite of a tenant's complaints. For example, the landlord may use the premises for himself. The code also permits him to increase the rent in spite of the tenant's previous complaint, under various circumstances, such as a substantial increase in taxes or other operating costs or a substantial capital improvement. The *Model Code* rejects the New Jersey method of enforcement through criminal sanctions. Instead it gives the tenant the right to recover three months rent or triple damages, whichever is greater, plus a reasonable attorney's fee, if the landlord evicts the tenant in violation of protective provisions.

EVALUATIONS OF TENANT REMEDIES

6.73 The various tenant remedies described in this chapter were created in response to the tenant's need for legal principles that define the responsibility of landlords and tenants in an urban society. The common law principle of independence of covenants and the lease provisions that require a tenant to pay rent in spite of the landlord's failure to maintain minimum standards have caused tenants to seek to surmount these obsolete legal impediments (see Chapter 5). The need for direct and concerted tenant action could be minimized by revision of the law to establish the dependency of the tenant's obligation to maintain minimum standards. Once this underlying *legal* cause of contention is resolved, constructive efforts must be made to improve the procedures by which rental income is used to repair and maintain the property.

Use of Existing Standards and Procedures
6.74 The National Commission on Urban Problems[39] has proposed a number of criteria for evaluating the usefulness of tenant remedies.

Use of Existing Standards and Procedures
6.75 It would be confusing to create different minimum standards than those already prescribed in existing housing and health codes. Whether those standards have been violated should be determined by the code enforcement agency rather than by the courts or by any other tribunal that may not have the necessary technical competence.

Sufficient Supervision of the Use of Rents for Repairs
6.76 The success of any technique of tenant remedy must ultimately be judged upon its effective use of rent monies to improve housing. It is questionable whether the tenants or the court have the competence to supervise the process of alteration and repair. If a receiver or administrator is appointed by the court he must have sufficient expertise to justify his compensation.

Making the Remedy Appropriate to the Conditions
6.77 Under some circumstances the threat of rent abatement may induce the landlord to maintain and repair the premises. Under other

circumstances the funds accumulated through rent escrow may be sufficient to improve the conditions. However, either remedy may cause the landlord to abandon the property if he has no incentive to continue his ownership.

Long-Range Improvement of Landlord-Tenant Relationships
6.78 The remedy selected should insure that the collective action results in reasonable and constructive tenant attitudes and their appreciation of the economic factors that have caused the property to deteriorate.

NOTES

1. *E.g.,* Schoshinski, *Remedies of the Indigent Tenant: Proposal for Change,* 54 *Geo. L.J.* 519, 523(1966).

2. 14 Wis. 2d 590, 111 N.W.2d 490(1961).

3. For court's language see 3.4, 3.5.

4. For a good discussion of this area see *The Indigent Tenant and the Doctrine of Constructive Eviction,* 1968 *Wash. U.L.Q.* 461.

5. Schoshinski, *supra* note 1, at 529.

6. 61 N.Y.S.2d 195(1946).

7. *Magen, supra* note 6, at 196-7.

8. See *e.g. Leases and the Illegal Contract Theory—Judicial Enforcement of the Housing Code,* 56 *Geo. L.J.* 920(1968).

9. Schoshinski, *supra* note 1, at 538.

10. *Mass. Ann. Laws* c. 239, Sec. 8a.

11. *Pa. Stat. Ann.* tit. 35, Sec. 1700-1.

12. Article 7a(1965).

13. *E.g.,* E. Gribitz, *New York City's Receivership Law,* 21 *J. of Housing* 297 (1964).

14. F. Grad, *Legal Remedies for Housing Code Violations* pp. 46-48 (The National Comm. on Urban Problems Research Report No. 14 1968).

15. New York Sess. Laws, L. 1937 c. 353.

16. 279 N.Y. 266, 18 N.E.2d 151(1938).

17. *N.Y. Mult. Dwell. Law,* Sec. 309, as amended by L. 1962, c. 492(1962).

18. 14 N.Y.2d 291, 200 N.E.2d 432(1964).

19. N.Y. Sess. Laws L. 1965 c. 144, & c. 919.

20. *Supra* note 14.

21. *Supra* note 14, at 43.

22. Henley v. Brockman, 124 Ga. 1059, 53 S.E. 672(1906).

23. Susskind v. 1136 Tenants Corp., 251 N.Y.S.2d 321, 43 Misc. 2d 588(1964).

24. Blumberg's Improved Gilsey Form of Lease is in widespread use in New Jersey and New York.

25. Pubringer v. Del Monte, 217 N.Y.S.2d 792(1961).

26. *Calif. Civ. Code* Sec. 1941-42; *Mont. Rev. Codes Ann.* Sec. 42-201(Supp. 1947); *N.Y. Cent.* Code Sec. 47-16-12, 13(Supp. 1960); *Okla. Stat.* tit. 41, Sec. 31-32(1952); and *S.D. Code* Sec. 38-0409-.10(1939).

27. Pines *supra* note 2.

28. R. Coulson, *The Tenant Union—New Institution or Abrasive Failure,* 14 *The Practical Lawyer* 23(1968); *Tenant Unions: Collective Bargaining and the Low Income Tenant,* 77 *Yale L.J.* 1368(1968).

29. Housing Act of 1949, 42 U.S.C. Sec. 1441(1964).

30. Econ. Opport. Act, 42 U.S.C. Sec. 2782(a) (1964).

31. Springfield, Bayside Corp. v. Hochman, 255 N.Y.S.2d 140, 44 Misc. 2d 882(1960); *But see* Dicta Realty Assoc. v. Shaw, 270 N.Y.S.2d 342, 50 Misc. 2d 267(1966).

32. Over 33,000 housing units were abandoned in 1969 in New York City where the vacancy rate is below 1 percent. The national vacancy rate is 4.6 percent. The Wall Street Journal, Dec. 2, 1970, at 1, col. 6.

33. 77 *Yale L.J.* 1368, 1395(1968).

34. *Protection for Citizen Complaints to Public Authorities—Prohibition of Retaliatory Evictions,* 48 *Neb. L.R.* 1101, 1106(1969).

35. 397 F.2d 687 D.L. Cir., *cert.* denied 393 U.S. 1016(1969).

36. 299 F. Supp. 501(S.D. N.Y. 1969).

37. D.C. Gen Sess. L & T, (1969).

38. Illinois, Maryland & *N.J. Stat. Ann.* 2A.170-92.1.

39. *Supra* note 14, at 146.

7 Public Landlords
and Their Tenants

CHARACTERISTICS OF PUBLIC LANDLORDS

CREATION OF THE PUBLIC HOUSING PROGRAM

7.1   The public housing program, created by the U.S. Housing Act of 1937, was part of the New Deal legislation designed to relieve unemployment and to stimulate the economy through increased construction. In addition, the public housing program was designed to provide adequate shelter for low-income families, or more accurately, the newly submerged middle-class.[1] It represented an attempt to close the gap in the private housing market, which private enterprise was unable to do without government subsidy.

7.2   The 1937 Act created the U.S. Housing Authority[2] as the administrative body of a decentralized program. The Authority was not to plan, build or manage the projects, but to provide loans to the local public housing agencies (PHA), for up to 90 percent of the development costs of a project.[3] The PHA, "and State, county, municipality, or other governmental agency which is authorized to engage in the development or administration of a low-rent housing or slum clearance,"[4] retained discretion concerning whether to enter the program and what number of units to build. The main contribution of the federal government was to provide financial assistance, primarily through annual contributions contracts, for the amortization of the costs of acquisition and development. Operating expenses were to be covered by the tenants' rent payments. In addition, the authority exercised some control over the form and administration of local housing programs.[5]

123

7.3　　　Altered several times since 1937, the present public housing program consists of a "conventional" program, established by the 1937 and 1949 Housing Acts, which provides for large projects planned and constructed through the PHAs; and "new" programs developed in the 1960s, including the scattered-site projects, acquisition of "used" housing for rehabilitation, leasing and Turnkey projects.[6]

GEOGRAPHIC DISTRIBUTION OF PUBLIC HOUSING AGENCIES

Nationally
7.4　　　The public landlord owns and operates housing in every state, and in the U.S. territories and commonwealths of Guam, Puerto Rico and the Virgin Islands. By the end of 1968, approximately 1,721 local authorities were managing public housing projects totaling 744,496 units or 1.3 percent of all the housing units in the country. If one includes low-rent programs whose applications are under consideration and those under planning prior to construction, the figure increases to 2,340 local housing authorities involved in providing 1,066,952 units of low-rent housing in 3,174 localities.

State Comparisons
7.5　　　The number of PHAs within a state is not always proportional to the number of units within that state. The greatest concentration of PHAs is generally in the southern states, while the states with the largest metropolitan populations usually have more units under management. While there are 69 local authorities in New York, 78 in Michigan, 80 in Illinois, 55 in Pennsylvania and 60 in California, there are 293 in Texas, 137 in Alabama, 193 in Georgia, 103 in Kentucky and 91 in Arkansas. There were 230,943 total units, or 31 percent of all units under management, in the four states of California, Illinois, New York and Pennsylvania, but five southern states (Alabama, Georgia, Texas, Kentucky and Arkansas) had only slightly more than half that total under management, (129,495 units). Furthermore, the states with the smallest number of local housing agencies are the northern New England states of Vermont, New Hampshire and Maine, and the north central states of Montana, Idaho, North Dakota. South Dakota and Wyoming. In addition, the District of Columbia has only one PHA, but about the same number of units as Connecticut or Maryland.

Comparison by Size of Cities
7.6　　　The Report of the National Commission on Urban Problems points out that participation in low-rent, public housing increases as the size of the city increases. Ninety percent of the cities with populations between 100,000 and 250,000 have, or are planning, public housing projects. Among the 52 cities with populations of 250,000 and over, only San Diego has no public housing.[8] All cities with one million or more persons are participating in the program.

Table 1

NUMBER OF LOCALITIES INVOLVED IN FEDERAL PUBLIC HOUSING,
DECEMBER 1967 (INCLUDING PUERTO RICO AND THE VIRGIN ISLANDS)
CLASSIFIED BY SIZE[9]

Population of Localities With Public Housing			Number of Localities With Public Housing	Percent of Localities With Public Housing
Under 2,500			1,177	8
2,500	to	5,000	473	22
5,000	to	10,000	406	29
10,000	to	25,000	401	35
25,000	to	50,000	198	46
50,000	to	100,000	133	66
100,000	to	250,000	74	90
250,000	to	500,000	31	100
500,000	to	1,000,000	15	94
Over 1,000,000			5	100
Total			2,913	14

Table 2

PUBLIC HOUSING UNITS UNDER MANAGEMENT IN THE 15 LARGEST CITIES
IN THE UNITED STATES (SEPTEMBER 30, 1967)[11]

City (Ordered by Decreasing Population)	Number of Units	Percentage of 15-City Total*
New York, New York	64,157	31.3
Chicago, Illinois	32,431	15.8
Los Angeles, California	9,198	4.5
Philadelphia, Pennsylvania	15,223	7.4
Detroit, Michigan	8,180	4.0
Baltimore, Maryland	10,314	5.0
Houston, Texas	2,562	1.2
Cleveland, Ohio	7,458	3.6
Washington, D.C.	9,773	4.8
St. Louis, Missouri	7,014	3.4
Milwaukee, Wisconsin	3,066	1.5
San Francisco, California	5,808	2.8
Boston, Massachusetts	10,857	5.3
Dallas, Texas	6,372	3.1
New Orleans, Louisiana	12,270	6.0
Total	204,683	99.7

*Units under management.

125

7.7 Similarly, the number of public housing units is proportional to the size of the locality. Cities with populations under 10,000 account for 13 percent of all public housing units; those with populations between 10,000 and 100,000 have 28 percent of all public housing. Cities with populations of 100,000 to 500,000 and those with more than half a million persons have 26 and 33 percent of the public housing units, respectively.[10]

7.8 A closer examination of 15 of the largest U.S. cities, all of which have populations over half a million, indicates wide variations in the number of their public housing units. New York and Chicago maintain the greatest number of units, with 64,157 and 32,431 units respectively, or 47 percent of the 15-city total. Furthermore, Boston and New Orleans, two of the smallest cities in this category, have larger programs than Houston or Detroit.

PUBLIC HOUSING AGENCY COMPARISON BY NUMBER OF UNITS

7.9 The size of the public housing program, in terms of the number of units administered by the individual local housing agency, is generally small or moderate. Table 3 presents the number of PHAs classified by the size of the program. Note that 30 percent of the local housing agencies administer programs with less than 50 units, while 36 percent administer programs with 100 to 500 units. Only one out of seven PHAs manages programs with more than 500 units.

Table 3

NUMBER OF PUBLIC AUTHORITIES CLASSIFIED
BY SIZE OF PROGRAM[12]*

Size of Program	Number of PHAs	Percentage
Less than 50 units	656	30.5
50 to 100 units	431	20.0
100 to 500 units	773	35.8
Over 500 units	296	12.7
Total	2,156	100.0

CHARACTERISTICS OF TENANTS
OF PUBLIC LANDLORDS

7.10 By the end of 1967, about 2.4 million persons, a little more than 1 percent of the total population or a little less than 2 percent of the population in the SMSAs, lived in public housing.[13]

126

INCOME

Statutory Qualifications Concerning Income Level

7.11   The 1937 Public Housing Act restricted occupancy to "families of low income," defined as "families who are in the lowest income group and who cannot afford to pay enough to cause private enterprise in their locality or metropolitan area to build an adequate supply of decent, safe and sanitary dwellings for their use."[14] The 1949 Act further defined these requirements by specifying a 20 percent gap between "the upper limits for admission to the proposed low-rent housing and the lowest rents at which private enterprise unaided by public subsidy is providing (through new construction and available existing structures) a substantial supply of decent, safe and sanitary housing."[15]

7.12   In addition, the financial requirements imposed upon local housing authorities forced them to set rents higher than some poor families or persons were able to pay. Eight to 10 percent of the urban population may be excluded because their income falls below qualifying levels.

Personal Income

7.13   The median incomes of all public housing tenants who have lived in public housing more than one year are shown in Table 4.

Table 4

MEDIAN INCOME OF PUBLIC HOUSING OCCUPANTS[17]

Year	Average Annual Income All Family Occupants of Public Housing	Constant Dollars of Purchasing Power (1957-1959 as Base Year)
1956	$ 2,256	$ 2,382
1961	2,418	2,321
1965	2,577	2,345
1966	2,709	2,395

INCOME DIFFERENTIALS

7.14   If the median income of the elderly and nonelderly families in public housing are compared wide disparities become evident (see Table 5). There is, however, little variation according to race.

7.15   Aside from the income differential between the elderly and nonelderly, there is a regional differential. Northern and western families living in public housing have higher incomes than similar families in the South.

Table 5

MEDIAN INCOMES FOR ELDERLY AND NONELDERLY FAMILIES IN PUBLIC
HOUSING RE-EXAMINED FOR CONTINUED OCCUPANCY DURING
JANUARY 1-SEPTEMBER 30, 1968, BY RACE[18]

| | | Race | |
	All	White	Negro and Other
Elderly	$ 1,658	$ 1,630	$ 1,715
Nonelderly	3,532	3,509	3,540

Conclusions[19]

7.16

1. The majority of residents of public housing are "poor," according to the 1968 Social Security Administration income limit of $3,553 for a family of four,

2. Public housing tenants have not benefited tremendously from cost-of-living increases; their real purchasing power has remained the same;

3. The vast majority of elderly tenants exist on extremely low incomes, relying heavily on relief money and social security payments. During the ten years between 1956 and 1966, the proportion of elderly tenants in the total inventory of public housing units increased sharply, thereby keeping the median income figures low.

WELFARE AND OTHER ASSISTANCE

Statutory Requirements

7.17 Regulations pertaining to welfare recipients' eligibility for public housing varied during the program's first 25 years. Initially, welfare recipients were excluded; in 1949, the law was amended to declare that local agencies must "not discriminate against families, otherwise eligible for admission . . . because their incomes are derived in whole or in part from public assistance."[20] This amendment was repealed in 1961, but the following data show that welfare tenants are accepted in sizeable proportions. However, as L. Friedman emphasizes, "the ideal remains strong that in a healthy housing project and in a healthy society members of the deserving, working poor predominate."[21]

Assistance and Benefits According to Age

7.18 Table 6 presents the proportion of public housing tenants receiving assistance and benefits by age. All but 5 percent of the elderly tenant families receive some form of assistance or benefits, primarily old age, survivors and disability insurance. Only 40 percent of the nonelderly families receive welfare or benefits, primarily family assistance. There are small variations with regard to race, but a slightly greater percentage of white than nonwhite elderly tenant families receive assistance or benefits.

Table 6

LOW-RENT PUBLIC HOUSING: ASSISTANCE AND BENEFITS RECEIVED BY ELDERLY AND NONELDERLY FAMILIES BY RACE, RE-EXAMINED FOR CONTINUED OCCUPANCY DURING THE PERIOD JANUARY 1-SEPTEMBER 30, 1968[22]

Assistance and Benefits	Total	White	Negro and Other
Nonelderly			
Receiving Assistance or Benefits	40	39	40
Assistance With or Without Benefits	30	27	32
Benefits Only	9	12	8
Not Receiving Assistance or Benefits	60	61	60
Elderly			
Receiving Assistance or Benefits	95	96	92
Assistance With or Without Benefits	38	32	49
Benefits Only	57	65	43
Not Receiving Assistance or Benefits	5	4	8

Note: *Assistance*—funds given on the basis of need by organization, some private, but primarily public. *Benefits*—nonsalary funds not given on the basis of need by government agencies.

OTHER PERSONAL CHARACTERISTICS

7.19   The initial public housing program of 1937 was designed for the temporarily submerged or potential middle class, those suffering from the misfortunes of the Depression. After the war, however, increased incomes and the advent of suburban housing and FHA/VA financing caused the middle class to abandon public housing and, subsequently, the character of the public housing tenantry changed. As the southern rural migration to the North and West increased, the proportion of Negro tenants also increased. Furthermore, public housing was attracting more of the dependent poor and "problem" families.

Age
7.20   The elderly have come to constitute an increasingly large proportion of the units in public housing. In 1963, the percentage of units occupied by the elderly was 25 percent; in 1968, 36 percent. This appears to be the predominant trend of the future. Looking at the number and kind of low-rent public housing starts in recent years, one finds that approximately 50 percent or more of them have been *specifically* for the elderly.[23] Certain states apparently emphasize this type of public housing. In Iowa, for example, 98 percent of total occupied units were occupied by elderly persons at the end of 1968. Other states with high percentages of elderly tenants are Idaho, 62 percent; Minnesota, 63 percent; Nebraska, 65 percent; and Vermont 75 percent.

7.21   The median age of the nonelderly head of household is 37 years. The white head of household is generally younger than the non-white, 35 and 39 years respectively. Less than 10 percent of all the heads of household are under 25.

Family Size
7.22   Elderly households are predominately one- and two-person households; the former are almost twice as prevalent as the latter. Only 15 percent of the elderly households include minors.

7.23   In contrast, the mean number of persons in the nonelderly household is 4.5 and the mean number of minors is three. However, among tenants with minors, 22 percent have five or more minors. There is a greater proportion of white than nonwhite households with no minors. In addition, nonwhite households have a larger number of minors per household. Among the public housing regions, Puerto Rico has the highest mean number of minors and persons per household, 3.4 and 5.3 respectively.[24]

Family Structure
7.24   There is an upward trend in the proportion of "broken" families with female heads. Among the tenants "reexamined" for continued occupancy in 1966, 42.4 percent were members of "broken" families, almost all of which were headed by a female head. Among the new entrants to public housing, the proportion was 48 percent.[25]

Prior Residence

7.25   The process of slum clearance was incorporated into the Housing Act of 1937 as a complementary process to low-rent public housing construction. It was not until the 1949 Housing Act, however, that those low-income families "displaced by any low-rent housing project" were to be given first priority among low-income families eligible for public housing.

7.26   Most families who moved into public housing from January 1 to September 30, 1968, previously lived in substandard housing, yet had not been displaced, one out of every four was previously without housing;[26] another 14 percent came from standard housing; and 8 percent of the former residences were unknown.

7.27   Eleven percent of the new families had been displaced from an urban renewal or HAA site, or another displacement program. A little less than half of these families were previously living in substandard housing; 43 percent were without housing; and less than 5 percent were in standard housing. Furthermore, over twice as many nonwhites as whites have entered public housing as a result of displacement.[27]

Length of Residence and Mobility

7.28   The rate of physical mobility for public housing tenants is below that of the population at large; it is slightly greater than 16 percent annually. These families presumably leave either because they have exceeded the maximum income limits for admission or are dissatisfied with this type of housing. This turnover is particularly high in certain cities, such as Los Angeles (39 percent), San Antonio (34 percent), Phoenix (46 percent), Kansas City (32 percent) and Jersey City (39 percent).   In contrast, New York and Chicago, the cities with the largest number of units, have the lowest tenant mobility rate, 5.7 percent and 9.9 percent respectively.

7.29   Among those families and individuals reexamined and determined to be within the income limits in 1968, slightly more than four out of every five persons, both elderly and nonelderly, had lived in public housing for ten years or more. Approximately 45 percent had lived in their units for three years or less. This data also showed that a larger proportion of nonwhites than whites have lived in public housing for ten years or more.[28]

Race

7.30   The proportion of public housing units occupied by Negro families has steadily increased since 1956. In 1967, 50.5 percent of all tenant families were black, compared to 43.6 percent in 1956 (see Table 7).

Table 7
PERCENTAGE OF NEGRO TENANTS IN PUBLIC HOUSING[29]

Year	Percentage Which Negro Families Formed of All Tenant Families.
1956	43.6%
1961	47.4
1965	49.7
1966	50.2
1967	50.5

The total nonwhite figure of public housing occupancy has been estimated at 55 percent of all families and between 59 and 60 percent of all persons.

7.31   A slightly different sample of all nonwhite residents highlights regional differences. While the Chicago and Philadelphia areas were slightly higher than the national average, San Francisco was very much below the average, and New York and Atlanta were slightly below the national average. As the Douglas Commission stated, these variations may be partially accounted for by the varying proportions of nonwhites in the different areas.[30]

7.32   There is some variation with regard to age. Of the elderly residents, a greater number are white; however, it is "more common for Negro families in the active years of life to have recourse to public housing than for whites."[31]

National Origin
7.33   The proportion of public housing tenants from minority groups (Negro, Mexican-American, Puerto Rican and other nonwhites) in projects in the continental United States is between 60 and 66 percent. The Douglas Commission further estimated that the proportion of persons of Anglo-Saxon and European background did not exceed 40 percent and might be as low as 33 percent. Anglo-Saxon and European backgrounds are common among the elderly, but occur in less than one-third of all the children.[32]

Social Criteria
7.34   Social criteria governing the admission of otherwise eligible applicants vary among local authorities. Although most authorities do not adopt arbitrary criteria for exclusion, many applicants with "questionable social histories" are thoroughly screened and "those with behavioral patterns or housekeeping standards which are considered potentially harmful or distasteful to other tenants" are excluded. For example, prostitution, drug addiction or "pushing," extreme alcoholism, child molestation, rape

or attempted rape, assault and battery, or pregnancy in unmarried girls under 18 (or 20) may lead to exclusion.[33]

TENANT ATTITUDES TOWARD THE PUBLIC LANDLORD

Housing Management

7.35   Many of the problems and complaints concerning public housing management and design have created resentment between the tenant and landlord. In a report prepared for the National Commission on Urban Problems, however, survey results indicated that the tenants believe these problems could be corrected by the local housing authorities and management within the existing financial formula. This same survey indicated that administrators and managers do not agree with the tenants; they do not believe that the problems are correctable within the existing subsidy formula and social policy of accepting all eligible applicants regardless of social behavior and life style.[34]

Condition of Premises

7.36   The major areas of dissatisfaction among tenants in public housing involve the absence of community facilities, the inadequacy of laundry facilities, delays in maintenance services, numerous service charges and, for those in highrise buildings, the inadequacy of elevator service. While the increased operating expenses and financial problems and deficits of many of the PHAs have caused cuts or delays in maintenance services, most other complaints stem from initial poor design or planning complications. Most criticisms of the size and type of projects and highrise building concern the needs of families with minors. In contrast, regardless of construction size or type, housing designed for the elderly elicits few criticisms.[36]

Administrative Practices

7.37   Another primary cause of tenant discontent with the public landlord stems from administrative practices that seem arbitrary to the tenants. The complaints focused upon

> . . . management procedures in issuing rent notices or instituting eviction procedures, the (frequent) demand for income reports, the system for computing incomes and setting rents, the alleged discourtesies of management staff and the failure of management to control the behavior of some tenant families or groups of teenagers.[37]

7.38   Tenants have organized themselves into groups to effectively support their claims and to bring lawsuits against unfair rules and unfair governance.[38] Although complaints are lodged against several administrative practices, most tenants do not appear discontented with the dwelling units or the rents charged. Almost all agreed that the dwellings and rents represented a "much better bargain" than the other alternatives available to them.[39]

133

Vandalism

7.39   Vandalism and the lack of security protection are frequent complaints of all tenants in public housing, but particularly among those in highrise projects. Some project tenants have formed their own nighttime security force.

NOTES

1. L. Friedman, *Government and Slum Housing: A Century of Frustration,* at 106 (1968).

2. The U.S. Housing Authority is now the Housing Assistance Administration.

3. The Authority was not barred from owning and managing projects, but it did not build them. Those units owned by HAA are primarily those inherited from the PWA. Friedman *supra* note 1, at 106.

4. U.S. Housing Act of 1937, 42 U.S.C. Sec. 1401 (1964).

5. Friedman *supra* note 1, at 106.

6. *More Than Shelter,* George Schermer Associates (Prepared for the consideration of the National Commission on Urban Problems Research Report No. 8, 1968).

7. Data gathered from HAA Tables 10 and 13, 1968 *HUD Statistical Yearbook* at 251, 254.

8. *Building the American City,* Report of the National Commission on Urban Problems to the Congress and the President of the United States, at 112 (1968(.

9. *Id.* at 112.

10. *Id.* at 113.

11. *Id.* at 113.

12. *Id.* at 113.

13. *Id.* at 114.

14. U.S. Housing Act of 1937, 50 Stat. 888, 42 U.S.C. 1402.

15. Housing Act of 1949, 63 Stat. 422 (1949), 42 U.S.C.A. Sec. 1415 (7)(b)(i). In 1966, these maximum income standards for occupancy caused the eviction of one out of every 30 families, *Building the American City supra* note 8, at 116.

16. *Building the American City supra* note 8, at 116.

17. *Id.* at 115.

18. HAA Tables 36 & 39, 1968 *HUD Statistical Yearbook* at 272.

19. *Building the American City supra* note 8, at 115, 116.

20. U.S. Housing Act of 1949 *supra* note 15.

21. Friedman *supra* note 1, at 109.

22. HAA Tables 30-35, 43, 1968 *HUD Statistical Yearbook,* at 268-272.

23. *Building the American City supra* note 8, at 114.

24. HAA Tables 30-35, 1968 *HUD Statistical Yearbook,* at 268-272.

25. *More Than Shelter supra* note 6, at 30.

26. The "without housing" category includes all those persons who were temporarily living in a hotel, where subtenants did not have a *bona fide* residence, whose homes were burned-out, who were given notice of eviction, who literally had no previous home, or who gave no definite knowledge of being without a home.

27. HAA Table 21, 1968 *HUD Statistical Yearbook,* at 261.

28. *Id.* Tables 44, 45, at 278; *Building the American City, supra* note 8, at 131.
29. *Building the American City supra* note 8, at 114.
30. *Id.* at 114.
31. *Id.* at 115.
32. *Id.* at 114.
33. *More Than Shelter supra* note 6, at 76.
34. *Id.* at 74.
35. *Id.* at 74.
36. *Id.* at 73.
37. *Id.* at 74.
38. Such activities have taken place in the larger metropolitan areas such as New York, San Francisco and Syracuse; Friedman, *supra* note 1, at 183.
39. *More Than Shelter supra* note 6, at 74.

8 The Government as Landlord

PUBLIC HOUSING PROGRAMS

THE STATUTORY FRAMEWORK OF FEDERAL POLICY

8.1   As early as 1937 the federal government outlined a policy "to remedy the unsafe and unsanitary housing conditions and the acute shortage of decent, safe and sanitary dwellings for families of low income . . . that are injurious to the health, safety and morals of the citizens of the Nation."[1] The object of this federal legislation was to provide public housing for people who, by the nature of their economic class,

137

were least capable of securing a "decent, safe and sanitary dwelling." Judging from the language of the 1937 Housing Act, the federal housing program was structured upon factors of economic class, regardless of the social background attached to class. Congress made this explicit when it defined the scope of the low-rent housing program as providing "safe, and sanitary dwellings within the financial reach of families of low income. . . ."[2]

8.2   Congress reasserted its concern for the housing conditions of the nation in a more definitive manner when, in 1949, it enunciated a "national housing policy."[3] In this more inclusive statement of federal intent, Congress expressed its legislative purpose as "the realization as soon as possible of the goal of a decent home and a suitable living environment for every American family. . . ."

8.3   Although the 1949 act indicated broad objectives, the language continued to emphasize Congressional concern with the blighted conditions of slum living.[4] Furthermore, the Congressional perspective was expanded to include the social environment and "community development"[5] as part and parcel of federal concern with domestic social policy.

8.4   After operating for over 15 years under a nascent policy directed toward public housing alone, Congress set forth a comprehensive statement of intent "to eliminate the paradox of poverty in the midst of plenty in the Nation by opening to everyone the opportunity to work, and the opportunity to live in decency and dignity."[6] In a much-heralded "war on poverty," Congress resolved to ameliorate a broad range of social conditions which contribute to poverty.

8.5   While the original legislation recognized only the lack of a suitable dwelling as a condition of deprivation, by 1964 Congressional policy identified poverty as inseparable from the physical decay of slums. Such a recognition must be interpreted as inferring a Congressional intent for active federal involvement in the operation of public housing. It is the discrepancy between this national policy, and the more parochial application of local authorities that is the focus of this chapter.

THE STATUTORY FRAMEWORK OF OPERATIVE PROVISIONS

8.6   The Housing Act of 1937, as amended,[7] provides for the administering of a low-rent public housing program. Under the 1937 statute, housing is built, operated and owned by a Local Housing Authority (LHA), which is established as a public corporation under state housing authority laws. Ownership and subsidy of housing exists in various combinations: locally owned and federally sponsored; locally owned and federally and state sponsored.

8.7   The federal housing program is administered through the

138

Housing Assistance Administration (HAA), an agency of the Department of Housing and Urban Development (HUD). HAA is the successor of the Public Housing Authority (PHA). The HAA and LHA enter into an Annual Contributions Contract (ACC), for the operation and maintenance of housing providing decent living conditions. The ACC translates the purposes and provisions of the law into specific contractual obligations and mutual responsibilities with respect to the development, operation and fiscal aspects of the program, as well as with respect to defaults, breaches, remedies and general provisions. The ACC establishes and defines specific contractual rights and obligations of HUD and the LHA in their joint undertaking to achieve and maintain the low-rent character of the projects. In return for loans and subsidies provided for in the ACC, the LHA agrees to comply with the requirements for maintaining decent, safe and sanitary dwellings,[8] in accordance with federal statutory policy.

FEDERAL DIRECTIVES, REGULATIONS

8.8   Public housing projects across the nation are not directly regulated by Congressional statute. Although the administration of projects must not contravene express statutory provisions, the federal legislation is sufficiently nonspecific to allow a great deal of discretion on the part of local officials.

8.9   Congress administers public housing programs through its administrative agencies. These agencies regulate local projects through administrative rules, regulations and guidelines. But administrative law does not always afford a right or impose a duty upon which a tenant may base a legal claim.

8.10   The responsibility for operating the housing project lies with the LHA.[9] However, HUD, in various publications, provides supervisory guidelines and mandatory directives which are further clarified by the HAA. Unfortunately, rather than developing coherent programs intended to cope with deterioration and obsolescence, the chief concerns of the directives, until recently, have been technical procedures and mechanics of repair and maintenance.[10]

DELEGATION TO THE LHA

8.11   The federal government, through the HAA, has pursued a policy of granting great discretionary authority to the LHA in matters of operation and maintenance. The overall policy of the HAA has been not to impose any rigorous standards for the operation of housing projects. This is partially due to the practical necessity of flexibility where detailed managing techniques are employed. Principally, however, the HAA has been concerned about promoting public housing as an economically viable operation. To operate with a degree of economic autonomy, LHAs have required maximum discretion to maintain solvency. HAA concern has focused, at least until recently, on the profitable operation of the projects, and the use of profits, termed "residual receipts," to reduce the government's annual guaranteed contributions.[11]

8.12   The principal HAA control against LHA mismanagement is periodic inspections and reports. However, the administrative policy toward enforcement of existing regulations in cases of noncompliance has been one of *laissez-faire*. The HAA operates under the theory that tenant complaints regarding improper maintenance can be more expeditiously resolved at the local level. If the HAA does become involved with tenant complaints, it prefers to encourage "voluntary compliance" by the LHA.[12] In practice, however, HAA intervention has generally been reserved for cases of blatant violation of federal statutory policy. Thus, failure to comply with regulations usually results in recommendations to the LHA and ultimately greater exhortation.

8.13   The laws determining tenant eligibility standards have also moved toward increasing federal noninvolvement. The 1937 act provided that certain tenants be given preferential admissions by LHAs,[13] such as hardship cases, including those displaced through urban renewal or housing condemnation. The Housing Act of 1959 amended this policy, adding that

> it is the policy of the United States to vest in the local public housing agencies the maximum amount of responsibility in the administration of the low-rent housing program, including responsibility for the establishment of rents and eligibility requirements (subject to the approval of the [Federal] Authority), with due consideration to accomplishing objectives of this Act while effecting economies.[14]

8.14   The trend towards greater LHA discretion in determining eligibility was consummated under the Housing Act of 2072.[15] With the abolition of explicit tenant selection preferences, the ACC wording merely provided that the LHAs should "give full consideration"[16] to such needy classes of applicants. The act had a more far-reaching implication, however, for LHA officials interpreted it as a grant of absolute discretion in determining general eligibility standards.[17]

8.15   To create an administratively flexible and economically viable housing program, Congress delegated much of the control over the managerial and operational aspects of housing projects. However, the 1959 and 1961 laws, which abolished preferences for certain classes of applicants, have been unjustly interpreted by local officials as conferring authority to disregard the economic needs of applicants and tenants. The statutory language generally seems to maintain income as the primary criterion for eligibility, despite the inferences of maximum administrative discretion. The legal specifications of preferences for eligibility were probably updated to eliminate obsolete classes of preference (i.e., veterans), while still maintaining the basic policies aimed at social and economic deprivation. They probably also are supposed to delegate more discretion in the operation and maintenance of public housing in order to make housing programs more self-sustaining. These two Congressional goals appear to have been thought interdependent. Local authorities, however, have emphasized the latter at the expense of the former.

8.16 Federal *laissez-faire* in the regulation of public housing has not transpired without the development of several undesirable local management practices.[18] In the first of these, eligibility criteria have been formulated at the local level which are at variance with the federal policy goals of public housing. In the second development, LHA admission standards and operating procedures to applicants have not been accessible to tenants. Third, LHAs have reserved the right to admit, retain and evict tenants, often with no opportunity for a tenant to challenge a decision, and without formal communication of the reasons for such decisions.

OPERATING PUBLIC HOUSING—FEDERAL ECONOMIC POLICIES

Fiscal Integrity Concept

8.17 The federally assisted public housing program has not been significantly altered since 1937. The single criterion for admission from 1937 to the present is that the individual or family that occupies the subsidized unit must be at the low end of the income scale.[19] Conversely, while eligibility is based on income, federal assistance is primarily targeted to the housing project, as opposed to the tenant. Although the amount of assistance may vary with the tenant's income, the *occupancy* of a specific unit creates eligibility for federal subsidies.[20]

8.18 The prevailing approach to public housing was formulated under the Housing Acts of 1937 and 1949. These statutes enable all, or nearly all, funds for public housing to be raised through the sale of local housing authority (LHA) bonds, backed by federal annual contributions in the private investment market.[21] As a result of substantial fiscal integrity through the federal annual contributions, the rent paid by low-income tenants only has to cover expenses for maintenance, repair, operation and administration of the project, in addition to local taxes, equalling not more than 10 percent of the project-rent.[22]

8.19 The 1937 Housing Act authorized the U.S. Housing Authority to make loans to the LHAs for up to 90 percent of the development cost of a project. LHAs sell short-term bonds, secured by federal loan commitments, in the private bond market in order to finance a project, including land and site development costs. A 40-year contract (ACC) between the federal government and the LHA provides the security for financing the total development cost of the project after it is built, including interest and amortization, through the sale of long-term serial bonds by LHA to private investors.

8.20 Since the LHAs are local public bodies established under state law, the bonds they sell on the private market bear interest which is exempt from federal income tax, making these especially attractive to private investors interested in tax-exempt securities. In addition, the LHA is exempt from local real estate taxes, but pays an amount up to 10 percent of the shelter-rent of the project.[23]

8.21 Despite the benefits of these direct and indirect subsidies, at the local and national levels, there exists a growing financial crisis in the public housing sector. This crisis stems from the premise that rent-income will be sufficient to meet operating expenses, overhead, replacement costs and payments in lieu of taxes. The assumption that LHAs can maintain fiscal integrity from rent-income suffers from several hidden contradictions of federal policy.

8.22 First, existing federal legislation employs a counterproductive economic logic, which adversely affects public housing policies.[24] Under the 1937 Act, U.S. Housing Authority loans to any LHA were calculated according to a fixed average cost per dwelling unit, or per room, with a standard allowance for cities of greater population.[25] Subsequently, the legislative limitation on cost per unit was eliminated, and the subsidy for each room was adjusted upward.[26]

8.23 Nevertheless, the maximum allowable cost per unit is still restricted as a matter of administrative regulation, imposed by the Secretary of HUD.[27] In the absence of an explicit intent by Congress to limit the cost per dwelling unit, federal housing officials have claimed that their administrative regulation is consistent with the intent of Congress to provide a certain number of public housing units within a specific budget figure.[28]

8.24 The maximum investment per room, however, has proved totally inflexible, since it encompasses all costs, including construction, land assembly, demolition and administration.[29] Congressional policy is a result of conflicting political goals, with economic efficiency suffering at the expense of political feasibility. Although it has accepted the idea of subsidization of low-rent public housing, Congress has attempted to conciliate unfavorable political opinion toward the notion of "a new house for low-income families."[30] Unwilling to endanger the entire public housing program by providing low subsidies Congress has limited the standards of quality for construction in order to prevent "elaborate or extravagant design."[31] In settling standards for construction by providing statutory cost limitations, Congress has tried to limit the amount of federal subsidy without endangering the entire public housing program.

8.25 Legal and administrative investment limitations have produced several undesirable consequences. For example, these restraints, which are figured as an average for each project, fail to reflect the added cost of building units for large families.[32] This is in marked contrast to the cost allowances provided in the construction of public housing for the elderly. As a direct result of the investment maximum, few two-bedroom units have been constructed. Also, cost limitations have made proposed public housing substandard according to some local zoning criteria.[33] Finally, the durability of any structure is severely lessened by the harsh proscriptions which are dictated by the values of middle-class taxpayers.[34]

8.26   Under present federal legislation, aggregate subsidization of public housing for low-income families (including the provisions of the ACC and the rent-supplement program) is based upon premises which virtually preclude economic efficiency. Assuming that the total amount of government assistance and the cost of the unit are constant, several significant economic consequences follow.[35]

1.   The number of units which can be subsidized by the federal government varies inversely with the average cost of the dwelling unit. For example, if a $10,000 subsidy finances ten units at the cost of $1,000 per unit, then only five units can be covered at a cost of $2,000 per unit.

2.   The amount of money needed by the LHA to cover expenses varies inversely with the rent an occupant can pay. For example, in a case where a tenant is able to pay only $1,500 toward a $2,500 per annum rent, the government must make up the difference of $1,000. However, if a tenant can only pay $500, the government subsidy must compensate for a $2,000 balance.

3.   The amount of rent an occupant pays varies directly with his income, based on a standard allocation of 20 percent of that income for rent.

4.   As the incomes of the occupants decline, the amount of the subsidy per unit from the federal government increases, and the total number of units which are subsidized declines.

Congress has often unwittingly undermined public housing programs by imposing income limits in order to assure that the neediest receive support. Without a corresponding increase in the subsidy, the legislation's impact is narrowed by the increased burden of cost.[37]

8.27   Income limitations for admission have impaired the ability of poor families, large and small, to take advantage of housing which does exist. In both traditional and leased public housing, as well as rent supplement housing, there is a discrepancy between the maximum income qualifying applicants for admission into public housing and the minimum income necessary to obtain standard private housing.[38] Because of the maximum incomes for residency in public housing, which are established with the explicit Congressional intent to create a 20 percent difference between the prices of housing on the public and private markets, a housing gap results in which people of moderate income either do not qualify under the income requirements for public housing or cannot afford the costs of private housing.[39] Furthermore, the rationale which justifies income ceilings for admission—the prevention of governmental intrusion into the private housing sector—is inappropriate since both governmental and private efforts have proved inadequate to meet the general demand for more housing.[40] It seems that a more realistic approach would be to adjust income ceilings upward until private investment found it profitable to provide housing for people of moderate income. As the National Commission on Urban Problems concluded, this need not conflict with the principle of granting top priority to the poorest applicants.[41]

8.28　　A halfway means of raising income limitations was provided in the Housing Act of 1968, which permits tenants who have qualified for public housing to retain their residence at a higher rent if their earnings increase to a level which would make them ineligible. Nevertheless, the 1968 Act does not affect the income standards for applicants seeking admission to public housing.

8.29　　Aside from the problematic economic logic in federal housing legislation, several administrative pitfalls militate against the economic feasibility of public housing. Until 1959, the federal government relied, to a great extent, on national direction of public housing administration. Under the Housing Act of 1949,[42] Congress had decentralized authority. Among the various measures which gave authority to the local and private sectors was the "[vesting] in the local public housing agencies, the maximum amount of responsibility in the administration of the low-rent housing program. . . ." In the current statutes, the only criteria mentioned for the proper administration of public housing were safe and sanitary dwellings and low rent.[43]

8.30　　At the administrative level, public housing suffered for lack of guidelines. Since the law emphasized the responsibility of the LHAs in the operation and supervision of public housing, the HAA for the most part limited itself to prescribing technical procedures and the mechanics of repair and maintenance.[44] Although Section 213 of the ACC requires LHAs to maintain the project in good repair and empowers the HAA with remedial authority, federal officials apparently felt that complaints were better left to the LHA, leaving the HAA to apply persuasion and gentle pressure.[45] As a result, the HAA policy has been to intervene only in cases of gross disrepair resulting from negligence, while improper maintenance has gone unremedied when LHAs do not take the initiative.

8.31　　Another factor which contributed to substandard maintenance has been lack of legislative provisions for financing repair and maintenance. The LHAs are expected to operate, according to the concept of fiscal integrity, on income derived from rent, which constitutes a profit known as residual receipts. Officials of the HAA and LHA have worked in conjunction, placing major emphasis on fiscal integrity and high residual receipts in order to reduce federal subsidies.[46] Although the amount of the ACC subsidy is reduced by the residual receipts of a project, HUD recently estimated[47] that the actual annual payment of future public housing bonds would equal 95 percent of the maximum contribution.[48]

8.32 The fiscal integrity concept is simply another aspect of the general ambivalence of federal policy toward low-income housing. While the government has emphasized self-sufficiency in the operation of housing projects, the income derived from fixed rent cannot be adjusted to meet the increasing costs of labor and materials for upkeep and rehabilitation.[49] Along with the federal policy of fiscal integrity, this has resulted in a perennial lack of funds for financing project improvement. The little money contributed towards reducing the subsidy has not been channeled back to the local level for maintaining projects.[50] Furthermore, deficit spending has rarely been permitted[51] except in cases of imminent health hazards. The only other alternative to LHAs seeking financing for project improvement—a HUD loan—is circumscribed by the requirement that repayment be made from the reserves of operating income.[52] Generally, public housing has lacked a preventive policy of federal direction, participation and subsidy.[53]

HUD Modernization Program: A Possible Shift Toward Subsidy
8.33 The HUD Modernization Program for public housing, a program administratively conceived in 1967 on the basis of Sec. 10 (b) of the Housing Act, was designed to assist LHAs in upgrading low-rent housing projects which, for reasons of physical condition, location and outmoded management policies, adversely affect the quality of living of the tenants.[54] The program's primary emphasis on upgrading physical facilities through federal funds targeted specifically for that purpose seems to be a significant departure from HUD's former concern with the economic autonomy of LHAs and a shift toward a subsidy approach.[55] The remaining upkeep of public housing could be achieved by applying residual receipts and operating income reserves to upgrading the physical plant of public housing projects.

ADMISSION TO PUBLIC HOUSING: CREATION OF TENANCY

SUBSTANTIVE STANDARDS FOR ELIGIBILITY
Federal Social Policy Versus Local Standards
8.34 Underlying much of the inequity and impropriety in the formulation and application of eligibility standards is the discrepancy between federal social policy and local LHA standards. Although a host of economic and administrative factors inhibit the proper allocation of housing, these factors only supplement the core problem of gross inequity.

145

The fact remains that the moral and social biases of local managers and administrators have too often thwarted the aims of federal housing programs.

Federal Requirements

8.35　　The express federal statutory criterion for eligibility is that tenants be "low-income families."[56] Nothing in the legislative history of the 1939 Housing Act and its subsequent amendments indicates that Congress intended to set any other standards.[57] The 1959 Act vested primary responsibility for the determination of eligibility in the LHA, but had no substantive effect upon eligibility requirements. The power of the LHAs was purely discretionary and was to operate within the legal standards. The laws merely decentralized and transferred responsibility for setting income limitations and establishing priorities among eligible families.[58]

8.36　　The ACC supports this legislative purpose by emphasizing the low-rent character of the housing project.[59] Furthermore, the wording of the contract indicates exclusive federal concern for eligibility according to income requirements.

8.37　　The 1937 Act, the *Low Rent Management Manual* and the ACC do not specify that the family be patriarchal. The *LHA Management Handbook*, however, attempts to define the social structure of a family as a guide to applying standards.[60] This in itself does not contribute to abuse of the national policy. The crucial factor is the absence of an express prohibition, in HAA directives, of considerations other than income. The only express requirement is that the admission standards be "reasonable."[61] The *Handbook* goes a step further, by expressly permitting eligibility standards not contained in the Act, "provided they would not be contrary to the purposes of the low-rent program."[62] Obviously, local officials will refer to the more parochial and particular administrative regulations, not to the broader statutory goals. Basically, the additional admission criteria adopted by LHA fall into two categories: standards for evaluating the desirability of an applicant; and residency requirements.

Restriction of "Undesirables" From Public Housing

8.38　　Placed in a situation where the number of applicants have far outnumbered the occupancy openings, LHA officials have tended to select tenants for subjective reasons rather than overriding social need. Protected by the administrative discretion clause and lack of tenant recourse, LHA officials have justified decisions actually based on subjective judgments by invoking the problem of supply and demand in housing. Underlying the official decisions has been concern with maintaining a healthy social environment within the project. This practice defeats any federal policy to have public housing provide opportunities for social rehabilitation.

8.39　　Most LHA criteria thinly disguise a condemnation of low income status.[64] By applying eligibility criteria which conform to personal standards of morality, local authorities have established requirements which deny admission to those classes of people who require housing most. Thus, the "badges" of the poor become the very standards by which they are denied the benefits which are intended for them by federal policy.

8.40　　Among the various standards of ineligibility are a record of eviction for nonpayment of rent, irregular work history, separation of husband and wife, frequent change of residence and a longstanding juvenile record. Every characteristic of low-income living has at some time been used to deny admission and permit eviction. Clearly, designation of the lower income life-style as a standard for exclusion has significantly hampered federal attempts to alleviate these conditions.

8.41　　But the most striking aspect of the substantive standards of local housing authorities is their breadth.[65] While the LHA claims to exercise judgment in the interest of resident tenants, officials often disqualify applicants on the basis of a dubious causal connection between an applicant's former activity and the welfare of tenants. In doing so, the LHA looks for activities which often have no reasonable relation to the applicants' associations with tenants. Here again, the applicants' social needs are secondary to their social acceptability. The burden is not that an applicant must prove acceptability, but, that certain types of behavior automatically classify an applicant as undesirable.[66]

8.42　　Ineligibility is most frequently based on family characteristics. Much exclusion results because desirability is evaluated on the basis of an aggregate family portrait. Even a satisfactory parental record might not qualify a family if the children have a history as extracurricular or scholastic disciplinary problems.

8.43　　One policy standard which results in frequent disqualification is applied against families with illegitimate children, or in which the parents are separated, or in which a common-law marriage exists. The standard rests upon an extremely dubious causal connection between moral judgment and the welfare of neighboring tenants. Such criteria discriminate against racial minority groups, which have a greater proportion of such familial-marital arrangements.

Restrictive Residency Standards
8.44　　Another substantive denial of housing occurs in the restriction of admission through residency requirements. Such standards may not only discriminate by denying housing, but also by restricting constitutionally protected freedoms of association and movement.

8.45　　The HAA by implication has permitted the application of resi-

147

dency requirements. In its advisory *LHA Management Handbook,* HAA mentions residency in an area for a minimum period as a possible criterion for admission.[67] HAA authorities delegated discretion in this area, claiming that it has traditionally viewed the administration of public housing for low-income families as a local function.[68] Preference for local residents has been considered consistent with local management.

8.46   LHA officials have exercised their discretion to its fullest extent in imposing residency requirements to discourage wholesale migration to areas where housing is available. Welfare authorities allege that a large influx of indigents would result in an unbearable drain on state and local municipal treasuries, since increased demands would be made on public welfare assistance, public health services and the public social services.[69]

8.47   The high degree of mobility and transience of the poor has been ignored by LHA officials. The effect of fixed residency requirements is to force needy families into slum housing for the particular time period established, even though they otherwise qualify for public housing.[70] While the shortage of public housing units ordinarily has the same effect as a fixed residency requirement, it produces hardship even where shortages do not exist.

Constitutional and Legal Rights
8.48   There are serious questions about the constitutionality of standards based upon moral and subjective judgment. The Supreme Court has not addressed itself to this question in the area of public housing, although it has ruled against such dubious standards for granting federal benefits in other areas. Recently, however, lower federal courts have begun to consider the issue. In *Colon v. Tompkins Square Neighbors,*[71] (see 2.76, 2.77) a private landlord was held to be, by his participation in government programs of financial aid, subject to the provisions of the Fourteenth Amendment. He had denied housing to tenants because they were recipients of welfare funds, but was forced to adopt "ascertainable standards" for the selection of tenants, subject to the Due Process Clause of the Fourteenth Amendment. The practices of LHA authorities raise an analogous question of constitutionality. Can the government as landlord withhold a benefit for arbitrary, irrational or unconstitutional reasons which are unrelated to the program under which it is administered? The Supreme Court has generally held that:

> the attempted classification must always rest upon some difference which bears a reasonable and just relation to the act in respect to which the classification is proposed, and can never be made arbitrarily and without any such basis.[72]

The reasonableness of any classification hinges on two criteria: the rights, if any, of the individual, which are infringed upon by the classification, and the purpose of the program, including the state's interest in the program.[73]

8.49   In the area of social welfare programs the Supreme Court has protected family life[75]—the right to "establish a home and bring up children"[76] and "the right to have children."[77]

8.50   These basic constitutional rights do not appear to be diminished under federal programs. Housing policy is directed toward the attainment of "a decent home and suitable living environment for every American family." On the face of it that statutory goal applies to all beneficiaries of federal legislation. A policy of excluding low-income families otherwise eligible for public housing on the basis of moral judgment would seem to be contrary to the purposes of public housing.[78] If anything, the "war on poverty" indicated congressional intent to accomplish social rehabilitation through federal welfare aid.

8.51   While the judicial and legislative statements conflict with the dubious moral judgments used in the admission to public housing, such judgments might be justified if overriding state interest demands them. A counterclaim has been raised that no right exists to have illegitimate children. However, the question is not the right to have illegitimate children, but the legality of discrimination against this condition, when a person would otherwise be eligible to receive a federal benefit.[79]

8.52   A second argument alleges that, in accordance with national goals of remedying injurious living environments, local authorities may attempt to exclude objectional moral types. The answer to this contention is twofold.[80] First, the public housing program is not supposed to maintain the moral fabric of the nation, but to improve it by eliminating *living conditions* injurious to its citizens. Second, statutes which create classes must base the distinction between the classes upon factors that are germane to the purpose of the legislation.

8.53   Federal policy in support of the first point has already been adequately advanced. According to the Supreme Court, overly broad classification can be prohibited and LHA policies invalidated, in light of the size of class affected. Given the high proportion of marital problems occuring in the lower-income class, it is significant that Congress did not condition eligibility criteria upon moral acceptability. Nor does state legislation impose any restriction in this area. Such restriction would contradict the purpose of federal programs for the lower class.

8.54   In view of the evidence that eligibility classification based on moral judgment is too broad, and its contradiction of federal and state statutory intent, LHA policy excluding socially stigmatized families would appear to be unconstitutional. The Supreme Court has often struck down statutes and regulations which in their broadness of scope, stifled constitutional rights and liberties.[81] Where personal liberties are involved, the state action may be justified only if it can show a "subordinating interest which is compelling,"[82] and the regulation is shown to be "necessary, and not merely rationally related to the accomplishment of a permissable state policy."[83] Given the express intent of federal rehabilitative programs, discriminatory local policies are merely expedient. In the context of constitutional requirements, the LHA must grant individual reviews of eligibility, and desist in excluding entire classes of families.

8.55 Despite compelling economic arguments for residency requirements, the validity of these measures is also questionable. As in the case of marital-familial rights, the Supreme Court has not yet resolved the exact constitutional status of restrictive residency requirements in public housing. However, the Court has held similar requirements in welfare assistance programs unconstitutional on the grounds that they infringe upon constitutionally protected freedom of movement in violation of the Equal Protection Clause of the Fourteenth Amendment.[84] Since the rights deprived and the rationale for enacting welfare residency requirements are analogous to those in public housing, a similar application by the Court may be predicted in public housing. The residency requirement in public housing is an equally direct burden on state-to-state freedom of movement as in the welfare statutes.[85]

8.56 There are at least two possible resolutions to the problem of residency requirements.[86] Congress is ultimately responsible for discrepancy between its legislative policy and the *LHA Management Handbook* guidelines, so explicit statutory protection of constitutional liberties must come from Congress. Furthermore, the HAA should require that the LHA prove ineligibility through formal, visable procedures. The LHA should also be advised of alternative approaches to determine eligibility, such as investigations, and residency or state citizenship requirements without a minimum period.

PROCEDURAL DUE PROCESS

8.57 Any proposed resolution of the problems in public housing will be futile if it does not safeguard due process.[87] Granting maximum discretion to local management will inevitably result in arbitrary decision-making unless procedural requirements are instituted. Presently, admissions, evictions and the like are generally decided without published guidelines, adequate notice of the charges against the tenant or applicant, an established standard of proof or a review by an impartial tribunal, and often without an opportunity for the tenant to appear before, and be heard by, the officials who make such decisions.[88] Such practices result, in the main, from the great discretion given LHA officials. This section undertakes to review some of the grievances which arise from admission procedures which are devoid of due process protections.

Availability of Regulations

8.58   *Federal requirements.* The statutory language requires the LHA to ". . . adopt and promulgate regulations establishing admission policies. . ." in order to be eligible for federal contributions.[89] The ACC requires that the LHA ". . . duly adopt and promulgate, by publication or posting in a conspicuous place for examination by prospective tenants, regulations establishing its admission policies."[90] This provison is part of the terms and conditions of the federal contribution, in the sense that the requirement of the ACC that admission standards be posted, is legally indistinguishable from the federal government's contractual duty to deliver its financial subsidies.[91] The *Low Rent Management Manual,* which contains the HAA's minimum requirements for fulfillment of federal responsibilities,[92] repeats the requirement for posting regulations.

8.59   *State requirements.* Some state laws require the publication of admission policies, but by filing regulations as "internal procedures," a housing authority may evade its obligation to publish eligibility standards.[93] By formulating broad statements of policy, an LHA can offer evidence in court against tenants, yet immunize its internal standards from perusal by the court, effectively shielding itself from public scrutiny. However, the state is not responsible for the LHA's abuse of publication requirements, but rather the HAA, which does not enforce compliance with local standards of publication.

8.60   *Implication of nonpublication.* The inability of an applicant to learn eligibility standards is one of several procedural deprivations. Given the discriminatory standards upon which many LHAs base admissions decisions, the applicant's lack of information permits the LHA to use arbitrary and unreasonable determinations of eligibility. Invisibility becomes the tenant's foremost obstacle to insuring his constitutional rights in a determination of eligibility. It is symptomatic of the secretive attitude of LHA management that due process is alleged to be administratively unfeasible and incompatible with the need to exclude "undesirable" applicants.[94]

Processing Applications

8.61   *Invisibility and vagueness of standards.* Although the 1959 Act prohibits local standards which conflict with its purpose, the parochial application of the *Low Rent Management Manual's* standard of "reasonableness,"[95] and the broad interpretation of discretion provided for in the *Management Handbook,* have led to the formation of classes of applicants by degree of eligibility. These classes are based on criteria of personal behavior. An applicant whose record contains evidence of certain behavior is formally categorized and is automatically ineligible for admission.

8.62 Furthermore, the LHA is not required to meet any administrative standards for the proof used to deny admission.[96] The information considered by the LHA comes from diverse sources, many of them unverifiable. The acceptance of hearsay exemplifies the lack of standards of evidence in LHA determination.

8.63 Finally, cataloging deviant behavior and accumulating applicants' records over an extended period is patently oppressive. An individual's deviant behavior is resurrected whenever he applies for federal housing, depriving him of any opportunity to prove his worthiness. If not allowed to argue on his own behalf when applying, a stigmatized applicant may be perpetually condemned by unpublished LHA classifications.

8.64 The problem of lack of standards for proof is intimately connected with the LHA failure to make admissions criteria available.[97] An applicant cannot contest the LHA rejection if he has no knowledge of the grounds upon which the decision was based. To this end, the LHA formulates broad or ambiguous categories of undesirability for applicants. The underlying criteria of these categories are often constitutionally suspect, and is consequently stated ambiguously, to prevent judicial scrutiny if the determination should be challenged in court.

8.65 *Lack of a hearing*—ex parte *decisions.* Most other problems stemming from lack of due process safeguards are minor compared to the lack of a hearing in the admission process. While many tenants are afforded a hearing in eviction proceedings, no such opportunity is normally available to an applicant. Even if the HAA explicitly ordered the elimination of all admission criteria other than income, an applicant would not have access to the LHA decision-making procedure to insure adherence to the HAA directive.

8.66 This determination of eligibility without a hearing is known as an *ex parte* proceeding. The term denotes the presence of one party in a hearing or determination in which the rights of an absent party are decided.[98] An applicant subjected to an LHA *ex parte* proceeding is unable to appeal the decision since he lacks knowledge of the grounds for the decision. In most cases, the opportunity to appeal simply does not exist.

8.67 In some of the more progressive states, such as New York, an applicant receives notification of the reasons for a denial or deferral, and may subsequently secure a personal interview for explanations of the determination. Additionally, some states give an applicant the opportunity to rebut LHA determinations by submitting additional evidence on his behalf, or to appeal the decision. In some instances, successive appeals to separate arbiting bodies can be made. The above provisions are the exception and not the rule, however.

8.68   *Surplus applicants and priorities for admission.* The problem of due process is complicated by the fact that most local authorities must select only a few of the total number of applicants, for want of adequate space. [99] An applicant who attempts to contest an unfavorable determination may be rebuffed by the answer that there are no vacancies.

8.69   Federal legislation provides that LHAs establish a system of priorities for admission based on financial need. Aside from this broad federal prescription, LHAs exercise discretion in the exact composition and ordering of priorities. Having received an application, the LHA processes and assigns a priority to each applicant, depending on the location requested and the number of units available in that housing unit. In a normal housing situation of greater demand than supply, the applicant, without an opportunity to present his case in a hearing, must rely on the LHA committee to assess his economic need accurately. Since the LHA retains priority assignments as classified information, the applicant is never informed of his listing.

8.70   The priority system may perpetrate arbitrary and discriminatory determinations of eligibility. Concealing the substantive basis upon which the priorities are assigned, the LHA can discriminate against otherwise eligible applicants. In a court proceeding, the LHA may simply contend that the challenging applicant was superseded by others of higher priority and equal qualifications. Such nonvisibility permeates every level of LHA decision-making and inevitably leads to determinations based on arbitrary and unreasonable standards.

Due Process Requirements: Constitutional Basis

8.71   Since LHAs are government agencies, by virtue of their existence through state implementing legislation, their activities must conform with requirements of due process of law. State-created housing authorities, as landlord, have been held to be subject to the Due Process Clause of the Fourteenth Amendment,[100] unlike private landlords, who are governed by common law. Thus, the government as landlord is prohibited from arbitrary action in violation of due process.

8.72   Furthermore, the standards of due process have been applied to the withholding of a privilege as well as to the withdrawal of a right.[101] Thus, the claims of applicants to the federal benefit of public housing are entitled to due process protection.

8.73   Guarantee of procedural due process in LHA decisions is an invaluable protection when constitutional rights and liberties are involved. Due process embodies a number of legal safeguards, such as adequate notice of specific charges,[102] a hearing by impartial officials,[103] an opportunity to present evidence,[104] a right to confront and cross-examine adverse witnesses,[105] and a decision based upon evidence presented and tested at the hearing.[106]

8.74   It may be argued that inconsistencies exist between the procedural right adjudicated in the above cases and the flouting of such rights by LHA authorities in their admission process. In the absence of express Supreme Court prohibitions to the contrary, LHA officials will probably continue to employ administrative immunity to shield the present inadequacy of eligibility standards and procedural provisions. Supreme Court and inferior federal court rulings would appear to be the most expedient method of securing procedural due process protection. However, the Court would moderate any position on due process requirements in public housing out of deference to administrative management and its concomitant laws and regulations. It is reasonable to believe that HUD would follow the lead of the Supreme Court and require minimal procedural standards in areas where the Court adjudicates substantive constitutional rights of applicants and tenants.

Remedies Available to the Applicant
8.75   A public housing applicant is seriously impaired in any challenge of the rationale and validity of LHA determinations. The finality of LHA determinations is presently dictated by the 1959 amendments to the Housing Act which gave the LHA primary responsibility for determining eligibility. This Congressional action, which transferred power to the LHA to set income limitations and establish priorities, was bolstered by HAA directives, which by implication permitted the local authority to employ additional substantive standards. In spite of Congressional policy statements to the contrary, HAA regulations specify only a minimum standard of "reasonableness" in formulating admission policies.[107]

8.76   In the absence of federal administrative prohibitions against LHA procedures, the average applicant is for all practical purposes unable to challenge LHA determinations. The developing case law[108] indicates that admission standards based on "reasonableness" may no longer be acceptable and that constitutionally protected rights and liberties might be limited only upon proof of a compelling government interest.

8.77   However, while admission standards may be challenged on the grounds that they are inconsistent with federal and state statutory policy and Constitutional rights and liberties, litigation on substantive rights of due process will be piecemeal and ad hoc. Thus, the procedural guarantees of due process can only be secured in a very haphazard and inconsistent manner of the litigation process.

8.78   While we do not contend here that the HAA should prescribe and administer the entire admission process, the present distribution of authority places too much discretion in the hands of the LHA. Understandably, the LHA must be allowed a sufficient amount of discretion to distribute available occupancies according to the demands of local conditions. This may require the legitimate application of criteria such as residency when the applicants are all of comparable credentials. However, if provisions for procedural due process are not embodied in the admission process, standards can be applied which bear no reasonable relation to the purpose of the public housing program, and are not justified by a compelling state interest.

8.79   From the viewpoint of the applicant, the ability to participate in a formal hearing on his eligibility is the surest safeguard against deprivation of his rights and liberties. If the LHA were required to open its administrative procedures to public scrutiny, applicants would be relieved of the burden of attempting to discover the fate of their application before the LHA admission board. As conditions stand, the applicant who has not received notification of the disposition of his application may file for a "writ of mandamus," requiring the LHA to process the application and reveal the grounds upon which the determination was based.

8.80   Two factors discourage the use of this procedure by applicants. First, the average applicant has no access to a lawyer who would institute such proceedings. Nor can most applicants afford such a costly course of action. Second, assuming that legal services and adequate financial means are available, the most that can be gained by "writ of mandamus" is a determination couched in the broad and vague language of admission categories. Since local officials have interpreted HAA directives[109] as prescriptions for internal processing of applications, eligibility standards are shielded from the applicant. As long as decision-making maintains its administratively immune status, a legal proceeding to determine the standing of an application can be consistently stymied by the contention that the applicant is eligible but not able to secure a residence because of a shortage of space. As long as the LHA is allowed to establish priorities on an *ex parte* basis, the tendency to shield discriminatory standards in decision-making will persist.

8.81   The procedures of LHA can also be challenged on due process grounds through a suit instituted by the applicant. In such cases, LHAs have often accepted the applicant for public housing, thus precluding a judicial determination which might have invalidated its administrative procedures.

THE PUBLIC HOUSING LEASE AND RIGHTS DURING OCCUPANCY

LEGAL BASIS OF TENANCY

The Monthly Tenancy

8.82   The public housing lease is an effective weapon in the hands of the LHA, formulated according to the caprice of local authorities, and often drawn with the intent to insulate local authorities against legal challenges by tenants. Both federal and state enabling legislation, as well as the ACC, are silent regarding the content of public housing leases, except for rent and income standards. Moreover, the recommendation of the *Management Handbook* that leases be drawn on a monthly basis have been interpreted to mean that most public housing leases should create a contract which gives disproportionate legal and bargaining advantage to the LHA.[110]

8.83   Although the rationale[111] for a monthly lease has been applied in other provisions of the public housing lease, the most devastating effect on the tenant has been the short duration of the lease itself. Under private leases, a monthly tenancy is terminated on a 30-day notice. However, most public housing leases terminate on a 15-day notice whenever housing officials adjudge a violation of the terms of the lease. Thus, the short-term, monthly lease creates insecurity, given the fact that the LHA functions as the sole judge of tenant conduct. Furthermore, under many leases, the tenant waives even the right to a 15-day notice. Under other public housing leases, the tenant loses his right to possession without legal notice or legal proceedings when his income exceeds the maximum established by federal law for eligibility.

The Standard Form Lease
8.84   Leases between the LHA and tenants are consummated in a standard form contract. Standard form contracts have been defined as contracts which are habitually made by one party, follow a particular form, and allow little, if any, variation.[112] Generally, this type of contract has been used in large-scale organizations to create a uniform legal relationship which ordinarily would have been established with an agreement specifically drafted for each individual party.

8.85   The use of a standard form lease has the advantages of uniformity, consistency and workability. According to the general theory of standard form contracts,[113] the offeror may insist upon the use of a standard form contract which he has drafted. Since both bargaining parties are considered to be on an equal footing, the offeree is expected to take it or leave it, seeking better conditions elsewhere if he is not satisfied.

8.86   It has been argued that this scenario does not accurately reflect the relative inequality of the two parties which the housing market creates in favor of housing officials.[114] The following passage indicates the inequity of bargaining in the housing market, and how a standard form contract may further imbalance the bargaining equilibrium:

> The weaker party, in need of the goods or services, is frequently not in a position to shop around for better terms, either because the author of the standard contract has a monopoly (natural or artificial) or because all competitors

156

use the same clauses. His contractual intention is but a subjection more or less voluntary to the terms dictated by the stronger party...[115]

Furthermore, the applicant for public housing will most likely be unable to comprehend many of the terms of a public housing lease, which to him is one of a large number of inscrutable standard form contracts which he must confront every day.[116]

8.87 It has been argued that standard form contracts should conform to the law of the jurisdiction in which they are applied.[117] The courts have not been tolerant of form contracts which are contrary to local law. Thus, although private contracting parties may create "law" which is tailored to a particular transaction, contracts drafted by state agencies must conform to and positively reflect a state's policies.[119] Furthermore, the question of public policy must be viewed in terms of the goals of federal legislation.

The Lease as a Contract of Adhesion

8.88 As noted previously, a practical imbalance in bargaining results from the application of a take it or leave it theory to negotiations between public housing authorities and applicants. The public housing lease closely approximates what is called a contract of adhesion, in which one party's participation consists of mere adherence, unwilling and often unknowing, to a document drafted unilaterally and insisted upon by what is usually a powerful enterprise.[120]

8.89 It has been argued that "all the elements of adhesion contracts and the characteristics surrounding their execution exist in the case of leasing by an indigent tenant."[121] The argument has been that the requisite elements of an adhesion contract exist with greater force in public housing than in private housing.[122] The standard lease is drafted unilaterally, with provisions which disproportionately favor the LHA. Furthermore, the indigent applicant for public housing cannot reasonably be said to have freedom of choice in the matter, since the acute shortage of public housing unjustly forces him to accept the terms of the lease if he does not wish to remain in slum private housing. Generally, the public housing lease has been called a "noncontract," since it permits no substantive bargaining (see 9.104).[123]

8.90 The question arises, therefore, as to why the courts have not nullified the inequality which arises under "freedom of contract" practices in public housing as they have in other fields.[124] Although not uniformly followed, the Appellate Court of the District of Columbia has ruled against public housing leases which grant inordinate bargaining power. Regarding an immunity clause in a public housing lease, the Court said:

Moreover, it is doubtful whether a clause which did undertake to exempt

157

a landlord from responsibility for such negligence would now be valid. The acute housing shortage in and near the District of Columbia gives the landlord so great a bargaining advantage over the tenant that such an exemption might well be held invalid on grounds of public policy.[126]

The Court's ruling interjects again the notion that public housing leases should be viewed in terms of federal and state laws and policies.

8.91   Several remedies could be applied to unconscionable public housing leases. Whatever remedy is provided, it appears likely that the courts would uphold the lease in general and either strike the unconscionable clause, refuse to enforce it, or wait until performance could be carried out under circumstances more conducive to free and equitable negotiations.

Exculpatory Clauses
8.92   The disparity in bargaining power between applicants for public housing and the LHA bears directly on the validity of exculpatory clauses (i.e. provisions that excuse the landlord from liability for injuries resulting from his own negligence) in public housing leases. Generally, when the bargaining parties are on equal terms, the lessee may exculpate his lessor from liability for negligence.[128] Although private tenement leases have normally been adjudged contracts between equals, exculpation contracts by tenement lessees have been overthrown upon contrary findings.[129] Furthermore, when the party exculpated is in a superior bargaining position, exemption has been almost universally denied, although most precedents have not been directly applicable to housing leases.[130]

8.93   Arguing by analogy, there is nothing even approaching equality in the relationship between the public landlord and tenant. Substantive bargaining is often impossible since the tenant must deal with a real estate agent or an apartment manager who has no authority to vary the terms of the lease.[131] The widespread use of modern standard form leases further aggravates the disparity of bargaining power. Add to these factors the take it or leave it assumption under which housing officials present the lease to applicants, and the relationship becomes one of decided advantage for the housing authority.

8.94   Exculpatory clauses in public housing leases seem to encourage indifference of the housing authority to the safety of tenants.[132] The prohibition of exculpatory clauses might make public housing landlords more conscious of tenant safety, since the absence of such insurance against culpability might very well lead to a judgment against public officials, or to higher insurance rates.[133] There is every likelihood that the exclusion of exculpatory clauses would induce LHAs to rely on liability insurance. Insurance companies' normal function as a watchdog for their clients' susceptibility to liability could lead to improvement

158

in the physical condition of many public housing units.[134] From the tenant's perspective the prohibition of exculpatory clauses would enable tenants, many of whom are too poor to insure themselves against injury, to be compensated by either the landlord or an insurance company.[135]

8.95 There are several grounds upon which exculpatory clauses regarding negligence may be attacked as unconscionable. The *LHA Management Handbook* expressly prohibits any attempt by an LHA to disclaim liability for negligence.[136] Clauses which allow LHAs to maintain units which are in physical disrepair, and thus potentially dangerous, may be in violation of federal statutory policy providing for decent, safe and sanitary dwellings for families of low income. Similarly, exculpation may be considered contrary to the public policy of the states, which very nearly duplicates federal statutory policy. Exculpation is legally suspect on the grounds that it violates local housing regulations aimed at public safety as well as local building codes.[137] As mentioned, exculpation has been judicially and statutorily condemned in the private sector.[138] Many of these same arguments are readily applicable to clauses which impose upon the tenant the duty to repair defective conditions.[139] Finally, the new HUD policy prohibits such provisions (See 8.101).

Waiver of Statutory Remedies
8.96 Public housing leases are replete with "waivers," as a result of which the tenant gives up many rights, privileges, exemptions and remedies which he would otherwise be accorded by law.[140] Here again, the courts sometimes sanction such waivers where there has been a freely negotiated contract between two relatively equal parties.[141]

8.97 However, it has been contended that a more cogent logic should be applied in reviewing the waiver of statutory remedies.

> It is obvious that when a right, a privilege, or a defense is conferred upon an individual by law, it is conferred upon him because it is believed to be in the public interest to do so. In many such cases it is believed to be contrary to the public interest to permit him to waive or to bargain away the right, privilege, or defense, and when it is so believed the attempted waiver or bargain is inoperative.[142]

This argument, that waivers should not be accorded traditional judicial sanction, is especially persuasive as applied to public housing leases, since a number of factors inhibit freedom of contract and equitable bargaining positions. Aside from the constitutional questions, tenants may not be aware of the rights they have waived in signing a lease.[143] Consequently, the waiver of rights granted by statute is questionable when that statute has been enacted specifically for protection of tenants.[144]

The Landlord as the Sole Judge of Tenant Conduct
8.98 Among the clauses commonly contained in public housing leas-

es, those giving the landlord nearly unfettered discretion in passing judgment on the conduct of a tenant are potentially the most destructive to the legal rights of tenants. In the absence of an explicit administrative sanction for the termination of tenancy at the option of the landlord, the policy of maximum discretion for local officials has been interpreted, however erroneously, as justification for such clauses.

8.99   It has been argued that the lack of express standards by which the tenant's liability is to be determined should render such clauses too uncertain and indefinite for administrative enforcement.[145] Furthermore, if the LHA should require a judicial remedy to remove a belligerent tenant, it has been said that, in the absence of limiting standards on the exercise of discretion by the LHA, the court would hold the LHA's authority unenforceable.[146] Generally, if internal administrative standards of reasonableness are not to be applied, there is a strong argument for substituting judicial determination for the present autonomy of LHA discretion concerning the conduct of tenants.[147]

New HUD Policies

8.100   Moving initially to strike particularly unconscionable provisions from low-rent public housing leases, HUD barred clauses which were considered to undermine the legal rights of tenants. The new policy stated as its rationale the prohibition of provisions which "focus more on the interests of the landlord than that of the tenant,"[149] and pursued greater balance in tenant-landlord rights. This particular aspect of the new HUD policy appears directed against turning the monthly tenancy together with maximum discretion into a broad sanction for drafting a lease which places the burden of performance on the tenant.

8.101   Among the provisions found to have created an imbalance in landlord-tenant relations were the following clauses: Confession of Judgment (prior consent by the tenant to any lawsuit the landlord may wish to bring regarding the provisions of the lease); Distraint for Rent or Other Charges (agreement that the landlord is authorized to seize the tenant's property and hold it as a pledge until the tenant performs some obligation); Exculpatory Clauses; Waiver of Legal Notice Prior to Actions for Eviction (agreement by the tenant that the landlord may institute suit without notice, thus preventing the tenant from defending against the lawsuit); Waiver of Legal Proceedings (authorizing the landlord to evict a tenant for breach of the lease without notice to the tenant or any action for judicial proceedings); Waiver of a Jury Trial; and Payment of Legal Fees by Tenant Regardless of Outcome.

8.102   Significantly, Norman V. Watson, Acting HUD Assistant Secretary for Renewal and Housing Management, found that the prohibition of all these clauses from public housing leases was in no way inconsistent with the federal policy of seeking "more efficient management and improved conditions in public housing."[150] Watson's remark, taken in the context of the sweeping prohibitions, seems to indicate that the maximum discretion granted to LHAs is not necessarily synonymous with autonomous decision-making and more properly means that local officials should have self-determination in technical matters, along with limited fiscal independence, subject to the explicit federal policies relating to tenant income. Although Watson's pronouncements of hope for a "partnership"[151] between tenants and landlords implied a future goal toward which HUD was negotiating, the immediate effect of the August 10, 1970 directive was merely to eliminate some of the more patently discriminatory aspects of LHA conduct, leaving important internal procedures which foster discrimination unaffected.

8.103　　HUD followed the August 1970 directive with a comprehensive policy formulation[152] regarding lease and grievance procedures affecting the rights of tenants in low-rent public housing and the balance of bargaining positions in tenant-landlord relations. Watson, commenting on the HUD policy, pointed out that the balance in landlord-tenant relations had traditionally been strongly in favor of the landlord, and that the new lease and grievance procedures would open up channels of communication in order to create tenant credibility in the management of public housing.[153]

8.104　　Taken collectively, the new HUD lease and grievance procedures have potential for dispelling many complaints which have been levelled against the management of public housing. Although the new lease and grievance procedure reflects the obligations and responsibilities of both management and tenants,[154] the substantive provisions[155] are drawn so as to emphasize managerial practices.

8.105　　Regarding the formulation of terms for a lease, the HUD circular cites the ACC,[156] which provides that "the Local Authority shall not terminate the tenancy other than for violation of the terms of the lease or other good cause." The circular establishes numerous provisions as requisite to the performance of the ACC, many of which promise radical alterations in management policy.

8.106　　In the broad area of rent collection, one of the most significant new requirements is that rental payments be computed separately from other fees or charges, and that the tenant's obligation to pay is fulfilled under the terms of the lease independently of fines or other affixed fees.[157] This provision alters the policy in which proceedings for eviction were commonly instituted against tenants who did not pay assessed fees, called "additional rent charges."[158]

8.107　　Although the procedure for re-examining income and redetermining rent must be specified and regularized, new HUD policy[159] does not prescribe the exact frequency of rent re-evaluation. While federal policy requires at least an annual review of a tenant's income,[160] some

LHAs also require tenants to report significant interim changes in their incomes.[161] Although the model form lease included in the HUD circular[162] suggests a yearly examination of a tenant's income, the minimal requirements of the circular do not preclude a bi-annual income inspection, provided that the schedule of rent re-examinations is specified in the lease. Thus, the criticism of interim rent examinations and the suggestion that income re-assessment be conducted on an annual basis in order to limit the number of over-income evictees[163] are not effectively dealt with in the new HUD circular.

8.108 There is federal statutory and administrative sanction for allowing over-income tenants to remain in public housing under specified circumstances.[164] However, the federal policy suggests other alternatives, including rent adjustment, transfer of overcrowded families to larger units and eviction.[165] Nevertheless, most LHAs[166] have granted over-income families a grace period ranging from three months to an indefinite amount of time in which to find suitable housing in the private sector. Given the shortage of decent housing in the intermediate price range in which most over-income tenants are situated, this grace period often becomes meaningless unless the LHA itself helps to relocate the over-income family.[167] It has been argued that evicting over-income tenants, only to have them return to slum private housing, is contrary to the federal policy of providing a decent home for the poor, since over-income evictions merely turn over residents in public housing without meeting the overall housing needs of the poor.[168]

8.109 Furthermore, the HUD circular merely requires the publication of standards by which rents and eligibility shall be judged,[169] and thus does not in any way preclude other standards which have been used in computing tenant income. Including secondary wage earners in the computation of tenant income is one of these standards, and has been criticized as deterring the wage-earning initiative of the poor, as well as discriminating against the large family.[170]

8.110 Regarding other LHA practices in rent collection, the HUD circular explicitly recommends that assessing penalties for late rent payments is counterproductive to tenant-management relations and should be discontinued. Implicitly, lease[171] provisions which provide for the automatic termination of tenancy and subsequent eviction because of untimely payment of rent[172] do not appear to qualify as a "good cause"[173] under the new lease provisions.

8.111 One of the key features of the new HUD requirements for public housing leases is the "responsibility of management to maintain the buildings, and any unassigned community areas in a decent, safe, and sanitary condition in accordance with local housing codes and HUD regulations."[174] Since the primary burden for maintenance and repair is placed upon the local authority, it could be argued that exculpatory clauses are now banned.

8.112   Complementing this clause, which gives management primary responsibility for meeting safe and sanitary standards of housing, is the requirement that the responsibilities of the tenant for upkeep and maintenance be specified, as well as his culpability for negligence.[175] Including the exact conditions under which a tenant is responsible for maintenance will undoubtedly benefit the tenant, since a major problem in tenant-landlord relations has been the tendency of management to hold tenants responsible for duties it wishes to shirk.[176]

8.113   Generally, there has been a lack of administrative guidelines, which has allowed project managers great latitude in the day-to-day operation of public housing.[177] The *Low-Rent Management Manual,* the only mandatory administrative directive given to LHAs, only dictates guidelines for income limits, rent and tenant eligibility, leaving a great deal of administrative flexibility in the tenant's relations with management. The discretion given the LHAs[178] has contributed to the leniency with which HUD and HAA, its administrative agency, have enforced regulations on the local level. An area in which management has often abused its discretion has been the assessment of fees and charges, especially for the cost of repairs. The policy of assessing tenants for failure to maintain their units in satisfactory repair is universally recognized in public housing[179] and has direct federal sanction.[180] The new HUD leasing provisions also reflect the need to assess damages where there is a clear case of tenant negligence.[181] The standards and procedures which local managements have used to assess monetary damages are of questionable validity under federal statutory and administrative policy. Many of the objections appear to have been resolved by HUD's directive regarding leases.

8.114   Among the questionable practices of management was the addition of fees and charges, termed "additional rent payments," to the normal monthly rent. Often the tenant would not be informed about such payments until the day the rent was to be paid, and summary action for eviction was often brought against tenants for failure to pay this "compound rent."[182] Dispossession for failure to pay such additional charges did not seem to be sanctioned by the federal policy, and particularly by the rent schedule of the *Management Manual.*[183] Nevertheless, clauses in many standard form leases for public housing provided that the tenant would pay "additional rent" for these charges. The new HUD directive requires that there be a separate legal process for collecting any monetary damages,[184] thus bypassing the question of the authority of local officials to attach additional fees to the standard rent. The new HUD requirements prohibit what has been characterized as an increase in rent without a complementary increase in a tenant's income.[185]

8.115   The more explicit allocation of responsibilities between management and tenant in upkeep and maintenance of public housing will prevent assessment of fees for services which should have been rendered as part of the management functions, or for the replacement of physical facilities which have depreciated from normal use. Coupled with management's primary responsibility for the upkeep of the project, specification of management's duties will help prevent penalizing the tenant for outside vandalism. Additionally, the opportunity for a hearing will help the tenant uncover any questionable fining practices which LHA management may employ.

8.116   The newly formulated grievance procedures could be of inestimable benefit to the tenant in challenging management practices in general, and the assessment of fines in particular. It has been found that the publication of regulations regarding fees and charges is generally included in standard form public housing leases, although often cast in small type.[186] Hence, many tenants often unwittingly agree to pay the cost or reasonable value of repair, as determined by the landlord, for any damages to the premises short of normal wear and tear.

8.117   Since the new HUD directive does not specify minimal standards for fines, legally questionable fines could still be included in public housing leases. Given the nature of standard form contracts, the possibility that a tenant may fail to comprehend the terms of the lease still exists. Hence, whether fines are questionable because of suspected practices of management or initial misinterpretation of a complicated standard form lease, the tenant now has an ultimate remedy in an administrative hearing.[187] Practices formerly shielded from examination by the tenant or review by the courts may now be challenged by a tenant in an administrative hearing and brought to light, and may ultimately be referred for scrutiny by judicial review.[188]

REDRESS OF GRIEVANCES

Common Law of Landlord and Tenant: Property
8.118   *Traditional landlord-tenant relations.* Common law remedies available to tenants whose landlords fail to keep the premises in good repair are notoriously inadequate.[189] These remedies are correspondingly of little effectiveness to public housing tenants, even though they possess any remedy available to private lessees, pursuant to a broad statutory waiver of LHA's immunity under most state enabling legislation.[190]

8.119   At common law the landlord has no duty to maintain the premises in a habitable condition unless he has covenanted to do so in the lease.[191] An express covenant to repair has probably never existed in any public housing lease.[192] However, the minimal HUD lease provisions[193] specifying the delineation of an LHA's responsibility to maintain the premises in accordance with federal statutory policy, local hous-

164

ing codes and HUD regulations, can be construed as such a covenant. The new lease requirements appear to have vitiated dubious proposals[194] that an externally imposed obligation to repair, either contractual[195] or statutory,[196] might be incorporated into the lease by implication.

8.120 But a viable remedy would hardly be achieved solely by changing the concept of the tenant as purchaser of an estate in land who is responsible for minor repairs of the premises. Even if the courts should interpret the new HUD lease requirements as imposing a duty on management to maintain the premises, common law precedent obligates tenants to pay rent regardless of the performance of management. Thus, a breach of an implied covenant to maintain the premises would not entitle the tenant to withhold his rent, and may be grounds for eviction.[198] The only remedy would be to institute an action against the LHA for damages measured by the rental value of the premises in their present nonconforming condition against the rental value had the proper standards of habitability been enforced.[199] But the award for damages has been estimated to be so insignificant in most cases that the remedy has been deemed useless.[200]

8.121 *Constructive eviction.* If the LHA's neglect of the premises is gross, a constructive eviction may result whether or not the duty to repair is part of the lease.[201] The standard for a constructive eviction has been "the substantial interference by the landlord with the tenant's right to quiet enjoyment" of his dwelling,[202] although the exact content of the term "substantial interference" is uncertain.

8.122 Unfortunately, the doctrine of constructive eviction dictates that the tenant vacate the premises to avoid future liability for rent.[203] Invariably, this remedy is wholly unsatisfactory to a low-income tenant, since the great demand for public housing and the shortage of decent private housing forces him to accept the status quo.[204]

8.123 Perhaps the only remedy that would be adequate for tenants in public housing would be a judicial ruling of "constructive eviction without abandonment,"[205] also called "partial constructive eviction."[206] This would involve combining the theory of "partial actual eviction," where an encroachment on the premises is grounds for the tenant to remain without paying rent,[207] with the traditional constructive eviction doctrine. Combining these two theories would allow the tenant to remain on the premises without paying rent, while still providing a partial "constructive" eviction.[208] The possibility of this doctrine being accepted is highly unlikely.[209] Another alternative, "equitable constructive eviction," argues that since most local housing codes obligate both public and private landlords to repair, and since leaving public housing is not reasonable due to a shortage of general housing supply, the tenant should argue that all remedies at law are inadequate.[210] Hence, under such circum-

165

stances the tenant should not be required to abandon the premises.[211] Unfortunately, proponents of this theory acknowledge its widespread judicial non-acceptance.

8.124   *Implied warranty of habitability.* Since the tenant is a purchaser of an estate in land, subject to the role of *caveat emptor,* common law has generally ruled that the lessor does not implicitly warrant the premises to be habitable.[212] The one exception to this rule in private property law is when a lease is attached to a furnished apartment.[213] It has been argued that since housing regulations apply to public housing, and are not limited to the renting of furnished apartments, it may be possible to conceive of an interpretation in which the public policy pursuant to both state and federal statutes creates an implied warranty of habitability.[214] Assuming such a theory is accepted, the tenant would then not only have to withhold rent, but would have to take the initiative in an action for damages against the housing authority.[215] This need for tenant activism has prompted the criticism that such a theory, even if judicially acceptable, would be wholly impractical, given the lack of awareness and expertise among tenants of the lower socioeconomic class.[216]

Common Law: Contracts
8.125   *Failure of consideration.* Leases have traditionally been treated as conveyances of interest in real property.[217] Consequently, contract principles requiring the dependency of promises have not been applied to leases.[218] However, an argument has been raised in support of the theory that modern leases are contracts as well as conveyances.[219]

8.126   According to this argument, a multiple dwelling lease resembles a contract for the purchase of space and services, in which utilities such as plumbing, heating, water and electricity are provided.[220] Since such services are purchased by contract, it has been reasoned that the obligation to provide them should be dependent on contract rules.[221] This theory should be applicable to public housing, which is subject to building code requirements which create the obligation to maintain the premises in good repair.[222] However, it has been recognized that this theory may only be applicable if the courts break from the traditional concept of independent covenants.[223] To date, this theory has little judicial support.[224]

8.127   *Illegal contract.* There is a well-established rule of law that a contract which violates a statute designed for police or regulatory purposes is illegal and unenforceable.[225] It has been argued that if local housing codes prohibit the renting of a habitation which is not safe, sanitary and in proper repair, a lease which fails to meet such standards should be illegal.[226]

8.128   Precedent for such an argument exists only in private contract law, and is not widely recognized. In an action for possession, the ten-

166

ant contended that the landlord had knowingly violated the District of Columbia Housing Regulations when he had leased a substandard unit, thus, it was argued, making the lease unenforceable because it was an illegal contract.[227] The Court of Appeals acknowledged the binding effect of the housing regulations prior to the lease agreement, holding that letting such premises made the contract illegal and unenforceable. In addition to the limited application of this holding, and its analogous relevance to public housing, the violation existed prior to the consummation of the lease. Consequently, a remedy under the theory of illegal contracts would not necessarily be available to tenants in housing where the breach was committed after the fact.

8.129 *Adhesion contracts.* LHAs standard form contracts formerly contributed to a disproportionate bargaining advantage in favor of management. While all the appropriate conditions exist to characterize the public housing lease as adhesive, courts have been reluctant to extend private contract precedents to the public sector. Courts which have ventured against contracts negotiated under unequal bargaining conditions have merely barred individual clauses which were unconscionable rather than the entire contract.

8.130 In the case of *Kay v. Cain,*[228] the District of Columbia Court of Appeals invalidated an immunity clause because a severe housing shortage created a disproportionate bargaining advantage for the housing authority. In *Vinson v. Greenburgh Housing Authority*[229] the court cited the nonnegotiability of public housing leases in granting the tenant's priority over the interests of the management.

8.131 Under HUD's new minimal lease provisions, the major objections to a standard form contract appear to have been vitiated. While the tenant still does not possess considerable individual bargaining power, it is highly unlikely that any court would now rule provisions of the lease invalid (indeed courts have been reluctant to do so up to this point) because of their adhesive nature. HUD's minimal guidelines for drawing the lease seemingly constitute adequate procedural guidelines. The current responsibility of management to maintain the upkeep of the project can be construed as creating an implied covenant to repair. The requirement for a separate legal process in the collection of fines will also eliminate the high incidence of abusive management practices.

8.132 *Tenants as third-party beneficiaries.* Since contract law permits a third party to enforce a contract made for his benefit,[230] it has been argued that the public housing tenant living in a substandard housing project should have a remedy for repair of the project.[231] Under the terms of the ACC, the LHA agrees to operate the project "wholly for the purpose of providing decent, safe, and sanitary dwellings . . . within the financial reach of families of low income."[232] The LHA further contracts

167

to maintain each project in "good repair, order and condition."[233] The object of these federal policies is obviously the low-income tenant.

8.133   There are two questionable aspects of the applicability of a third-party beneficiary theory to tenants in public housing.[234] It is possible to interpret public housing tenants as "donee" rather than "credit" beneficiaries. In other words, public housing tenants can be construed as being the beneficiaries of a gift, rather than discharging an obligation, under the federal statutes. Although originally only credit beneficiaries were entitled to recover as third-party beneficiaries, this distinction has become of little legal significance.[235]

8.134   The second question has to do with whether a tenant beneficiary can be ascertained at the time ACC legislation was drafted. This does not present a problem, since the housing program identifies the low-income socioeconomic class as the distinct group to be benefited, while the individual tenants are clearly identifiable beneficiaries.[236]

8.135   The case of *Shell v. Schmidt*[237] seems to be directly apposite to the circumstances of tenants in public housing. In this case, a group of veterans were allowed to recover damages, since the contract between the FHA and a local building contractor was construed as being made for the benefit of veterans as an ascertainable class of persons. The court held that the presence of the government, as one of the contracting parties, did not affect the applicability of the third-party beneficiary doctrine.[238] Although in *Shell* the court awarded only damages, specific performance is also available to third-party beneficiaries,[239] and would unquestionably be more appropriate for tenants in public housing, given the lack of an adequate supply of decent housing to tenants in this income range.

8.136   A subsidiary question under the third-party beneficiary theory is the precision of the terms "decent," "safe," "sanitary" and "good repair" for judicial determination.[240] Due to new HUD lease provisions requiring that the LHA spell out its responsibilities for maintenance,[241] the need for ad hoc judicial determination of the LHA's duties[242] is now unnecessary.

8.137   A strong argument in favor of the third-party beneficiary theory is its mere feasibility, given the scarcity of alternative remedies available to public housing tenants.[243] Since administrative remedies are now available to tenants in public housing, it is doubtful that courts will apply contract law to public housing. It is also highly unlikely that a court would consider a tenant's case on the grounds of a third-party beneficiary theory unless the administrative remedy of an LHA hearing had been exhausted. Consequently, the success of HUD's new lease and grievance procedures could determine the vitality of other proposed judicial remedies.

Administrative Remedies

8.138 *HUD grievance procedures.* It has been argued that the HAA should in some measure be made responsive to the complaints of public housing tenants when local authorities do not maintain projects in accordance with federal statutory and administrative goals.[244] The HAA possesses several sanctions to be levelled against nonconforming LHAs— all rather burdensome, in addition to being drastic remedies not commensurate with the minor problems of maintenance with which most public housing tenants are forced. Until recently, the HAA could reduce payments or completely terminate the grants under the ACC,[245] increase interest on loans to the LHA (loans which were seldom sought since they had to be repaid from the reserves of operating income), or convey the title of possession until a remedy was provided by the LHA. The lack of a mediatory remedy can be attributed to the failure of the Housing Act of 1937 to provide formal administrative procedures through which tenants could seek satisfaction when grievances arose.[246]

8.139 Because of the discretion granted to local authorities, and a perennial lack of funds for conducting adequate inspections, the HAA has rarely intervened directly in landlord-tenant disputes. Instead, it has restricted itself to the application of indirect pressure and verbal exhortation. In order to have had the HAA use its power to make the LHAs act, tenants would have had to ask the courts to review the HAA's inaction under the Administrative Procedure Act (APA).[247] However, there are several obstacles to this remedy.[248] First, there is some question as to the extent to which the HAA may be subject to judicial review due to the traditional judicial respect for administrative discretion. If the courts were to grant review the scope of inquiry would be narrow.[249] Conceivably, the tenant-plaintiff might argue that the HAA as an administrative agency must act pursuant to the federal statutory goals, although it is doubtful that a tenant would be granted relief for a minor grievance. Second, in order to obtain standing to sue the tenant must show that he has suffered a "legal wrong"[250] from the HAA's failure to require compliance with federal statutory policy providing for decent, safe and sanitary housing. Here again, the vague language in the federal statutes would have led the courts to fashion ad hoc remedies where there was an absence of specific guidelines. The term "legal wrong" was included in the APA to provide grounds for contesting the HAA if the state and federal statutes were silent on the standing issue.[251] Furthermore, federal courts have widely accepted the doctrine of conferring standing to a class of persons whose private interests are adversely affected, and who are supposed to be protected through congressional regulatory agencies.[252] Finally, the tenant must establish a basis for federal jurisdiction. While a tenant's action might never involve sufficient controversy to warrant federal jurisdiction, the APA does confer an independent ground for jurisdiction.[253] On this matter the courts hold diverse viewpoints.[254]

169

8.140 The new HUD lease and grievance procedures appear to provide the long-needed intermediate remedy for unsatisfactory housing conditions. An administrative hearing[255] will allow the tenant to initiate internal procedures, not only if the landlord has acted wrongly, but if he has failed to act in accordance with the new lease provisions. Consequently, tenants will have a self-regulatory mechanism[256] which is not subject to bureaucratic lethargy or judicial delay. Substantively, the internal procedures for an administrative hearing will enable tenants to secure a judicial remedy when the grievance involves insignificant monetary restitution.

8.141 Invaluable procedural requirements are also built into the provisions for an administrative hearing; they will balance the statuses of landlord and tenant and be conducive to fairer and more equitable management of public housing. The requirement that tenants be informed of the disposition of the LHA before a hearing[257] now allows the tenant adequate opportunity to prepare a case. Perhaps the most important procedural feature of the new requirements is the right of the tenant to bring in witnesses in his own behalf, and confront and cross-examine adverse witnesses.[258] This will help prevent questionable, nonvisible practices of management, such as retaliatory evictions, the assessment of "additional rent payments," and the levying of unsubstantiated fines. The collective procedure now guaranteed to the tenant promises to lend new balance to landlord-tenant relations and to enable the tenant to hold management accountable for its performance.

EVICTION FROM PUBLIC HOUSING; TERMINATION OF THE TENANCY
LEGAL BASIS
Federal Law: Over Income

8.142 The statutory criteria for eviction from public housing are almost identical with the federal standards established for admission. The legislative history of the 1937 Housing Act and its subsequent amendments indicates that Congress never intended to set any standards for eligibility other than low income.[259]

8.143 The 1937 Act, as amended, requires "periodic re-examination" of tenant income, in the course of which the LHA must:

> . . . require any family whose income has increased beyond the approved maximum income limits for continued occupancy to move from the project unless the public housing agency determines that, due to special circumstances the family is unable to find decent, safe and sanitary housing within its financial reach. . . . [260]

8.144 In the Housing and Rent Act of 1947[261] and the Housing Act of 1948 (federal rent control),[262] a section was added which is now incorporated into the original 1937 Act[263] empowering the LHA:

. . . to maintain an action or proceeding to recover possession of any housing accommodations operated by it where such action is authorized by the statute or regulations under which such housing accommodations are administered. . . . [264]

8.145   Although in several cases courts have relied upon this federal act as conferring power upon a local authority to evict regardless of or without a reason, its legislative history indicates that the act was intended only to allow local housing authorities to evict tenants whose incomes exceeded the prescribed limits.[265]

8.146   In 1959, amendments to the original Housing Act gave power and discretion to the LHA to determine eligibility standards.

8.147   State enabling statutes, like federal statutes, specify no standards for occupancy other than income limitation. State statutes express a legislative intent to preserve the low-rent nature of each project in the administration of standards for tenant selection, continued occupancy and rent formulation.

8.148   Under the terms of the ACC, which repeats the language of the 1937 Housing Act statute, the only criterion for eligibility is financial need. While the ACC does not specify conditions for eviction, its language emphasizes the low-rent quality of the project as the minimum condition for performance of the contract.

8.149   Nevertheless, several HAA directives previously mentioned[266] have been applied narrowly, without reference to the policy statement of federal statutes. These advisory directives have been interpreted as granting additional substantive power by local officials, to be applied in both admission and eviction determinations.

8.150   HAA advisory directives have become important only through their selective reading by the LHAs. Several HAA regulations and directives do define the issue of continued eligibility. The *Low-Rent Management Manual* sets forth low income as the only qualification for continued residency in a public housing project.[267] The *Management Handbook* broadens the eviction power of the LHA to include cases in which income is misrepresented or the terms of the lease are violated.[268]

8.151   Despite the policy intent of federal statutes and the silence of state enabling statutes on all criteria other than income limitations, courts have rejected arguments for the invalidity of LHA determinations based on standards other than income. Despite all legislative history to the contrary, courts interpreted federal statutes as authorizing evictions on the basis of nonfinancial criteria.

Month-to-Month Lease Governing Tenancy

171

8.152   It has been argued that since the LHA contracts under the ACC to operate each project "in such a manner as to promote serviceability, efficiency, economy and stability,"[269] officials are implicitly authorized to exclude or evict from residence in public housing those people who would be detrimental to its operation. To a certain degree this argument concedes to the proponents of decentralization decision-making in eviction determinations. Indeed, the LHA must be able to exclude tenants who constitute a habitual social nuisance if it is to have control over the project's welfare. However, the argument is not nearly as persuasive for admission determinations since a history of social deviance will not always indicate the way a person would relate to neighbors in a housing project. Furthermore, the power to evict should be fettered by constitutional and legal prohibitions.

8.153   The HAA has facilitated the eviction of a tenant by recommending that the lease between tenant and local authority:

> . . . be drawn on a month-to-month basis whenever possible. This should permit any necessary evictions to be accomplished with a minimum of delay and expense upon the giving of a statutory Notice to Quit.[270]

On its face, the *Handbook* must be interpreted as empowering the LHA to discontinue a lease on 30 days notice. Federal legislation stipulates income limitations as the sole criterion for eviction. Federal directives prescribe no other standards, but do grant administrative discretion. Thus, a review of judicial opinion on the extent of administrative immunity is the only gauge of LHA authority under the leasing recommendations of the *Handbook*.

The Early Case Law
8.154   The recommendations governing the terms of the lease, with the authority for eviction vested in the LHA by the provisions of the Housing Act, have given courts valid cause to reject any contention that the tenant has indefinite tenure or a vested right to an apartment. However, the courts have gone a step further by ruling that in the absence of a statutory prohibition, the LHA has general eviction power to be governed by the local law of landlord-tenant relations. This has generally enabled local authorities to evict without fear of judicial review. The prevailing legal principle in most public housing cases has been that the terms of the lease circumscribe any rights the tenants might claim. The language in the following opinion is typical.

> Any property right acquired by the plaintiffs was circumscribed by the terms and conditions upon which it was founded. True, as tenants, they acquired the right of possession, but this right was limited by the terms of the lease by which such right was obtained . . . It is our opinion that (the) provisions with reference to the termination of the tenancy are valid and bind-

ing upon plaintiffs in the same manner as though the lessor had been a private person rather than a Governmental Agency.[271]

8.155   The *Brand* case quoted above outlined the major suppositions which have been so detrimental to tenants attempting to bring suit against local authorities. First, the Court enunciated the principle that the rights and duties of the federal government in a contract are governed by the law applicable to private individuals.[272] As mentioned, this private law of landlord-tenant relations has traditionally allowed local authorities to evict without reason, and without fear of judicial review.

8.156   Second, the federal court in the *Brand* case rejected the argument that tenants were entitled to a hearing, since such a claim is actually subject to the sole discretion of the owner of the property.[273] This second point reveals an underlying judicial theory of landlord-tenant relations in public housing: a presumption of validity in the matter of administrative regulations, even where procedures have circumvented due process requirements. In most cases, courts are reluctant to invalidate administrative regulations, since it is easier to find that under the facts of the particular case, the local authority failed to apply properly its otherwise valid regulations.[274] This respect for existing administrative regulations has curbed judicial incursion to the extent that the only limitation imposed by the courts on the power to evict was that an LHA could not use a legally or constitutionally invalid reason for eviction, if a reason was stated.[275] Thus, the statement of a reason by the LHA became the only grounds upon which a tenant could challenge an eviction. Even then, the courts would not uphold a tenant's claim unless the underlying reason for eviction, as stated by the LHA, was adjudged to be unconstitutional or contrary to public policy. In the 1954 case of *Rudder v. United States,*[276] the right of the tenant to challenge the validity of an eviction determination was upheld on the grounds that the LHA had cited a basis for eviction which involved constitutionally protected rights of the tenant. Shortly thereafter, the Public Housing Administration (now HAA) issued an advisory circular which implied criticism of LHA eviction proceedings which gave no reason for the determination.[277]

8.157   This 1954 circular set an historical precedent which has, until recently, influenced LHA procedures. It reinforced administrative immunity by prescribing an alternative method for eviction. The circular recommended the use of the terms in the lease as the sole basis for eviction. As explained by the circular, the citation by a landlord in a Statutory Notice to Quit of a provision contained in the lease, "permits termination within a specified time without reference to any other provision (in the lease)."[278] Thus, the terms of the lease become the defining factor in judicial scrutiny of any claim by a public housing tenant. Further-

173

more, invoking the Statutory Notice to Quit has the effect of a legal red flag which causes courts to defer to administrative discretion. Based upon the terms of the lease, the court in *Brand* rejected the contention that the status of a tenant entitles him to a continuing right of tenure.[279]

DUE PROCESS DEPRIVATION

Month-to-Month Lease: New HUD Policy

8.158 More recent statements in HAA directives indicate an inclination to ameliorate the harsh effects of eviction procedures under the terms of the month-to-month lease. Possibly, the new HUD emphasis can be attributed to heightened awareness of tenant problems, or to concern with the vulnerability of administrative prerogatives under increasing due process challenges.[280]

8.159 In a set of circulars recently issued, the HAA announced a new policy governing LHA eviction determinations. In May 1966, HAA indicated an enlightened view of tenant challenges to LHA evictions which did not cite a reason for eviction.[281] It was "strongly urged" that the reason for eviction be communicated in a "private conference."

8.160 In a circular issued in February 1967, a detailed set of procedures was outlined for eviction proceedings.[282] The importance of a "private conference" was reiterated. Furthermore, it was the "belief" of federal officials that the aggrieved tenant should be afforded an opportunity to "make such reply or explanation as he may wish." The publication prescribed a model format for records of eviction, which the circular stated, "each Local Authority shall maintain... to be available for review... by HUD representatives...."

8.161 The circular was published under the auspices of HUD, as distinguished from the 1966 circular issued by the HAA. The detail in which the former circular was framed regarding internal regulation, indicates an alteration in federal policy, presumably toward more stringent regulation of eviction procedures by the federal agencies.

8.162 The federal courts have recently reaffirmed that the public landlord must give sufficient notice of good cause for eviction to the tenant. In *McQueen v. Drucker,* the court held that a private landlord receiving government assistance, in the form of an urban renewal site, an FHA mortgage and real estate tax exemptions, must give his tenant a good cause notice, in line with those required for public housing tenants.[283]

Enforceability of Federal Regulations by Tenants: Vagueness of HUD Circular

8.163 The 1967 HUD circular is ambiguous as to enforcement and the legal standing of public housing tenants. It makes the filing of records mandatory. But it appears to maintain previous administrative immunity in internal procedures, since the circular clearly states that "such records are to be available for review . . . by HUD representatives. . . ." The language leads to the conclusion that tightened regulation was intended by federal administrative scrutiny of LHA eviction proceedings, through the investigation of detailed records.

8.164   Closely related is the ambiguity about the legal effect of provisions urging the notification of the reasons for eviction. The circular states that federal administrative authorities "believe it is essential that . . . (a) tenant be given . . . the reasons for eviction. . . ." However, the interpretation of the "belief" as implying a nonmandatory recommendation is reinforced, when compared to the use of the legally mandatory term "shall," regarding filing records for eviction. The distinction between the terms "shall" and "belief," supports the conclusion that the circular enunciated tighter regulation of LHA internal procedures by federal administrative authorities, while preserving local administrative discretion in evictions.

Mandatory Nature of Administrative Regulations
8.165   The circumstances surrounding the issuance of the circulars gives an interesting insight into the possible underlying motives of HUD and HAA. The May 1966 circular indicated awareness of suits challenging LHA eviction determinations. Two months prior to the issuance of the February 1967 circular the Supreme Court accepted the case of *Thorpe v. Housing Authority*[284] for review.

8.166   The petitioner challenged an eviction proceeding in which notice had been given pursuant to the lease, but without reason or provision for a hearing. The petitioner raised the constitutional questions that her First Amendment rights had been abridged as a result of her eviction. She also claimed that a constitutional right to a notice of eviction existed, as well as a hearing upon such eviction. In other words, a plea was made to the Court to grant due process protection in administrative determinations as a matter of constitutional right.

8.167   While this case was pending, HUD issued its circular of February 1967. In view of the intervening circular the Supreme Court remanded the case to the state supreme court for further proceedings. In passing, however, the Court, in a per curiam opinion, refused to comment on the legal status of the circular, the extent to which it bound local authorities, and the effect of the circular upon the petitioner.[285] The circular thus forestalled a decision of the Court upon questions of due process requirements in administrative proceedings which could have had far-reaching implications.

8.168   When the state supreme court held that the circular had no retroactive effect, the Supreme Court accepted an appeal for rehearing. In holding that the circular applied in the current case, the Court cited correspondence of HUD officials as proof of the generic mandatory nature of the circular.[286] Furthermore, the Court acknowledged deference to federal administrative discretion, saying that "when construing an administrative regulation, a court must necessarily look to the administrative construction of the regulation if the meaning is in doubt....[287] In comparing the two successive circulars, the Court was led to conclude that the distinction in language was evidence of a mandatory effect of the latter circular.[288]

8.169   The Court rebuffed a strong contention by the LHA that the circular conflicted with the rule-making power of HUD,[289] which, it was contended, was limited to "vest(ing) in the local public housing agencies the maximum amount of responsibility in the administration of the low-rent housing program, with due consideration to accomplishing the objectives of this (1937) Act while effecting economies." In disposing of this claim, the Court emphasized the minimal effect of the HUD circular, in support of which it mentioned the brief of the LHA as concurring in this matter.[291] The brief of the respondent LHA is noteworthy, for it indicates the narrow effect of the Court decision by illuminating what the Court interprets the circular to exclude:

> It does not . . . purport to change the terms of the lease . . . nor does it purport to take away from the Housing Authority its legal ability to evict by complying with the terms of the lease and the pertinent provisions of the State law relating to evictions. It does not deal with what reasons are acceptable to HUD . . . Moreover, the Circular clearly does not say that a Housing Authority cannot terminate at the end of any term without cause as is provided in the lease.[292]

In other words, the LHA may evict a tenant for any reason, except his participation in constitutionally protected activities,[293] as long as it states that reason. However, in cases raising a novel constitutional question, the tenant would have to challenge the reason for an eviction in judicial proceedings.

8.170   What prompted the propitious issuance of the 1967 HUD circular is uncertain. However, its practical effect is clear enough. When a petitioner argued the necessity of a Court ruling which would guarantee her "a hearing that comports with the requirements of due process . . ."[294] the Court invoked a longstanding doctrine of judicial self-restraint in refusing "to decide any constitutional question in advance of the necessity for its decision. . ."[295] Thus, interposing the administrative circular precluded Supreme Court adjudication of due process requirements in administrative procedures. The Court indicated this when it outlined alternative administrative remedies available to the petitioner in light of the provisions of the circular. The *Thorpe* opinion indicates that the Supreme Court will resolve the due process question only when all other remedies, both administrative and judicial, have been exhausted.

8.171   The effect of the *Thorpe* decision upon the rights of a tenant threatened with eviction are, in several respects, ambiguous. Previously, the courts looked only to the terms of the lease in cases involving public housing. The only restriction which courts previously imposed was that the local authority was prohibited from evicting in violation of a constitutional right or statement of public policy.[296] The statement of a reason for eviction was the legal prerogative of the LHA. After the PHA circular of 1954, evictions were routinely accomplished under the terms of the Statutory Notice to Quit, thus obviating the possibility of judicial review. A tenant thus evicted was faced with the burden of discovering a retaliatory motive on the part of the LHA, and the additional problem of proving that the notice violated his constitutionally protected rights.[297] A tenant challenging an eviction notice often found that local landlord-tenant proceedings did not allow him to raise a legal or constitutional defense to the eviction, the limit of his defense being the terms of the lease.[298] *Thorpe* supersedes previous case law to the extent that evictions may not be accomplished solely by invoking the terms of the lease. The *Thorpe* decision establishes the mandatory effect of the 1967 HUD circular, requiring the statement of a basis for eviction. On the basis of *Thorpe,* an eviction which allegedly infringes constitutional rights may be adjudicated by a local court.

8.172   But the standards of procedure secured by *Thorpe* are hardly adequate to protect a tenant against invidious discrimination by local officials. Notification of a basis for eviction and an opportunity for a tenant to give a reply are not always crucial protections against evictions when the underlying motive is constitutionally or legally suspect. Indeed, the greatest incidence of retaliatory evictions has been the practice of terminating a tenancy without reason.[299] While *Thorpe* effectively invalidates that procedure, a number of other practices ceded to administrative discretion may be used in eviction determinations to shield unconscionable discrimination from judicial review.

8.173   The mandatory provisions of the 1967 HUD circular, as interpreted in *Thorpe,* require only that a "tenant be . . . told by the Local Authority, in a private conference or other appropriate manner, the reasons for the eviction, and given an opportunity to make such reply or explanation as he may wish." Clearly, *Thorpe* barely provides for the entire class of procedural due process guarantees which are basic to judicial proceedings.[300]

8.174 An administrative proceeding need not embody all of the traditional due process requirements, although certain minimal standards are essential.[301] First, the basis for an eviction is communicated, in many LHA determinations, so vaguely as to make the *Thorpe* requirement only a theoretical safeguard. As long as the LHA is allowed to notify tenants through classifications of ineligibility which are unduly broad and vague, the notification requirement can be circumvented for discriminatory motives. Access to a complete dossier of a tenant's behavior would be in accordance with due process to prevent discriminatory evictions.

8.175 A second basic procedural deprivation which *Thorpe* fails to ameliorate is the *ex parte* quality of eviction determinations. While the HUD circular provides for notification of the tenant, the "private conference" fails to affect the independent nature of LHA decision-making in eviction hearings.

Importance of a Due Process Hearing

8.176 Traditionally, the rights to cross-examine and confront adverse witnesses have been the procedural methods of insuring against *ex parte* determinations in judicial proceedings. These due process safeguards have had the additional effect of enabling the determination of truth and the uncovering of falsehood. By analogy, these two procedural safeguards are part and parcel of a tenant's presence at his own eviction hearing, and enable him to challenge the evidence brought against him.

8.177 The counter-argument made by the LHA is that confrontation between tenant and witnesses must be conceded to two more important values—the necessity of protecting informers from possible reprisals and the desire to avoid placing an overwhelming administrative burden on the eligibility committee.[302] However, since the Supreme Court has indicated that due process of law requires appropriate safeguards in adjudicatory or summary administrative proceedings,[303] the only defense to administrative discretion would be the existence of a compelling governmental interest,[304] and there is convincing evidence to refute any such contention.

8.178 While the two due process guarantees are most vital to insuring tenants' rights, other administrative procedures employed by LHAs contribute significantly to the deprivation of tenants' rights. In some instances local authorities allow tenants to be present at their hearings. Since administrative procedures usually dictate that the source of information be protected from identification, much of the evidence brought against the tenant in an eviction proceeding is compiled through written statements. This constitutes hearsay evidence against the tenant

178

and, in general, a lack of proper standards of evidence. A provision for a hearing can be meaningless if informal standards are employed.

8.179   Furthermore, the 1967 HUD circular merely provides an opportunity to reply to a reason for eviction, which is meaningless unless a formal process of appeal is available to the tenant. Without appeal to an independent arbitrating body, a power of summary determination is vested in the decision-making body.

NOTES

The author gratefully acknowledges the assistance of G. Jeffrey Pancza in the preparation of this chapter.

1. U.S. Housing Act of 1937, 42 U.S.C., Sec. 1401 (Supp. 1968).

2. *Id.,* Sec. 1402(1).

3. U.S. Housing Act of 1949, 42 U.S.C., Sec. 1441(1964).

4. *Id.*

5. *Id.*

6. Economic Opportunity Act of 1964, 42 U.S.C., Sec. 2701.

7. U.S. Housing Act of 1937, *supra* note 1, Secs. 1401-22.

8. Department of HUD, Low-Rent Public Housing Program: Consolidated Annual Contributions Contract, Pt. II, Sec. 213 (May 1967).

9. U.S. Housing Act of 1937, *supra* note 1, Secs. 1401, 1404, 1409, 1410 (Supp. 1968).

10. Schoshinski, *Public Landlord and Tenants; Survey of Developing Law,* 1969 *Duke L.J.* 399, 405(1969).

11. *Id.* at 407-8.

12. *Id.* at 162.

13. 42 U.S.C. Sec. 413.

14. U.S. Housing Act of 1959, 42 U.S.C. Sec. 401(1964).

15. 75 Stat. 149.

16. U.S. Housing Act of 1961, 42 U.S.C. Sec. 401(1964).

17. Rosen, Michael, *Tenants' Rights in Public Housing* at 161 *Housing for the Poor: Rights and Remedies* (1967).

18. Schoshinski, *supra* note 10, at 157-8.

19. Welfeld, *A New Framework for Federal Housing Aids,* 69 *Colum. L. Rev.* 1355, 1360(1970).

20. *Id.,* at 1361.

21. *Building the American City,* Report of the National Commission on Urban Problems to the Congress and the President of the United States, at 109(1968).

22. *Id.*

23. 42 U.S.C. Sec. 1410(h) (Supp. IV, 1965).

24. Welfeld, *supra* note 19, at 1361.

25. *Building the American City supra* note 21, at 108.

26. Welfeld, *supra* note 19, at 1369.

27. *Building the American City, supra* note 21, at 121.

28. *Id.*

29. *Id.*

30. Welfeld, *supra* note 19, at 1368.

31. *Id.*

32. *Building the American City, supra* note 21, at 121.

33. Welfeld, *supra* note 19, at 1369.

34. *Id.*

35. *Id.* at 1361.

36. *Id.* at 1362.

37. *Id.*

38. *Building the American City, supra* note 21, at 117.

39. *Id.*

40. *Id.*

41. *Id.*

42. 42 U.S.C. Sec. 1401 (Supp. 1964).

43. 42 U.S.C. Sec. 1402(1) (1964).

44. Schoshinski, *supra* note 10, at 404.

45. *Id.* at 405.

46. *Id.* at 402.

47. *Message from the President of the United States, First Annual Report on National Housing Goals, H.R. Doc.* No. 91-63, 91st Cong., 1st Sess. 95(1969) (Appendix D—Technical Note on Preparation of Cost Estimates) in Welfeld, *supra* note 19, at 1362.

48. Welfeld, *supra* note 19, at 1362.

49. Schoshinski, *supra* note 10, at 402.

50. *Id.*

51. *Id.* at 405.

52. *Id.* at 406.

53. *Id.* at 409.

54. *Low-Rent Housing Handbook, RHA* 7485.1 a (1).

55. Schoshinski, *supra* note 10, at 409.

56. 42 U.S.C. Sec. 1401 (1964).

57. Schoshinski, *supra* note 10, at 418.

58. *Id.* at 419.

59. ACC, *supra* note 8, Secs. 201(1), 202, 204, 207.

60. *Local Housing Authority Management Handbook,* Sec. 1, para. 3, sub-Sec. b (July, 1965).

61. *Low-Rent Management Manual,* Sec. 35(Oct. 1967).

62. *LHA Management Handbook, supra* note 60, Pt. IV, Sec. 1, 2(f).

63. Schoshinski, *supra* note 10, at 420.

64. Rosen, *supra* note 17, at 225.

65. Schoshinski, *supra* note 10, at 227.

66. *Id.* at 227.

67. *LHA Management Handbook, supra* note 60, Pt. IV, Sec. 1, 2(f).

68. Schoshinski, *supra* note 10, at 422.

69. *Id.* at 423.

70. *Id.* at 425.

71. 294 F. Supp. 134 (S.D.N.Y. 1968).

72. Gulf, Colorado and San Francisco R.R. v. Ellis, 165 U.S. 150, 155(1896).

73. Rosen, *supra* note 17, at 234.

74. Sherbert v. Vesner, 374 U.S. 398(1963). *But see* Wyman v. James, 400 U.S. 309 (1971) where the court held that a home visit, prescribed by state statutes and regulations as a condition for assistance under AFDC program, although possessing some of the characteristics of a search in criminal law sense, did not fall within Fourth Amendment's proscription against unreasonable searches and seizures, where visit was made by a caseworker and was not permitted outside working hours, and forcible entry and snooping were prohibited.

75. Griswold v. Connecticut, 381 U.S. 479 (1965); Meyer v. Nebraska, 272 U.S. 390(1923); Skinner v. Oklahoma, 316 U.S. 535(1942).

76. Meyer v. Nebraska, 262 U.S. 390(1923).

77. Skinner v. Oklahoma, 316 U.S. 535(1942).

78. Rosen, *supra* note 17, at 236.

79. *Id.* at 236.

80. *Id.*

81. *See* Shelton v. Tucker, 364 U.S. 479(1960); NAACP v. Alabama, 377 U.S. 288(1964).

82. Bates v. City of Little Rock, 361 U.S. 516, 524(1960).

83. McLaughlin v. Florida, 379 U.S. 184 196(1964).

84. Shapiro v. Thompson, 394 U.S. 618(1969).

85. Schoshinski, *supra* note 10, at 424.

86. *Id.* at 425.

87. Id. at 447.

88. *Id.*

89. 42 U.S.C. Sec. 1401 (g) (2) (1964).

90. *ACC, supra* note 8, Sec. 206, para. 8 (April 1966).

91. *See* 42 *C.J.S.* 543(1944).

92. *Low-Rent Management Manual,* Preface, iii (April 1962).

93. Schoskinski, *supra* note 10, at 166.

94. *Id.* at 167.

95. *Low-Rent Management Manual,* Sec. 35(Oct. 1967).

96. Rosen, *supra* note 17, at 168.

97. *Id.* at 169.

98. 32A *C.J.S. Ex parte* (1964).

99. Rosen, *supra* note 17, at 172.

100. Rudder v. U.S. 226 F.2d 51 (D.C. Cir. 1955).

101. Greene v. McElroy, 360 U.S. 474 (1959).

102. In re Gault, 387 U.S. 1, 31-4 (1967).

103. In re Murchison, 349 U.S. 133, 136-7 (1965).

104. Gonzales v. Freemen, 334 F.2d 570, 578 (D.C. Cir. 1964).

105. Greene v. McElroy, *supra* note 101, at 506-8.

106 Burlington Truck Lines, Inc. v. U.S. 371 U.S. 156, 169-70 (1962).

107. *See* note 61 *supra.*

108. Shapiro v. Thompson, 394 U.S. 618 (1969).

109. *See Low-Rent Management Manual,* Sec. 3.8; para 6, p. 6 (May 1966).

110. Schoshinski, *supra* note 10, at 466.

111. Notwithstanding possible common law standardization of private leases on this matter, the Federal Statutory Authorization for a yearly review of a tenant's income seems to conflict with the notion of a monthly tenancy.

112. Sales, *Standard Form Contracts,* 16 *Modern Law Review* 318 (1953).

113. Note, *Standard Form Leases in Wisconsin,* 1966 *Wisc. L. Rev.* 583 (1966).

114. *Id.*

115. Kessler, *Contracts of Adhesion—Some Thoughts About Freedom of Contract,* 43 *Colum. L. Rev.* 629, 632 (1943).

116. *Supra* note 113.

117. *Id.* at 585.

118. *Id.*

119. *Id.* at 585-6.

120. Schoshinski, *supra* note 10, at 468.

121. Schoshinski, *Remedies of the Indigent Tenant: Proposal for Change,* 54 *Geo. L.J.* 519, 555 (1966).

122. Schoshinski, *supra* note 10, at 468.

123. *Id.*

124. Schoshinski, *supra* note 121, at 544.

125. Kay v. Cain, 154 F.2d 305 (D.C. Cir. 1946).

126. *Id.* at 306.

127. Schoshinski, *supra* note 121, at 566.

128. Note, *The Significance of Comparative Bargaining Power in the Law of Exculpation,* 37 *Colum. L. Rev.* 248, 262-3 (1937).

129. *Id.* at 263.

130. *Id.* at 249.

131. Note, *Exculpation Contrary to Public Policy Where Landlord is Public Housing Authority,* 44 *Washington L. Rev.* 498, 502 (1969).

132. *Id.* at 503.

133. *Id.*

134. *Id.*

135. *Id.* at 504.

136. Housing Assistance Administration, Department of Housing and Urban De-

velopment, *Low-Rent Management Manual,* Pt. IV, Sec. 1, para. 6(d) (2) (July 1965).

137. Schoshinski, *supra* note 121, at 557.

138. Schoshinski, *supra* note 10, at 469.

139. Schoshinski, *supra* note 10, at 469; Schoshinski, *supra* note 121, at 557.

140. Schoshinski, *supra* note 10, at 470.

141. *Id.*

142. *Id.*

143. *Id.*

144. *Id.* at 471.

145. *Id.*

146. Schoshinski, *supra* note 121, at 557.

147. Schoshinski, *supra* note 10, at 471.

148. See HUD Bulletin No. 70-643 (Sept. 1, 1970); HUD Circular RHM 7465.6 (August 10, 1970).

149. HUD Bulletin, *supra* note 148.

150. *Id.*

151. *Id.*

152. See HUD Bulletin No. 70-90; HUD Circular RHM 7465.8 and RHM 7465.9 (Feb. 22, 1971). The validity of HUD's model lease and grievance procedure is still in doubt. *See* Housing Authority of the City of Omaha v. United States Housing Authority, Civ. No. 71-0-287 (U.S. District Court, District of Nebraska, 1972); *But see* Glover v. Housing Authority, 444 F.2d 158 (5th Cir. 1971).

153. HUD Bulletin, *supra* note 152.

154. HUD Circular RHM 7465.8, Sec. 2, para. 6.

155. HUD Circular RHM 7465.8, Sec. 3; RHM 7465.9, Sec. 3.

156. ACC, *supra* note 8, Sec. 203(b).

157. HUD Circular RHM 7465.8, Sec. 3, para. b(2).

158. Note, *Fines in Public Housing, 68 Colum. L. Rev.* 1538 (1968).

159. HUD Circular RHM 7465.8, Sec. 3, para. b(4) (a).

160. 42 U.S.C., Sec. 1410 (g) (3).

161. *Public Housing. 22 Vand. L. Rev.* 875, 947 (1969).

162. HUD Circular RHM 7465.8, Appendix 1, Sec. 5.

163. Schoshinski, *supra* note 10, at 456-7.

164. 42 U.S.C. Sec. 1410 (g) (3) (1964); ACC. *supra* note 8 Sec. 207 (b).

165. *Public Housing, supra* note 161, at 946.

166. *Id.* note 286, at 946.

167. *Id.*

168. *Id.*

169. HUD Circular RHM 7465.8, Sec. 3, para. b(4) (c).

170. Schoshinski, *supra* note 10, at 457.

171. HUD Circular RHM 7465.8, Sec. 4, para. b.

172. *Public Housing. supra* note 161, at 950.

173. HUD Circular RHM 7465.8, Sec. 3, para. b(12).

174. *Id.*, Sec. 4, para. b(8).

175. *Id.*, Sec. 3, para. b(6).

176. Schoshinski, *supra* note 10, at 456-8.

177. *Id.*

178. 42 U.S.C. Sec. 1401(1964).

179. Schoshinski, *supra* note 10, at 458.

180. Public Housing Administration, *Local Housing Authority Management Handbook,* Pt. II, Sec. 6, para 3(a) (Feb. 1966).

181. HUD Circular RHM 7465.8, Sec. 3, para. b (5) (6) (7).

182. *Fines in Public Housing, supra* note 158.

183. Schoshinski, *supra* note 10, note 272 at 456; Schoshinski, *supra* note 121, at 458; *Fines in Public Housing, supra* note 158, at 1543-4.

184. HUD Circular RHM 7465.8, Sec. 3, para. b(7).

185. Schoshinski, *supra* note 10, at 458.

186. *Fines in Public Housing, supra* note 158, note 19 at 1541.

187. HUD Circular RHM 7465.9, Sec. 3, para. a.

188. *Id.*, Sec. 3, para. g.

189. Note, *Remedies for Tenants in Substandard Public Housing,* 68 *Colum. L. Rev.* 561, 562 (1968); for a fuller discussion of the landlord's obligation to deliver and keep the premises in habitable condition, see 3.2-3.14.

190. *Remedies for Tenants, supra* note 189, note 20 at 562-3.

191. *Id.* at 563; *Public Housing, supra* note 161, at 976; *See also* 2 R. Powell, *The Law of Real Property,* Sec. 233, at 300 (1967).

192. *Id.*

193. HUD Circular RHM 7465.8, Sec. 3, para. 8.

194. *Remedies for Tenants, supra* note 189, at 563, and Schoshinski, *supra* note 121, at 523-8.

195. According to the terms of the ACC, *supra* note 8, Sec. 213.

196. Pursuant to 42 U.S.C. Sec. 1402(1) and the terms of various local housing codes and state enabling legislation; *See also* 2 R. Powell, *supra* note 191, para. 233(2), at 309-21.

197. *Remedies for Tenants, supra* note 189, at 563; *Public Housing, supra* note 161, at 976; *See also* 2 R. Powell, *supra* note 191, Sec. 230(3), at 262-3.

198. *Remedies for Tenants, supra* note 189, at 563; *Public Housing, supra* note 161, at 976.

199. *Remedies for Tenants, supra* note 189, at 563; Schoshinski, *supra* note 121, at 527.

200. *Remedies for Tenants, supra* note 189, at 564.

201. *Id.*

202. *Id. See also* discussion of constructive eviction, 7.7-7.9 and 4.2.

203. *Remedies for Tenants, supra* note 189, at 564; *Public Housing, supra* note 161, at 976-7.

204. *Remedies for Tenants, supra* note 189, at 564; Schoshinski, *supra* note

121, at 530.

205. *Public Housing, supra* note 161, at 977.

206. *Remedies for Tenants, supra* note 189, at 564.

207. *Id.*

208. *Id.,* Schoshinski, *supra* note 121, at 529-32.

209. *Remedies for Tenants, supra* note 189, at 546; Schoshinski, *supra* note 121, at 530-2.

210. *Public Housing, supra* note 161, at 977.

211. *Id.*

212. *Id.* at 978; for a fuller discussion of implied warranty of habitability, see 4.2-4.8 and 7.5, 7.6.

213. *Public Housing, supra* note 161, at 978.

214. *Ud,*

215. *Id.*

216. *Id.*

217. *Id.* at 979.

218. *Id.*

219. *Id.*

220. *Id.*

221. *Id.,* Schoshinski, *supra* note 211, at 534.

222. *Id.*

223. *Id.*

224. *Id.*

225. *Public Housing, supra* note 161, at 979-80.

226. *Id.* at 980.

227. Brown v. Southall Realty Co., 237 A.2d 834 (D.C. Ct. App. 1968).

228. 154 F.2d 305 (D.C. Cir. 1946).

229. 29 App. Div. 2d 338, 288 N.Y.S. 2d 159 (1968).

230. 4 *A. Corbin, Contracts,* Sec. 782, at 78-80 (1951); 2 *S. Williston, Contracts,* Sec. 356, at 828 (3rd ed. 1959).

231. *Public Housing, supra* note 161, at 981; *Remedies for Tenants, supra* note 189, at 576-9.

232. ACC, *supra* note 8, Pt. II, Sec. 201.

233. *Id.,* Sec. 213.

234. *Public Housing, supra* note 161, at 980; *Remedies for Tenants, supra* note 189, at 577; *See also Restatement (Second) of Contracts* Sec. 133 (1967).

235. *Public Housing, supra* note 161, at 980; *Remedies for Tenants, supra* note 189, at 577.

236. *Public Housing, supra* note 161, at 982; *Remedies for Tenants, supra* note 189, at 577.

237. 126 Cal. App. 279, 272 P.2d 82 (1954).

238. *Id.* at 290, 272 P.2d at 89.

239. *See 4 A. Corbin, Contracts,* Sec. 810, at 230-2 (1951).

240. *Remedies for Tenants, supra* note 189, at 578.

241. HUD Circular RHM 7465.8, Sec. 3, para. 8.

242. *Remedies for Tenants, supra* note 189, at 578.

243. *Id.* at 578-9.

244. *Public Housing, supra* note 161, at 988-9; *Remedies for Tenants, supra* note 189, at 565.

245. 42 U.S.C. Sec. 1415 (3) (1964).

246. *Public Housing, supra* note 161, at 988.

247. 5 U.S.C. Sec. 702 (1966); *see Public Housing, supra* note 161, at 988 and *Remedies for Tenants, supra* note 189, at 566.

248. *Public Housing, supra* note 161, at 988; *Remedies for Tenants, supra* note 189, at 566-7.

249. *Remedies for Tenants, supra* note 189, at 566.

250. 5. U.S.C. Sec. 702 (1966).

251. *Remedies for Tenants, supra* note 189, at 566.

252. *Id.*

253. *Public Housing, supra* note 161, at 988.

254. *Id., note* 588, at 989.

255. HUD Circular RHM 7465.9, Sec. 3, para. a.

256. *Id.,* Sec. 3, para. b.

257. *Id.,* Sec. 3, para. c, d.

258. *Id.,* Sec. 3, para. e.

259. Schoshinski, *supra* note 10, at 418.

260. 42 U.S.C. Sec. 1410 (g) (3) (1964).

261. 61 Stat. 193 (1947).

262. 62 Stat. 1268.

263. 42 *U.S.C.* Sec. 1404 (a) (1964).

264. U.S. Housing Act of 1948, Sec. 502 (b).

265. Rosen, *supra* note 17, at 182.

266. *See* text accompanying notes 13-18.

267. Sec. 3.6 (Oct. 1967).

268. *LHA Management Handbook, supra* note 60, Pt. IV, Sec. 1, para. 8(g).

269. ACC, *supra* note 8, Pt. II, Sec. 201(1).

270. *LHA Management Handbook, supra* note 60, Pt. IV, Sec. 2, para. 6.

271. Brand v. Chicago Housing Authority, 120 F.2d 786, 788 (7th Cir. 1941).

272. *See* Lynch v. U.S., 292 U.S. 571 (1934).

273. Brand, *supra* note 271, at 788.

274. Rosen, *supra* note 17, at 242.

275. Schoshinski, *supra* note 10, at 441.

276. 226 F.2d 51 (D.C. Cir. 1955).

277. PHA Circular, July 28, 1954.

278. *Id.*

279. 105 A2d 741, 789.

280. Rosen, *supra* note 17, at 204-5.
281. PHA Circular, May 31, 1966.
282. HUD Circular, Feb. 7, 1967.
283. 317 F. Supp. 1122 (D. Mass. 1970). *See* discussion of *McQueen,* 2.76, 2.78.
284. Thorpe v. Housing Authority, 386 U.S. 670 (1967).
285. 386 U.S. at 673.
286. Thorpe v. Housing Authority, 393 U.S. 268, 276 (1969).
287. *Id.*
288. *Id.*
289. U.S. Housing Act of 1937, Sec. 8.
290. U.S. Housing Act of 1959, 42 U.S.C. Sec. 1401.
291. 393 U.S. 268, 277.
292. Brief for Respondent, cited 393 U.S. at 281-2.
293. 393 U.S. at 282.
294. *Id.* at 283.
295. *Id.*
296. Schoshinski, *supra* note 10, at 441.
297. *Id.* at 445.
298. Rosen, *supra* note 17, at 198.
299. Schoshinski, *supra* note 10, at 441.
300. *See* notes 102-6 *supra.*
301. Schoshinski, *supra* note 10, at 451-2.
302. *Id.* at 451.
303. Hannah v. Larche, 363 U.S. 420, 422 (1960).
304. Schoshinski, *supra* note 10, at 452.

9 Mutual Ownership Landlords and Their Tenants

9.1　　Growing tenant dissatisfaction with the legal and economic consequences of the traditional landlord-tenant relationship has brought increased interest in various forms of mutual ownership of housing accommodations. Mutual ownership offers tenants the security of residential permanence, the pride of home ownership, the tax and investment benefits of real estate ownership and an opportunity to participate in the management of their residential community. It has been suggested that this fundamental change in the landlord-tenant relationship may be the primary basis of successful housing reform.[1]

9.2　　This chapter will examine the alternatives to the traditional landlord-tenant relationship resulting from mutual ownership of living facilities and describe the characteristics and advantages and disadvantages of the three legal devices in common use (the stock corporation cooperative, the condominium and the home ownership association corporation.

THE STOCK-COOPERATIVE

9.3　　A stock-corporation cooperative is a legal entity that holds title to the land and building(s) and is responsible for management of the corporation and all corporate financial obligations. These obligations include the mortgage and real property taxes assessed to the project as a whole. The corporation issues stock to the tenant-shareholders and provides each cooperator with a proprietary lease.[2]

CHARACTERISTICS OF THE STOCK-COOPERATIVE

Ownership

9.4　　In a stock-cooperative the corporation, which is composed of the resident tenants, holds the building and land in fee simple and is the surrogate landlord.[3]

9.5　　The tenant-cooperator is required to pay an initial cash investment[4] which secures two inseparable documents—shares of stock and proprietary lease.

9.6　　The lease defines the relationship between the cooperator and the corporation, specifying the former's rights and obligations regarding the use and management of his apartment and the common facilities.

> Because the ownership of stock automatically carries the right to tenancy, under a specific lease format and interlocking bylaws that require operation for the sole benefit of tenants, the lease is proprietary in nature and certainly confers a *preferred status as compared to that of an ordinary tenant.*[5]

9.7　　There are some exceptions, however, to the common practice of granting proprietary leases to tenant-shareholders, especially in publicly assisted projects. The nonproprietary lease is a short-term occupancy agreement for a two- or three-year duration. In these cases coopera-tors are generally not given a right of automatic renewal; however, in the case of FHA-sponsored projects, the right of renewal is an option of the cooperator.[6]

9.8   Ownership and occupancy within the cooperative can be ei-ther of two forms: residential, or a combination of residential and com-mercial. The tax benefits available to the corporation and its tenant-shareholders,[7] however, tend to limit the amount of commercial partici-pation. The corporation and its tenant-shareholders are eligible for de-ductions of real property taxes and interest paid on the amortization of the mortgage only if 80 percent or more of the gross income for that taxable year is from residential tenants.[8]

9.9   The lease commonly runs for the life of the corporation; at the end of the term, generally 20 to 50 years, the lease is automatically renewable or extended at the pleasure of the owners.[9]

Types of Housing Cooperatives
9.10   There are three recognized types of stock-cooperatives.

> [the management project]: organized as a non-profit cooperative corpora-tion or trust to provide for the construction of permanent cooperative hous-ing for its stockholder participants;

> [the management *conversion project*]: organized as a non-profit coopera-tive corporation or trust to acquire and recast or rehabilitate existing rental housing for conversion to permanent cooperative ownership;

> [the investor-sponsor project]: organized as a business profit corporation by its principals with the intention of selling the completed project to a non-profit cooperative corporation or "trust" within two years after its com-pletion if the cooperative subscribes to 97 percent of the dwelling unit.[10]

9.11   The two management types can be further classified as either builder-sponsor or consumer-oriented sponsor. The former is responsible for the project's construction, while the latter contracts for a builder in behalf of the cooperative.[11]

Governmental Aid
9.12   Government-financed cooperatives are chartered under spe-cific enabling legislation that commonly mandates corporate organiza-tion[12] and are generally restricted to limited-profit and non-profit spon-sors. The potential coverage of such financial aid includes the monthly carrying charges and/or the purchase price of stock ownership. These cooperatives can benefit from aid in any of the following forms: direct financing, mortgage insurance, tax abatement or direct subsidy to spe-cific income groups. In contrast, the conventional stock-cooperative has no profit restrictions other than those imposed by the marketplace.[13]

MANAGEMENT OF A COOPERATIVE: FHA MODEL FORM OF BYLAWS

9.13 Tenants with diverse interests require management of common facilities and areas to protect community needs and personal rights of the cooperative participants. The bylaws establish guidelines for the management of the corporate organization. They govern the cooperative's membership, its administrators and the board of directors. Specifically, the bylaws provide for a centralized governing body which has the responsibility for managing the project and for policing delinquents.[14] The landlord's position is assumed, therefore, by the cooperative's board of directors, elected officers and appointed committees.

9.14 The bylaws are subject to amendment by an "affirmative vote of the majority of the entire regular membership of record at any regular or special meeting." The amendments may be proposed by the board of directors or by a petition signed by a minimum of 20 percent of the members.[15]

9.15 Membership is granted to those persons who have been approved by the board, paid the initial subscription fee, received stock certificates and reside in the building.[16] The incorporators of the project are also given membership until the first annual meeting of the regular membership. At that time, in order to retain their membership, the incorporators must have purchased stock in the corporation and, in some cases, the FHA requires the incorporators to execute occupancy agreements.[17]

9.16 The regular membership must meet annually, but it can also meet at special times to consider important issues. The bylaws usually require a quorum for the transaction of general business and specific majorities for approval of important decisions, such as the yearly budget and the hiring of a new managing agent.

9.17 The organization of many cooperatives includes a provision for restricted voter rights. Each stockholder is limited to one vote "despite the fact that the value of individual cooperators, ownership interests may vary greatly."[18] Existing business laws were inadequate for the incorporation of residential cooperatives, because they did not permit restricted voting rights. As such, the cooperative laws of a state, which were originally designed for the creation of farm cooperatives, provided the initial legal foundation for the organization of residential cooperatives. Only recent revisions in the business corporation laws allowing the restricted vote have provided a more realistic foundation for residential cooperative incorporation.[19] Voting rights may be split if membership is owned jointly by husband and wife; however, no member is eligible to vote or be elected to the board of directors if his payments are delinquent for more than thirty days.[20]

TERMINATION OF MEMBERSHIP

By the Tenant

9.18   Membership is not transferable except in the following situations:

> 1.   When a member dies his membership shall then pass to a member of his immediate family, legatee or distributee. If this obligation is not assumed, the corporation has the option to purchase the membership from the deceased's estate within thirty days. If the corporation does not exercise this option, the estate may sell the membership to any "duly approved" person.
>
> 2.   If a member desires to leave the project, the corporation has the option of purchasing his membership. The corporation determines the transfer value of the membership minus any amounts due to it and/or the costs of deferred maintenance. Membership purchase by the corporation immediately terminates that member's rights and he must vacate the premises.
>
> 3.   When the corporation does not exercise its options in the above cases, a member may sell his membership to any person "duly approved by the corporation as a member and an occupant." The retiring member must pay all amounts due to the corporation to date before he is released from his obligations under the occupancy agreement.[21]

By the Corporation

9.19   Membership may be terminated by the corporation for cause. The legal methods available to enforce compliance with contractual obligations are the traditional remedies of the landlord: summary proceedings for nonpayment; and eviction for behavioral deviation.[22] Termination requires a member to leave his apartment and permits the cooperative to resell his membership at a sales price acceptable to the corporation.[23] The delinquent member is then entitled to the amount of the sale minus: any amounts due to the corporation under the terms of the lease; costs or estimated costs of deferred maintenance; and legal and other expenses incurred by the corporation in conjunction with that member's default and resale.[24]

THE BOARD OF DIRECTORS

9.20   The board of directors governs the corporation; it is elected by the regular membership and serves without compensation. The composition of the board may vary from three to nine members, and a majority must be members of the corporation. Initially members serve for varying terms in order to stagger the expiration of the terms of office. After the initial term of office, each director is elected for a three-year term.[25]

9.21   The board of directors "shall have all the powers and duties necessary for the administration of the affairs of the corporation and may do all such acts and things as are not by law or by these bylaws directed to be exercised and done by the members." These powers include, but are not limited to, the following:

1. The right to accept or reject applications for membership and admission to residency within the cooperative.

2. The right to establish monthly carrying charges for common expenses based upon the operating budget formally adopted by the board.

3. The right to employ an agent or employees for the management of the project under terms determined by the board.

4. The right to authorize the release of "patronage funds" from any of the corporation's residual receipts only as shown to be appropriate in the annual report.

5. The right to terminate membership and residency for cause.

6. The right to issue rules and regulations regarding the use and occupancy of the facilities as necessary. These rules must be consistent with the project's bylaws and document of incorporation.[26]

9.22 After the first organizational meeting of the newly elected board, to take place within ten days after the election, the directors are obligated to meet a minimum of four times during the fiscal year. Other special meetings may be called when necessary for a special purpose. The majority of the board members constitutes a quorum for business decisions.[27]

9.23 A director may be discharged with or without cause, at any regular or special meeting properly called, by an affirmative vote of the majority of the full regular membership if a replacement is elected at the same time to fill the newly created vacancy. Furthermore, a director may be automatically removed if he is more than 30 days delinquent in payment of his pro rata share of the carrying charges; the board's remaining membership may then fill the vacancy by appointment.[28]

Officers
9.24 The corporate officers are elected annually from the board of directors, by that body, and serve "at pleasure of the Board." There are four principal officers: the president, the vice-president, the secretary and the treasurer. Aside from these officers, the board has the power to appoint other officers as necessary for the project's management. Any officer may be removed by a majority vote of the board.[29]

1. The president is the chief executive of the corporation. He presides over all board meetings and regular membership meetings, appoints committees from among the membership for the conduct of the corporation's affairs, and holds general powers and duties associated with the corporate office of president.

2. The vice-president acts as surrogate chief executive and performs the latter's duties when he is absent or unable to act. The

194

board further delegates to him other necessary duties.

3. The secretary performs all customary duties, including recording the meeting minutes, keeping custody of the corporate seal and charge of the stock transfer books.

4. The treasurer has the responsibility of keeping "full and accurate" accounts of the transacted receipts, disbursements, deposits, credits, etc., for the corporate funds and securities.

9.25 As in corporate law, the problem arises of whether these officers can, by their actions, bind the corporation. Is the stock-cooperative responsible for the contracts made in its name by the officers? Is the stock-cooperative responsible for the torts of agents appointed by the officers? A fatuous answer might be "yes," if all the officers have agreed: "probably not" if it is the secretary; and "probably not" if it is the treasurer unless the transaction particularly concerns the duties of the treasurer.[30]

9.26 The duties of the officers are those of both the landlord and a fiduciary. All the officers in the corporation must be loyal to both roles.

ADVANTAGES AND DISADVANTAGES

To Individual Participators

9.27 The stock-cooperative offers some advantages to the tenant-shareholder that are commonly associated with home ownership, such as tax deductions, residence security and development of an equity. However, leasehold cooperatives and nonproprietary leases through which parties other than the resident cooperators retain legal and discretionary power over the cooperators, strain the limits of the cooperative's function and demean the "preferred status" of the tenant-shareholder. Also, the tenant-stockholder is responsible to the corporation for carrying charges as stated in the provisions of the proprietary lease. The carrying charges cover the unit's pro rata share of the costs of maintenance, management, mortgage amortization, tax obligations, real property insurance and other miscellaneous expenses. If he is unable to meet these payments, other cooperators must assume his assessment.[31] Thus, the very existence of the stock-cooperative depends upon the mutual solvency and good faith of its tenant-shareholders.

9.28 The stock cooperative does provide some security against the defaulter; corporate stock is sold subject to a lien retained by the corporation for unpaid carrying charges. This lien may not, however, protect the cooperative from a "pyramiding of arrearages" which may occur when economic hardship shrinks the supply of new cooperators and causes a wave of defaults.[32] In such circumstances, a tenant-cooperator can lose his down payment, accrued equity and apartment, even though he has not been delinquent in his own payments.[33] To curb the number of individual defaults, stock cooperatives have restricted the sale of stock by requiring a lengthy examination of the potential buyer's credit and a larger initial cash outlay. Higher monthly payments, the residue to be paid to a separate fund, also help soften the threat of multiple defaults.

Of the Corporate Form

9.29   Under a state's business corporation laws, the stock corporation benefits from limited liability. All services performed in behalf of the tenant-shareholders are performed in the name of the corporation, thereby insulating the tenant-shareholders from personal liability arising from contractual liabilities of the corporate management, or torts of the corporation, the management or its agents.[34] The tenant-shareholder would only be personally liable for occurrences within the apartment under his personal control.[35]

9.30   There are concomitant disadvantages to the corporate form, such as nationwide service, which may require the corporation to defend against an adverse claim in a distant state. Litigation may be costly.

CONDOMINIUMS

9.31   The word "condominium" is derived from the sixth century B.C. Roman Law of Condominium, which governed joint ownership. It means to have control (dominium) over a certain property jointly with (con) one or more persons.[36]

9.32   Condominiums relieve the resident from the traditional landlord-tenant relationship, allow him to participate in the home ownership market and build up equity, and permit him to enjoy the psychological advantages of an economic interest in real property and in community relations. A condominium is created by the execution and registration of the declaration and operating bylaws.[37]

CHARACTERISTICS OF CONDOMINIUMS

Property Interest

9.33   The property interest in a condominium comes from two principles: the ownership of discrete parts of a single building and the creation of estates in airspace. The latter approach recognizes the division of estates above the soil as an extension of the common law principle that recognized the division of estates beneath the soil.[38]

9.34   Although the exact nature of the property interest remains an "unresolved issue," two characteristics of the condominium interest are constant and inseparable: the fee simple interest in an apartment, and an undivided interest in the common areas and facilities of the project.[39]

196

Various Forms of Condominiums

9.35   The basic structure of condominium ownership necessitates two forms of tax assessment: multiple assessment for common property and facilities, and separate assessments for the apartment units. This separability of tax obligations and the two elements of property interests contributes to the diverse use of space. This diversity can be achieved by interchanging three variables: physical arrangements, special common facilities and primary functions. The following outline presents one line of division of the condominium's inherent possibilities:

a. Types of Activity
    1.   Residential high rise and garden apartments, "cluster arrangements," town houses and detached homes.
    2. Commercial developments of buildings for office use, industry and commerce.
    3. Recreational developments of housing and sport facilities.
    4. Educational-governmental facilities for use and ownership jointly by several independent localities.
    5. Combinations of the above.
b.   Distribution of rights
    1. Entirely residential ownership.
    2. Mixed condominium ownership of residentially and commercially utilized space.
    3. Residential areas under condominium ownership with commercially utilized space owned by the condominium residents but operated by commercial tenants under leases.
    4. Residential under condominium ownership only; commercial space reserved for sponsor or other owner. Easements and other reciprocal obligations existing between the two sets of owners.[40]

9.36   A condominium can also provide an investment outlet for its participants through rental space without the tax constraint upon similar action in a stock cooperative.[41] Leasehold condominiums, however, strain the principles underlying this form of mutual ownership.

Deed

9.37   The condominium's master deed or document of ownership contains certain "covenants, conditions and restrictions" which necessarily bind the property interests.[42] This deed enunciates the tenant's undivided interest in each unit and provides for the management of the common areas and facilities, and enforcement of the condominium's restrictions through an elected governing body of owners.

Need for Statutory Authorization

9.38   Recognition in common law of the separate ownership of discrete parts of a building and the creation of air estates has provided, in the absence of special legislation, a foundation for many condominiums, such as California's "Own Your Own Apartment" plan.

9.39   Although some condominiums have existed under common law, business communities have been somewhat reluctant to accept condominiums supported solely by common law. Legislation, in addition to removing many of the legal and practical stumbling blocks of condominium government and maintenance,[43] lends credence to the concept of ownership of airspace estates. This legislation stimulates the interest of developers and major institutional lenders in condominiums.

9.40   Condominiums face legal hurdles which are overcome by legislation which functions:

(1) to provide a procedure for the establishment and dissolution of a condominium and to secure a uniform pattern of legal documentation;

(2) to accommodate existing legislation dealing with taxation recording procedures, liens, land use control and security regulatory techniques to the special needs of the condominium; and

(3) to anticipate judicial antagonism involving such matters as bars on partition and covenants real.[44]

9.41   The existing FHA requirements for the insurance of condominium apartments under Section 234 of the National Housing Act have provided a major impetus toward the creation of enabling legislation. The FHA requires that the state in which the subject property is located must provide protection of the condominium form. While there is no uniformity of enabling statutes, in order for condominiums to qualify for FHA insurance,[45] local law must provide at least three things: recognition of an "air lot" estate fee; means for separate unit assessments and taxation rather than a single levy against the entire condominium property; and registration of a master document or plan that established separately deeded apartments, thereby providing an exemption for the condominium project from normal platting and subdivision ordinances.[46]

OWNERSHIP OF A CONDOMINIUM

9.42   The declaration of the condominium subdivides the ownership of land and airspace. To transfer ownership of the separate units, the sponsor-owner must convey each unit to the prospective unit-owners through separate deeds in accordance with the provisions of the enabling legislation and declaration.[47]

9.43   To insure the physical and legal unity of the project, statutes prohibit the separation of the unit ownership from the undivided interest in the common elements. The statutes prohibit the partitioning of the project's common areas while the building remains intact and continues to be governed by the condominium administration, and impose restraints upon the unit owner's right to transfer ownership or to rent his unit.[48]

Individual Ownership of an Apartment

9.44   The individual unit-owner holds his apartment in fee simple which provides him with all the rights of real property—the right to convey, to mortgage and to lease the unit—subject to the provisions of the enabling legislation, project declaration and bylaws.[49] The fee simple deed permits financial independence. The owner undertakes independent financing[50] and incurs responsibility only for that mortgage and not for the defaults of neighboring cotenants as in a stock-cooperative.

Individual Ownership of the Common Areas

9.45   With the title to an apartment, the cotenant receives an undivided interest in the common facilities.[51] This fractional interest is the ratio of the value of the apartment unit to the value of the whole project, and it is significant because it functions as an evaluative tool:

> It fixes permanently the unit owner's pro rata burden of the common expenses and his share in any profit or distribution of capital.[52] It is also the measure of his voice in the management. Because taxing officials will need a formula for apportioning a project's total value among the separate units. the fraction may be used to compute each apartment's assessment. And finally, the fraction may provide a basis for limiting the unit owner's individual liability for liens and for claims of the project's creditors.[53]

Advantages and Disadvantages of Ownership

9.46   *Advantages.* As with home ownership, the unit owner benefits from the annual income tax deductions available for interest paid on the amortization of the mortgage and the real property taxes. Furthermore, condominium ownership provides a voice in the management of the owner's community and elimination of the landlord's profit.

9.47   The ownership structure of the condominium eliminates the traditional landlord-tenant relationship. By eliminating the traditional landlord remedies of summary process and eviction notices, the condominium provides a greater degree of tenurial security than the proprietary lease of the stock corporation.

9.48   Another advantage is the potential for diverse activity within the organization and its resultant ability to reduce the costs of housing to its members through the leasing of commercial space. Despite the flexibility and ownership possibilities for added investment not available to the stock cooperator, there are certain tax consequences of the rental income received by a condominium.

9.49   If the condominium's income exceeds its expenditures in any given year, it may be subject to income taxation, but if the annual expenditures equal annual assessments, there will be no taxable income. And if excess revenues are from assessments against its members, tax liability is avoided by refunding any surplus to them at the year's end.[54] However, if the unincorporated association of owners receives excess income from the *rental* of commercial property under the common ownership of the unit owners, and/or apartments owned by the association,

199

several questions must be answered. What are the funds thus received to be used for? Are they taxable income? And if they are taxable income, to whom will they be taxed?

9.50   The receipts received could be used: to pay a proportion of the common expenses, reducing proportionally the unit owner's monthly assessment; to provide additional community facilities; or to provide for a combination of the above.[56]

9.51   Taxable income from the rental sources can be minimized by using proper depreciation methods and apportioning expenses and taxes to these facilities.[57] Yet another method of eliminating the "double taxation" on the income of rentals and commercial use suggested by several writers is to offset the operating expenses of the condominium against the derived commercial income.[58] However, two circuit courts have been at variance regarding the use of offsetting expenses.[59]

9.52   In addition, the Internal Revenue Code does not recognize a distinction between "association" and "corporation." The association of owners could be taxed as a partnership or corporation. The Code states that an "association" will be taxed as a corporation if it has a preponderance of corporate characteristics; these include the existence of associates, the objective to carry on a profit-making business and divide the gains, continuity of life, centralized management, limited liability and free transfer of ownership.[60] While the members of the typical condominium do not enjoy the right of limited liability and do not operate the organization for business profit, they are associates and the association has continuity of life and a "modified free transferability" in the form of a right of first refusal of potential owners. If the association is taxed as a "corporation," it will have to pay a corporate tax on this income and any remaining income would most probably be interpreted as a "constructive dividend" to be allocated proportionally to the individual unit owners. It might be beneficial to add the income directly to the income of the individual owner as "tenant-in-common" of the property instead of using the double taxation process mentioned above.[61]

9.53   While "associations" probably would be considered "corporations" for tax purposes,[62] there is still uncertainty regarding full income tax liability. However, neither the cooperator nor the condominium unit owner experiences disadvantageous tax consequences; in fact, each benefits from tax deductions not available to the ordinary apartment renter.

9.54   As an organization of common property interests, the condominium does seem to provide a greater degree of flexibility than the stock-cooperative. Unit owners will not lose tax deductions if more than

20 percent of the condominium's cooperative, tenant-shareholders would lose these benefits.

> And although the condominium association and the cooperative corporation may not be able to avoid the "double taxation" inherent in the corporate income tax, it may still be financially desirable for the low and moderate income condominium to include commercial facilities in the commonly owned property. . . . The personal income tax on constructive or actual dividends received by the low and moderate income occupants will be assessed at a low rate. In addition, the first $25,000 of "corporate" income is taxed at the relatively low rate of 22 percent.[63]

9.55   *Disadvantages.* The bylaws of the condominium obligate all owners to pay, in proportion to the pro rata unit value, monthly assessments determined by the association of owners, to cover the costs of administration, repair or replacement of the common areas and facilities and to include any reserves required for "unforeseen contingencies." The unit owner cannot defer or avoid liability for any of these expenses by abstaining from using these areas and facilities.[64]

9.56   Common ownership may create problems if one owner defaults and the reserves are insufficient and the default cannot be resolved by enforced payment. In this situation the other unit owners are liable for the defaulter's common expenses.

9.57   Covenants and liens employed by the condominium for recovery of the expenses due do not match the celerity of summary procedures for lease termination used by the stock cooperative. The stock-cooperative's remedies are the landlord's remedies and are not acceptable to the home-owning condominium resident.[65] The unit owner who owes rent has more independence and is more secure in his apartment than the stock-cooperator. Thus, this security can be both a benefit and a detriment. Although the project may seem to accept a greater risk, the collective body of unit owners may be covered by FHA mortgage insurance. In these cases, the FHA reviews the credit of each applicant. Individual mortgage financing and FHA review do provide a problem for low-and moderate-income families who wish to own a home but are handicapped by an irregular credit history.

9.58   Additionally, decisions regarding common areas and facilities are collective and do not provide the degree of independence characteristic of the single-family homeowner.[66]

9.59   Finally, unlike the stock cooperative, the condominium unit owner is personally liable for the condominium's debts and subject to tort judgment, although the homeowner does not have to defend claims against the condominium in distant states.

Physical Destruction of the Condominium: Effect on Ownership

9.60　　A major consideration of condominium ownership is the effect of physical destruction.

9.61　　In the absence of statutory provisions for rebuilding, the unit owners have the right to decide whether to rebuild. The project declaration specifies the method of voting and the number of votes necessary for a decision, the FHA Model Statute requires that the declaration stipulate this.[67] The initial costs of rebuilding or repairing would come from the insurance; additional funds would have to come from proportional assessments to the common owners.[68]

9.62　　If the decision is not to rebuild, the surviving property is dealt with in one of three ways[69]:

1. "Under some condominium administrations, each unit owner has a *cotenancy* in the premises with an additional exclusive *right of possession* in that part of the building that comprises his apartment." Upon destruction of his apartment, however, the exclusive right to possession is also destroyed; the unit owner has no remaining property interest in the space that was formerly his apartment. The only remaining interest he has is a "cotenant's interest in the land and rubble and a share in the insurance proceeds." An example of this type of situation is the California "Own Your Own Apartment" plan.[70]

2. The unit owner would be granted an exclusive *estate* in his apartment; a property interest in the air space described by his apartment deed. Upon destruction of the building the air space is still negotiable. However, situations may arise creating marketability problems of the condominium title. After destruction, conveyance of the title to the premises may be "hindered by the refusal of some owners to relinquish dominion over their air space or by the difficulty of identifying and locating the holders of all the outstanding interests."[71]

3. The FHA Model Statute provides that the unit owner receives a *fee simple absolute* estate in his apartment; upon damage or destruction of the premises a "timely" decision to rebuild must be made or the separate fees terminate and the individual units are "deemed to be owned in common by the apartment owners."[72] Upon sale of the property title, the owners would receive these proceeds, plus the insurance monies, in an amount proportional to their fractional interests.[73]

MANAGEMENT OF CONDOMINIUMS

9.63　　The ownership of common property within the condominium requires management for general maintenance and administration of the project. The bylaws authorize the creation of an association of owners to be governed by a board of directors; unit ownership automatically bestows association membership, the right to vote for a board of directors, and the right to participate in the business meetings of the condominium.

Association of Owners
9.64　　　The association of owners is usually unincorporated, but it is not limited to this form. To provide relief from the fear of limitless liability, the condominium may decide to incorporate. There are, however, disadvantages to incorporation in that it might tend to "blur the distinctiveness of the condominium for those consumers acquainted with cooperatives."[74]

9.65　　　Voting power is proportional to the value of each unit. The FHA rationale for this procedure highlights a crucial difference between the condominium and the stock-cooperative.

> FHA desires to assure itself of adequate protection for its guarantee of unit mortgages. Foreclosure against a cooperative would result in control of the whole project. On the other hand, if the mortgagee were to foreclose on an individual unit in a condominium, the FHA would get control of only that unit. In such cases, the FHA wants a voice equal to its financial interest in the property.[75]

9.66　　　The association of owners has the "responsibility of administering the project, approving the annual budget, establishing and collecting monthly assessments and arranging for the management of the projects. . . . " The decisions and resolutions of the association require approval by a majority of owners, which means owners holding 51 percent of the stock, not 51 percent of the unit owners. In extraordinary decisions, i.e., amending the bylaws, larger majorities are normally required.

The Board of Directors
9.67　　　The governing structure of the condominium is similar to that of the stock-cooperative; the main differences concern the member's franchise and the methods of policing delinquents. Like the cooperative, the central governing body of the condominium usually consists of five members who are elected by the unit owners at the annual meetings. Initially, the directors serve for varying terms of office to stagger their term expiration dates; after the initial term, each director is elected for a three-year term.[76]

9.68　　　After the first organizational meeting of the newly elected board, which is to take place within ten days of the election, the directors are obligated to meet at least twice during the fiscal year. Other meetings may be called for special purposes. The majority of the board members constitutes a quorum for the transaction of business.[77]

9.69　　　The board of directors "shall have all the powers and duties necessary for the administration of the affairs of the association and may do all such acts and things as are not by law or by these bylaws directed to be exercised and done by the owners." These responsibilities include: maintenance and repair of the project's common areas and facilities; determination and collection of monthly assessments from the unit owners; and employment and dismissal of personnel to manage and maintain the project's common areas and facilities.[78]

9.70 In many condominiums the board is also given the right of first refusal of prospective owners and tenants. The professed aims of this provision are to "reduce the risk of financial interdependence by excluding the unreliable" and to "promote the project's inner harmony by striving for compatible members."[79] The right of first refusal requires that the owner disclose his proposed buyer and the terms of the proposed sale to the board before consummating a sale or lease. Thus, within a stated period of time, the board must either approve the buyer or match the offer. This arrangement is beneficial to both the association and the unit owner; the former has a veto over all prospective buyers, while the latter retains the financial advantage available to the individual homeowner—to sell his property at a fair market value.[80] However, the right of first refusal may strain the budgets of many condominiums if they are pressured to match selling prices when they would prefer another buyer.[81]

9.71 Aside from the functions of management and control of admissions, the board has the responsibility of "policing" the financially delinquent unit owner and exercising some measure of control over those who violate house rules. Should the unit owner fail to fulfill his financial obligations for the support of the common areas and facilities, enabling statutes commonly grant the managing board two remedies:
1. The power to sue for failure of payment, "obtain a judgment, and levy execution against his real and personal assets, including, if necessary, his unit interest"[82] or
2. The power to impose a lien; a "right to be paid from the value of the property on which it is imposed, unless the value is exhausted in paying a prior lien."[83]

The form of lien may vary from a moderate sanction enabling the condominium management to extract from the sale proceeds any unpaid unit assessments to a more severe form whereby a lien is filed immediately after foreclosure if the delinquency continues.[84]

9.72 The fee simple title to real property insulates the condominium unit owner from the stringent remedy of summary process available to the stock corporation cooperative and the landlord. Thus, the board must rely on the lien foreclosure process; although a "tedious" method for recovering the delinquent's outstanding charges, it gives the unit owner more tenurial security than the stock-cooperator. Furthermore, it is a more realistic alternative to single-family home ownership than the cooperative for low-and moderate-income families and minority group members who have often been subject to "frustrating and degrading" tenant-landlord relations.[85]

9.73 Most enabling statutes or condominium declarations, including the FHA Model Statute, provide for the lien procedure. Once the validity of this procedure has been established, the problem shifts to the relative priority of a lien upon the property. In addition to the common expense lien, tax liens, mortgage liens and mechanics' liens are among the most common types of liens.[86] Under the FHA Model Statute, the common expense lien of the condominium takes precedence over all other liens, regardless of its date of registration, except for prior first mortgages and liens for unpaid taxes; failure to pay an assessment would give the association a right to foreclose on the defaulting party's interest.[87]

9.74 While the judicial lien-foreclosure procedure can be long, the collective body of condominium owners may be able to effectuate a power of sale to the lien as an additional legal resource:

> A notice of sale will be as effective a weapon against recalcitrant owners as notice of eviction. If the defaulting party is simply unable to pay, the . . . power of sale provides a period of grace commensurate with the intended advantages of home ownership.[88]

9.75 While given powers to control conduct violations, the board of a condominium does not have access to the legal method of eviction procedures commonly available to the stock-cooperative. Typically, the condominium association is given the right to "recover damages for breach of covenant or nuisance and the right to injunctive relief."[89] The realistic problems involved with such procedures, including the expense and difficulty of proving nuisance actions, has caused writers to suggest other methods of policing delinquents that would be within the powers of a condominium administration and not in violation of the basic elements of home ownership. One writer has suggested the use of a system of internal fines and penalties determinable by the board of directors and secured by a lien on the nonconforming party's unit interest.[90] Clearly, the main concern of any policing procedure is the degree of arbitrariness and discrimination:

> A review of only legal issues or "clearly erroneous" fact determinations is not likely to detect the subtleties of prejudice . . . the best protection against prejudice is a carefully selected Board of Directors.[91]

9.76 A director may be discharged with or without cause, at any regular or special meeting properly called, by an affirmative vote of the majority of the full regular membership. A replacement must be elected at that meeting to fill the vacancy. Furthermore, a director may be automatically removed from office if he is more than 30 days delinquent in paying his share of the common expenses. The board's remaining membership may then appoint a successor to fill the vacancy.

Officers[93]: The Managing Agent

9.77 The bylaws give the board of directors the authority to hire professional management or direct indigenous management.[94] It is the responsibility of the board and the proposed managing agent to work out a contract covering the duties, rights and conditions of employment and service. The following list is indicative of the major items of importance but it should not be construed to be exhaustive.

1. Designation of the areas to be managed.
2. Specification of how, when and by whom instructions are to be given to the managing agents.
3. Differentiation and enumeration of the managing agent's functions.
4. Explication of the term of the agreement, conditions for acceleration of its termination and notice, if any is required, for its renewal. Also, the terms of commissions, if any, to be paid to the managing agent for the initial sales and resales of units.
5. Authorization for the managing agent to spend funds, and any constraints to be imposed upon the dimensions of the expenditures and under what conditions.
6. Disclosure by the agent of cases where services or supplies obtained for the condominium represent companies in which the managing agent has a financial interest.
7. Determination of the duties and pay of the managing agent upon the event of physical destruction of the condominium or dissolution of the condominium.
8. A statement of the managing agent's terms of compensation and provision for suspension of the contract after a period of time thought sufficient to test the agent's performance.
9. Provision for whether or not liability insurance in the name of the agent would be carried by the condominium.[95]

THE HOME ASSOCIATION

9.78 In general, the cooperative movement functions to help reduce housing costs and to provide an alternative to the traditional tenant-landlord relationship. Another aim is the provision of a "quality living environment" to include green open spaces, child care centers and recreational facilities. One response to today's housing demand is characterized by new techniques of physical arrangement and mixed forms of tenure in contrast to the conventional single-family home ownership communities. Several of these alternatives presently being developed include: cluster subdivisions of detached homes and townhouses; developments of townhouses; and planned unit developments with owner-occupied homes and a variety of other land uses, including multifamily properties, churches, commercial facilities and even industrial concerns.[96]

ESTABLISHING THE ASSOCIATION

9.79   Preceding the recording of the subdivision plat and first lot sale, a nonprofit automatic-membership home association should be established and incorporated according to the laws of the state. The covenants should detail a member's rights to the use and ownership of the common property, his voting rights and his obligation to pay specified assessments. Bylaws and articles of the homes association should also be developed.

Registering the Documents

9.80   A final subdivision plat (the map or plan of the land) of the development and the associated set of covenants and restrictions should be prepared and registered. These documents establish land-use restriction on the individual and common parcels, and define the rights and obligations of the developer, the homes association and the subsequent land owners, and are binding with the land. Furthermore, the plat and covenants should explicitly define the land to be dedicated to the homes association and/or the public in an effort to avoid any subsequent doubts about *implied* dedication. Specifically, the subdivision plat and covenants identify:

> (a) property to be transferred to public agencies. . . . (b) the individual residential lots, (c) the common properties to be transferred by the developer to the homes association, and (d) any other parcels, such as a church site or shopping center, to be kept by the developer or transferred to others.[97]

9.81   The dedication procedure should also enumerate the recorded documents other than the subdivisions plat and establish the conditions and time for the conveyance by the developer of the common areas.

Conveying the Land

9.82   The sale and conveyance of the land and homes by deed confirms the rights and obligations specified in the previously mentioned development documents,[98] which necessarily include the responsibility for the association's management and maintenance operations.

9.83   The preceding discussion highlighted the important steps to be taken to insure an adequate basis for the homes association. To qualify for FHA approval, a planned unit development established with a homes association must:

> (a) Legally create an automatic-membership non-profit homes association;
> (b) Place title to the common property in the homes association, or give definite assurance that it automatically will be so placed within a reasonable definite time;

207

(c) Appropriately limit the uses of the common property;
(d) Give each lot owner the right to the use and enjoyment of the common property;
(e) Place responsibility for operation and maintenance of the common property in the homes association;
(f) Place an association charge on each lot in a manner which will (1) assure sufficient association funds and (2) provide adequate safeguards for the lot owners against undesirable high charges; and
g) Give each lot owner voting rights in the association.[99]

Developer's Control

9.84   The developer's role at the early stages of homes association formation is analogous to the landlord's. To protect his investment and the future condition of the common areas and facilities, three phases of the developer's control are significant. These are: control during the construction stage; organization of a homes association; and transition of ownership to the homes association.

9.85   *Construction stage.* Control during most, if not all, of the construction phase empowers the developer to create the full development according to plan, make improvements on the common grounds simultaneously with the construction of individual homes, protect his financial interests and aid in creating an effective homes association. Similarly, if such improvements are not complete prior to the organization and operation of the homes association, its covenants should protect the homes association interest by providing that the developer be committed to adequate improvements of common areas and conveyance of them to the association at a specific time.

9.86   *Organization of the association.* The developer should organize the nonprofit automatic-membership homes association prior to the sale of lots and houses to insure owner acceptance of the rights and responsibilities of the association and its common property (as required by FHA). Without prior understanding of this arrangement, the development can be critically handicapped if the individual owners refuse to establish an association.

9.87   *Transition of ownership.* The developer should retain title to the common properties until they are adequately improved. However, subsequent ownership given over to the association need not eliminate the developer's influence. To insure the successful merchandising of the development's units, the owner should retain voting control in the association until enough units are sold; this will also spread the initial costs of maintaining the common properties.[100] To aid in establishing a viable homes association writers maintain that developers should transfer control to the homeowners, but at the same time assist in the early operation of the association. However, control and its termination should be specified in the covenants controlling the voting rights of the owners.[101]

OWNERSHIP OF THE PREMISES

9.88   Individual owners of units in the planned unit development (PUD), whether townhouses or single-family units, hold in fee simple with all the associated rights of real property.[102] Rental units within a PUD would subject the tenant to the normal tenant-landlord relationships; the landlord would then be subject to the development as the fee simple landowner. In a homes association it is the landowner who has membership rights and whose lot is subject to the assessments for a proportionate share of the costs of maintaining the common property and operating the homes association.

9.89   Full fee title to the common land and facilities is held by the homes association. While FHA requirements have made the deeding of the common parts of the development to the association a prerequisite for mortgage insurance, *the common interests are not indivisible from unit ownership as a matter of statutory provision* as in the condominium.[103] Fear that the homes association may sell off the open spaces has been a handicap in the acceptance of cluster housing; however, legal remedies do exist to avoid such situations.[104]

9.90   As an alternative, the developer may grant the homes association only a leasehold arrangement on the entire common areas or individual areas. This arrangement, as other previously mentioned covenants,[105] allows the developer to retain substantial control over the future of the common areas. Furthermore, while the homes association may have only a leasehold on the property, it may be nevertheless obligated to pay for maintenance, repair and replacement of the common area facilities.[106]

LEGAL FOUNDATION OF A HOMES ASSOCIATION

9.91   The development of a viable homes association is dependent upon certain elements: a firm legal foundation for the residential community; protection for the investments of the individual owners and mortgage lenders; and an effective management and financial stability for the homes association. The rights, obligations and restrictions of the association and its members are detailed in the project's legal documents—namely, the subdivision plat and associated set of protective covenants. While in condominiums and cooperatives this information is normally incorporated in that organization's bylaws, the establishment of a homes association necessitates that the information be contained in the documents that run with the land. The document then makes *explicit* the full title rights associated with the homes association's ownership of the common areas.[107]

TYPES OF HOME OWNERSHIP ASSOCIATIONS

9.92   The homeowner association is the most common organization for the maintenance and management of common areas in PUDs.
A homes association is an organization specifically provided for in the
covenants, deeds or other recorded legal documents which affect the
title to the land within the development.[108] Some, but not all, of the
development documents will stipulate membership rights and the association's source of funds. Consequently, two basic types of homes associations can be distinguished, each having two secondary types.[109]

Automatic Homes Associations
9.93   The clearly automatic homes association is the most typical
of all homes associations and is the type required by FHA mortgage
insurance provisions. Its distinguishing feature is that the source of
maintenance funds is specified in the recorded covenants incorporated
into the land owner's deed. The source is usually an annual assessment
levied against each parcel of land in the development; the assessment is
binding and secured by a lien against the land.[110] Membership within the
association is automatic because it cannot be denied to an owner whose
land is charged with the obligation of assessment payments. The specification in the legal documents that affect the title to the land and super-
sede provisions in the bylaws of articles of the association classify this
type of association as automatic. The bylaws are not as significant as in a
stock-cooperative or condominium because they cannot create an obligation which would "run with the land"; furthermore, the bylaws and
articles are subject to amendment on the question of membership.[111]

9.94   Undetermined homes associations call for an association of
homeowners that will be responsible for the maintenance of the common
facilities and areas, but they do not specifically stipulate the membership rights or the method of financial fund raising for the association.[112]

Nonautomatic Homes Associations
9.95   Optional homes associations provide for association membership, but not automatically because there is no provision for assessments
that would "run with the land" and thus bind all land owners. Therefore, no land owner can be held to a continuing obligation for the payment
of dues or assessments, which are the principal sources of maintenance
funds, if he renounces his membership right.

9.96   In discretionary homes associations, the ability to grant
membership rights is a discretionary power of the association. Covenants
do not bind the land owners to payments of assessments or dues, and it
is not possible for the covenants to so provide where membership can be
withheld from the owner. Furthermore, by resigning or renouncing membership, an owner can avoid future financial obligations for dues or assessments.[113]

PLANNED-UNIT DEVELOPMENTS[114] AND HOMES ASSOCIATIONS

9.97   Traditionally, homes associations were composed of upper-income owners of detached and attached single-family homes. They were customarily limited in size and facilities to small developments. The legal relationships of these associations were "loose" and community ownership of property was not a principal feature. These homes associations were characterized by:

> trite and largely disregarded contents of reservations and covenants in tract development deeds, which placed on purchasers of homes mutual restrictions and obligations relative to such matters as signs, fencing, and the transfer of ownership (often with racial overtones that have been continually rendered ineffective by the courts).[115]

Modern Use of Homes Associations

9.98   Today's home ownership associations are generally formed for purposes of common property maintenance in housing developments that provide community open space and recreational facilities. The interest in cluster housing and conservation of open space has stimulated these associations and necessitated the revision of their legal structure. Aside from providing the association member with facilities not commonly enjoyed by the single lot homeowner or apartment renter, the housing developments aim at serving broader economic and social groups than the previous home ownership organizations. New organizational and management techniques have been developed to accommodate modern-day needs.

9.99   Prior experience has confirmed the success of the home ownership association among owners of detached homes[116]; while providing townhouses and garden apartments, builders are continuing to build a majority of single-family homes (detached) within the new developments. However, the availability of individual ownership of townhouses, even as a small proportion of single-family houses, offers the benefits of home ownership to many at lower costs than a detached home.

> Large lot size and other amenities found in competitive properties which cannot be provided in townhouses, for example, must be provided for in other features and offered at a lower relative price.[117]

Planned-Unit Developments

9.100   There are three integral parts of a PUD: the association-owned common property, the public streets and the individual residences.[118]

9.101   PUDS are characterized by mixed forms of tenure and physical arrangements. To accommodate the needs of varying income and age groups, the residential environment of a PUD can potentially include single family ownership of detached houses or attached townhouses,

211

rental apartments, and/or cooperative or condominium arrangements. A main focus however, continues to be the subdivision of land predominately for owner-occupied homes with some property and facilities commonly owned and maintained by the homeowners themselves through an automatic homes association.[119] The environment of the common facilities is the principal benefit of the PUD.

Builder Preference

9.102   The home owner association, rather than the cooperative or condominium, has been most often chosen by builders as the preferred type of community organization since homes are relatively simple to sell.[120] The buyer of an individual home requires less explanation of common ownership concepts of property than does the buyer of a condominium unit interest or stock shares of a cooperative.

Organizational Form

9.103   The homes association within the PUD is generally an incorporated, nonprofit organization operating under recorded land agreements. However, the organization may take one of several legal forms: an unincorporated association, unincorporated trust, nonprofit nonstock corporation, or nonprofit corporation that issues stock to members.[121] The choice of a proper legal form is dependent upon several criteria:

> (1) The organization must be capable of holding title to the real estate; (2) it must be capable of offering to its members a substantial degree of control over management without exposing the members to individual, unlimited liability; (3) it must be able to allow its officers to incur the necessary obligations on its behalf in connection with its daily activities without exposing individual officers to personal liability except in cases of clear breach of authority or personal negligence; and (4) it must be an organization which does not incur unnecessary tax burdens . . . The legal form best suited to the homes association is the nonprofit, nonstock corporation.[122]

9.104   The conceptual foundation of the PUD offers many advantages to the developer, buyer and involved community.

9.105   *Financial advantages.* PUD offers a prospective buyer an attractive package of housing amenities. Through more efficient planning with smaller networks of utilities and pavements, cost savings are possible.[123] The nature of the homes association ownership often makes PUD subject only to a nominal real estate tax rather than a high local tax on developable property.[124] And, by incorporating as a nonstock corporation, the homes association benefits from incorporation while avoiding the difficulties of security registration and income tax.[125]

9.106   *Amenities and aesthetics.* One of the main objectives of PUD is to create a "quality living environment" through the provision of privately owned community facilities and services for the common enjoyment of its residents. Large common areas of green open spaces for neighborhood settings and recreational facilities such as swimming pools, etc., can be provided at lower-than-normal prices due to shared costs.

9.107   Aesthetically, PUD offers a greater potential for innovative design in the physical arrangement of buildings and open space than can the conventional subdivision. In addition, the privately owned common areas of PUDs assure the local governmental agency that the common spaces are permanent and that maintenance will be paid by the benefited properties in the development, rather than out of public funds.[126] Concurrently, public funds need not be used for special benefits to specific areas; developers and, hence, home buyers need not place under public control common open space ultimately related to individual homes.[127]

9.108   *Social advantages.* The potential diversity of tenurial forms in PUDs and of reduced housing costs makes the development of a residential community accessible to mixed economic and age groups. Furthermore, the existence of a homes association for maintenance and management of common facilities is effective in the stabilization and preservation of the development plan and consequently the value of the home properties over long-term periods.

9.109   The small private yards of individual homes or townhouses are devoid of large lot maintenance responsibilities and allow a maximum of time and energy for recreational activities.[128]

9.110   *Disadvantages.* The homes association governing large areas of land benefits from a solid legal foundation, but it, unlike a condominium, is not guided by any specific statute. Thus, problems arising from the expanded usage of the concept cannot be readily resolved.[129] Furthermore, the underlying covenants of many associations establishing the structure of management and policy decisions are either unalterable or require the developer's consent. Bylaws often cannot be altered by the vote of reasonable majorities.[130]

9.111   Many of the early problems associated with the collection of assessments for maintenance are now alleviated by a stipulation detailing the homeowner's financial obligations.

9.112   Homeowners are unable to obtain title insurance covering both the ownership of their individual home and their interest in the homeowner association. Furthermore, title insurance for the association is not a common practice.[131]

9.113   Similarly, supporting documents provide less protection for the community after major hazards than in condominium statutes. Associations rarely carry hazard insurance because there is a question of the determination of the amount of hazard insurance to be carried and the values of common areas separated from the rest of the development. Consequently, destruction of a cluster of houses in a homes association has a less likely chance for community action in reconstruction than in a condominium.[132]

9.114 The main areas of concern can be enumerated as follows:

1. Adequate planning to provide a community of homes at "reasonable" sales prices and without excessive common area maintenance charges;

2. The time schedule and plan for development construction and transfer of the ownership by the developer;

3. The source and management of funds for the creation of the common properties;

4. The comparative analysis of the advantages of ownership and administration of common properties by a public agency as opposed to a private homes association.[133]

5. The specification of covenants adopted by builders affecting the exclusive right of these builders to "record supplementary bundle of new or amended covenants." These covenants may extend the home ownership association to new developments without further expansion of community facilities.[134]

MANAGEMENT OF THE COMMON PROPERTY

9.115 As with cooperatives and condominiums, the common ownership of property, especially open greens and recreational facilities, necessitates continual maintenance and repair by some organizational mechanism to preserve its value and use. Furthermore, community and individual needs must be balanced, but this is not as critical in a home ownership development as in condominiums and cooperatives where multifamily dwelling units are commonplace.

9.116 The PUD must be planned, brought into existence and operated *as a single project*.[135] Management for the development is operative through the membership meetings, a board of directors and its officers. Depending upon the quantity of work, paid management may be necessary. Aside from the basic property maintenance, management may serve a range of functions from administering private covenants for land use and architectural controls to municipal-type operations and services in new communities remote from urban facilities. The limits of the association's services are determined by the members' willingness to carry out the programs through the association.[136]

THE FUTURE OF MUTUAL OWNERSHIP

9.117 The preceding part of this chapter contains discussions of the various forms of cooperative housing in an attempt to suggest an alternative to the single-family homeowner/apartment renter bind. Each form provides tenurial security and advantages of common ownership of open spaces and tax deductions.

9.118   The potential use and problems of mutual ownership for low-income families will be discussed below. Response to the stock-cooperative and condominium has been primarily concentrated among the middle- and upper-income brackets,[137] and, as previously mentioned, homes associations have traditionally appealed to the same groups. In addition, many of these housing forms are being implemented in newly developing recreational centers as second family homes[138] which, of course, are available only to the more affluent.

SOCIAL BENEFITS OF COOPERATIVE FORMS OF HOUSING

9.119   At several points the relative merits of the cooperative forms of housing have been presented and reviewed in a comparative fashion. This section will mention a few other elements highlighted in the *Report of the National Commission on Urban Problems.*
    1.   Stock-cooperatives have appeared to be successful in promoting racial integration; they have "pioneered in residential integration and point to success in bringing members of all races and religions together as neighbors."
    2.   Cooperatives and condominiums are governed by democratic methods and thus provide equal opportunity for residents to govern their own affairs.
    3.   Ownership in cooperatives or condominiums instills a pride of ownership which promotes residential stability and effective management of the physical premises.
    4.   The development of ownership pride also engenders tenant responsibility. Vandalism, crime and delinquency are reportedly low or completely absent.[139]

POTENTIAL FOR LOW-INCOME FAMILIES

9.120   However, past results do not indicate that cooperative forms of housing have potential for low-income families. The traditional tenant-landlord relationship is frequently characterized by antagonism. Participation and an economic interest in a common housing project replace the older relationships and help create common interests among resident owners. Improvements in federal statutes and administrative principles, in addition to the expanded research on condominiums, have provided a new stimulus. The more favorable financial schemes available in the condominium project and the psychological attributes of real property interest make the condominium a more realistic vehicle for low-and moderate-income home ownership than the stock cooperative.

215

The separability of the fee simple interest and the greater protection of personal rights afforded by such an interest are major advantages of the condominium, especially when its price can be brought within the reach of moderate-and low-income families.

Reduced Costs
9.121   Housing costs can be separated into two major parts: development and construction costs, and operating expenses. The former consists of the costs of acquiring and improving the site, and construction and marketing of the housing. Operating expenses are incurred for administration of the units. They include payroll expenses for management and other personnel, fuel and utility charges, maintenance and repair, taxes, insurance, debt service, and costs associated with vacancies, bad debts, and profits.[140]

9.122   Condominiums, however, can achieve savings in both elements of housing cost. Development and construction costs, as reflected in the individual acquisition cost of a unit interest, can be reduced by effective large-scale purchasing and production in multifamily structures with limited or nonprofit sponsorship and governmental aid. Land costs may be lowered by government subsidy. Similarly, operating expenses can be reduced by government subsidy and mortgage insurance for both the project and individual unit, elimination of the landlord's rental profit, and through sweat equity and residential management. It is these two last elements that hold particular potential for the low-income family and on which the discussion will now focus.

Residential Management
9.123   Although theoretical costs and benefits of residential management in low-income condominiums are not sufficiently defined and supported by experimental case studies to warrant a definitive statement regarding its realistic merit as compared to the management agent scheme, it does appear to differ from the stock-cooperative. The bias against indigenous labor in stock-cooperatives is based upon the financial interdependence of the corporation's shareholders. Since the co-operator's monthly assessments include his pro rata share of the mortgage burden, as well as repair and maintenance and other miscellaneous costs, successful management of the collection of the carrying charges is essential to the continuity of the project. As has been emphasized earlier, if the cooperators are to remain solvent they need a businesslike management operation that is structured with the least interpersonal conflict.[141]

9.124   Several other interests—FHA, institutional lenders seem similarly disposed toward professional management for the condominium. This judgment is based primarily upon experience with cooperatives and middle-income community apartments.[142] They also believe that residents lack the experience, become involved in fractional disputes and fail to evict delinquent tenants promptly.[143]

Counter-Arguments

9.125 The above accusations have been attacked on the following grounds:[144]

1. Low-income apartment communities should be given the right to manage their own affairs and to decide whether they prefer professional or indigenous management.

2. Low-income apartment communities cannot as readily afford professional management as middle-and upper-income projects. Management duties such as administrative paperwork, maintenance and repair, and hiring and firing of other personnel could be handled by residents and provide a form of sweat equity, thereby reducing their individual monthly assessments. Other tasks that require professional abilities, such as the accounting and auditing of the books, would probably be contracted for.

3. Self-management must be viewed for the inherent social advantages of creating a basis of constructive pride and community management. Further, the community will never learn self-government if it delegates the responsibility.

4. There is no reason that the responsibility for policing financial and behavioral delinquents cannot be performed effectively by low-income families if the ground rules are clearly stated in the condominium's bylaws and the project has a competent board of directors.

DRAWBACKS TO COOPERATIVE OWNERSHIP

9.126 There are several elements handicapping the spread of cooperatives. The large initial cash investment required in a stock-cooperative is an obvious obstacle for the low-and moderate-income family without savings. This problem is compounded several years after the cooperative has been in existence because the initial cash investments are larger unless restraints have been imposed on the resale procedure. Without restraints on the resale price, the new purchaser must bear the costs of prior profits.[145] Secondly, strong, knowledgeable organization is needed to sponsor a cooperative venture.

Housing cooperatives do not organize themselves. They are not created by spontaneous generation. The tasks of enlisting members, arranging for financing, dealing with the government, letting contracts, and supervising construction are altogether too complex for individual members. The fact that people want and need a home does not give them the knowledge and experience to design, finance, and produce housing at a price they can afford.[146]

9.127   Additionally, the Douglas Report suggested that lack of interest on the part of some FHA regional offices has affected the growth of cooperatives.[147]

Constraints on Alienation
9.128   Although cooperative forms of housing move toward the freedoms of home ownership, certain constraints exist. Constraints may take one of two general forms: restraints upon resale profits imposed by many projects, particularly those with FHA insurance; and restraints designed to screen prospective members. These constraints may vary between condominiums and stock-cooperatives; there are no restraints in a homes association.

9.129   *Stock-cooperative.* In a stock-cooperative the restraints upon resale profits in the determination of the unit's transfer value may take one of two basic forms. First, a member who moves may receive his initial cash investment. The potential profits are theoretically enjoyed by the current and future members in the form of low initial down payments and monthly carrying charges. After a member receives his down payment, the unit is offered at the *original* sales price.[148] However, this restraint denies "the cooperator the opportunity to trade on a favorable leasehold and prevents him from recovering the cost of mortgage amortization."[149] Second, the selling member is obligated to offer the cooperative the right of first refusal at a price including the departing member's down payment, his share of equity in the project and an adjustment for the cost-of-living. This method is employed by almost all cooperatives under the federal programs.[150] However, the corporation need not exercise this option; it can "condition its approval of applicants upon the requirement that the seller pay all or a percentage of any profit to the corporation."[151] Furthermore, if the market value of the membership declines below the original sales price, the corporation can force the departing member to take a loss if it does not buy the membership.[152]

9.130   *Condominiums.* Condominium owners are not usually restricted in their profits from resales; however, the condominium administration does maintain control over new members through the right of first refusal. The *fee simple* interest of the unit owner provides protection of the ability to sell at a market price:

> Considering the property rights of the condominium owner, resale price restrictions on a condominium unit might be held invalid restraints on alienation by the courts (except in cases of government subsidy).[153]

9.131   While the condominium provisions are definitely more conducive to investment, there is a conflict of goals between condominium ownership for low-income families and restraints on resale profits. Is the goal to be housing for low-income groups or to integrate low-income families into the economic mainstream of our society? Obviously both goals are interrelated and consolidated in the idea of condominium unit ownership for low-income families. It may be expected that future statutes will express priorities. If there are no controls upon the resale profits, such housing will not be available to similar families at a later date at the same advantageous price. If there are restraints, housing will remain available, but the advantages of home ownership in government-assisted condominiums will be reduced.

NOTES

The author acknowledges the assistance of Lynne B. Sagalyn in the preparation of this chapter.

1. Gomberg, Quirk and Wein, *A Draft Program of Housing Reform,* 53 *Cornell L. Rev.* 361(1968).

2. The definition employed by the Internal Revenue Bureau Code, Section 216(b) is as follows:

> The term "cooperative housing corporation" means a corporation: having one and only one class of stock outstanding; each of the stockholders of which is entitled, solely by the reason of his ownership of stock in the corporation, to occupy for dwelling purposes a house, or an apartment in a building owned or leased by such a corporation; no stockholder of which is entitled (either conditionally or unconditionally) to receive any distribution not out of earnings and profits of the corporation except on a complete or partial liquidation of the corporation; and 80 percent or more of the gross income of which the taxes and interest described in subsection (a) are paid or incurred is derived from tenant-stockholders.

3. A leasehold cooperative is that corporation which holds a long-term leasehold for 50 to 99 years on the property, rather than a full fee ownership. In these cases, "landlord profiteering may remain"; security from rent increases is not as prevalent as in the fee ownership cooperative. Furthermore, allowable tax deductions may vary from the corporate fee ownership depending upon the conditions of the leasehold and the status of the building. *Clurman, D.* and *Hebard, E., Condominiums and Cooperatives* p. 170, 177 (1970) (hereinafter cited as *Clurman*).

4. The initial cash investment represents the primary cost of the apartment which is dependent upon the number of shares of stock allocated to it. The carrying charges and other obligations are also dependent upon the stock held by each tenant. The total cost of the apartment must, however, be figured to include the monthly mortgage assessments. *Id.,* p. 168.

5. *Id.,* p. 183 (emphasis added).

6. *Id.,* p. 182.

> The short-term leasing method gives government dominated cooperatives some flexibility in the provision of protection against exposure to possible cutoffs of government subsidies in below-market financing. Additionally, these cooperatives have better control over undesirable tenants as well as a policy regarding stock-holder income limitations.

7. The IRS Code, Section 216(b) defines a tenant-stockholder as an

individual who is a stockholder in a cooperative housing corporation, and whose stock is fully paid up in an amount not less than an amount shown to the satisfaction of the Secretary or his delegatee as bearing a reasonable relationship to the portion of the value of the corporation's equity in the house or apartment building and the land on which such individual is entitled to occupy.

8. *Clurman*, p. 174.

9. *Id.*, p. 166, 170.

10. The existence of Federal Mortgage Insurance for stock-cooperatives under Sec. 213 of the National Housing Act has provided the basis for classification. *Id.*, p. 202.

11. *Building the American City*, Report of the National Commission on Urban Problems p. 137 (1968) (hereinafter cited as *American City*).

12. *Clurman*, p. 181.

13. *Id.*

14. Teaford, *Homeownership for Low Income Families* 21 *Hastings L.J.* 253, 255 (1970) (hereinafter cited as *Teaford*).

15. Federal Housing Authority Form #3245, Article VIII, Sec. 1 (hereinafter cited as *FHA*).

16. *FHA* Article III, Sec. 1.

17. *Id.*

18. Pohoryles, The FHA Condominium, 31 *g.w.l. rev.* 1014 (1963) (hereinafter cited as *Pohoryles*).

19. *Clurman*, p. 181.

20. *FHA*, Article IV, Sec. 7.

21. *Id.*, Article 3, Sec. 8(a), (b), (c).

22. *Teaford*, p. 260.

23. *FHA*, Article III, Sec. 9.

24. *Id.*

25. *Id.*, Article V, Sec. 3.

26. *Id.*, Sec. 2.

27. *Id.*, Sec. 7, 8, 9, 11.

28. *Id.*, Sec. 5.

29. *Id.*, Article VI, Sec. 1, 2.

30. As a general rule, a corporation is liable for the torts and contracts incurred within the scope of the officer's employment.

31. Walbran, *Condominium*, 30 *Mo. L. Rev.* 532(1965). "The exact nature of the choice to which the solvent cooperator is put varies with the liability defaulted by the corporation and the provisions of his proprietary lease" (hereinafter cited as *Walbran*).

32. *Id.*, p. 532.

33. *Teaford*, p. 255.

34. *Id.*, 265.

35. *Pohoryles*, p. 1027.

36. Harrison, *The FHA Condominium*, 11 *N.Y.L. Forum* 460 (1965) (hereinafter

cited as *Harrison*).

37. The declaration describes the nature of the condominium enterprise, specifying the division of ownership and affirmation by unit owners of the shared rights and obligations for the use and maintenance of the project's common elements. Furthermore, it will customarily include restraints upon the unit owner's freedom to transfer ownership, provision for the establishment of a management body, arrangements for blanket casualty and liability insurance, and procedures regarding the aftermath of project destruction or obsolence. The declaration acts as a surrogate for the subdivision map; it details the condominium plans and includes a legal description of the underlying land, and a description in layman's terms of the building, apartment units and common facilities.

The bylaws function as the internal administrative mechanism to regulate building maintenance, budgeting, unit-owner assessment and collection, capital improvements and occupant control. Berger, *Condominium,* 63 *Colum. L. Rev.* 987, 1004-06 (1963) (hereinafter cited as *Berger*).

38. *Walbran,* p. 534.

39. Aside from the fee simple condominium ownership, several states permit leasehold condominiums in which "the developer or assignee reserves ownership of the entire land area, or of the land and building in entirety," or some part of the property and charges rent for its use by the unit owner. Unit leases, which are similar to proprietary leases, are issued; however, unlike the leasehold stock cooperative, the unit owner benefits from the condominium's other features—individual tax assessments and separate unit leasehold mortgages.

The advantages to the consumer of a leasehold condominium may be the decreased cost of land. However, a seller's market may obliterate the potential economic benefits and stimulate "prices that have little relationship to the distinction between leasehold and fee ownership." Furthermore, the leasehold condominium is a "speculator's dream"; ownership may be divided among the units while the land is sold to another part. Or, a "sandwich lease" may be created between the owners and the condominium which in actuality relinquishes only a *sublease* to the unit owners. *Clurman,* p. 146-47. See pages 148-61 for further discussion.

40. *Id.,* p. 10-11.

41. *Berger,* p. 994-95.

42. *Teaford,* p. 246.

43. *Berger,* p. 1002-03.

44. *Berger,* p. 1003.

45. This does not mean that in order to qualify for FHA mortgage insurance under Sec. 234 of the National Housing Act, the state in which the condominium is located must enact special enabling legislation for the creation of condominiums. It means that the laws of the locality and state must in some way permit the three elements enumerated above. *C. Ramsey, Condominiums, The Mortgage Banker,* p. 52 (1962).

46. *Pohoryles,* p. 1018.

47. *Clurman,* p. 14.

48. *Berger,* p. 1005.

49. *Walbran,* p. 537.

50. There are additional advantages to independent financing not available to the

stock-cooperator. Primary among these is the ability to finance the down pay-ment costs with relative flexibility. The stock of a cooperative is not a negotiable security for a mortgage loan. Thus institutional lenders do not like to finance the buying of stock and many are limited in the amount of such transactions. In comparison, a condominium purchaser can obtain a conventional or insured mortgage loan because the fee simple title to an apartment is evidence of the purchase of real estate. This difference in financing flexibility is crucial to the po-tential low-and moderate-income apartment purchaser who does not have cash reserves for a down payment in a cooperative corporation.

Separate financing also provides flexibility for the unit owner who needs to refinance his mortgage for cash emergencies, financing an education, etc. Because a mortgage in a stock cooperative is a blanket mortgage covering the entire project, it is not possible for an individual cooperator to refinance his pro rata share for needed cash. However, it should also be noted that separate financing involves extra costs for servicing and appraising separate units in comparison to the single cost for a stock-cooperative.

51. Common facilities include all areas other than the individual apartments—the land, the roofs, floors, main walls, elevators, staircases, lobbies, halls, parks, playgrounds, and parking spaces as well as other community and commercial facilities.

52. Consent of all unit owners may change fractional shares as provided in the project documents.

53. *Berger*, p. 1005.

54. *Teaford*, p. 271.

55. *Harrison*, p. 482.

56. *Id.*

57. *Pohoryles*, p. 1035.

58. *Teaford*, p. 271.

59. Anaheim Union Water Co., v. Comm'ss., 321 F.2d 253 (9th Cir. 1963) (Up-holding offset); Chicago & W.I.R.R. v. Comm., 303 F.2d 796 (reversed on re-hearing) 310 F.2d 380 (7th Cir. 1962) (disallowing offset). *See Harrison*, p. 481-88 for discussion of these cases.

60. Treas. Reg. Sec. 301.7701-02 (1960).

61. *See Harrison*, p. 482-88; *Berger*, p. 1007-10.

62. *Teaford*, p. 270; *Pohoryles*, p. 1035; *Contra Harrison*, p. 488.

63. *Teaford*, p. 271.

64. *Walbran*, p. 554.

65. *Berger*, p. 1011.

66. *Id.*, p. 995.

67. FHA Model Statute, Sec. 11.9.

68. *Pohoryles*, p. 1031.

69. For a discussion of the fourth way, defeasible fees, *see Berger*, p. 1014.

70. *Id.* at 1013 (emphasis added).

71. *Id.*

72. FHA Model Statute, Section 26 (a).

73. *Berger*, p. 1014.

74. *Pohoryles,* p. 1026.

75. *See Berger,* p. 1007-10 for discussion of this issue; *see also Harrison,* p. 487.

76. FHA Form #3277, Article IV, Sec. 5.

77. *Id.,* Secs. 8 & 9.

78. *Id.,* Sec. 3.

79. *Berger,* p. 1018. The urgency of a review of a prospective buyer's financial position is questionable because the economic interdependence in a condominium is minimal and the purchaser's reliability would be appraised by the mortgage lender and possibly FHA. While a "disruptive" neighbor may not be desirable, it is doubtful that the board can be a sensing device of these persons. Furthermore, while the criteria of religion and race have been forbidden by law, they are nonetheless applied; "in general, managements of cooperatives, by rejecting without opinion or by finding some legitimate pretext, have been able to be discriminating in their selection without serious challenge."

80. *Teaford,* p. 263.

81. *Clurman,* p. 103.

82. *Berger,* p. 1010.

83. *Walbran,* p. 555.

84. *Berger,* p. 1010.

85. *Teaford,* p 259.

86. *Walbran,* p. 555.

87. FHA Model Statute, Sec. 23. If secondary mortgages are subordinated to the condominium lien, it assists the management by eliminating the need for the management to contest the "fradulent" secondary encumbrances. However, this is disadvantageous for the unit owner because it discourages him from legitimate secondary borrowing and detracts from the "freedom to exploit the borrowing power of one's equity," an attraction characterizing the condominium purchase. *Berger,* p. 1011. In contrast, Teaford argues that for the low-income condominiums, prior second mortgages and mechanics' liens should not be subordinate to the association's lien so as not to discourage secondary borrowing for home improvements, etc. *Teaford,* p. 261.

88. *Teaford,* p. 261.

89. *Id.*

90. *Id.*

91. *Id.*

92. FHA form #3277, Article IV, Sec. 7.

93. The provisions are the same as for the stock-cooperative.

94. For a discussion of some of the problems of residential management see 10.115-10.130.

95. *Clurman,* p. 109-13.

96. PUD is an extension of the individual elements of land use control, combining zoning, subdivision, master planning, and housing and building codes. PUDs are essentially land subdivisions in which common land is a major element in the development and in which the common elements are owned by an association of all homeowners. PUD often is a staged development process; each stage represents a specific land area to be developed in accord with an overall plan. PUD empha-

223

sizes a mixture of land uses by establishing a minimum of two land uses within each development; it is not geared to the single lot types of development and thus there is no single ordinance for dictating land development. PUD is also characterized by a grant of "sweeping administrative discretion" given to the developers and the planning board by the local governing body. The aim of this provision is to establish few preset standards and thus maximize the bargaining process between the planning board and the developer. It is further hoped that this will stimulate innovation in land development and design. Burchell, Robert W., *Planned Unit Development* (PhD thesis Rutgers University, 1971).

97. *FHA Land Planning Bulletin #6*, p. 52.

98. *The Homes Association Handbook, Urban Law Institute* p. 197 (1964) (hereinafter cited as *Handbook*).

99. *FHA Land Planning Bulletin #6*, p. 52.

100. *Handbook*, p. 233.

101. *Id.*

102. It is possible for the PUD to include condominiums and/or cooperatives; the ownership rights of these housing ventures would then constitute subunits in the overall scheme of property ownership within the development.

103. *Clurman*, p. 223.

104. *Id.*

105. *Id.*

106. *Clurman*, p. 224.

107. *Id.*, p. 221.

108. *Handbook*, p. 5.

109. *Id.*, p. 5-9.

110. *Id.*, p. 7.

111. *Id.*

112. *Id.*

113. *Id.*

114. This discussion will not encompass the aspect of the physical development process.

115. *Clurman*, p. 218.

116. *Planned-Unit Development With a Homes Association*, US Department of Housing and Urban Development. *FHA Land Planning Bulletin #6*, p. 13.

117. *Id.*

118. *Id.*, p. 28.

119. *Id.*

120. *Clurman*, p. 222.

121. *Handbook*, p. 338.

122. *Id.*

123. *FHA Land Planning Bulletin #6*.

124. *Handbook*, p. xii.

125. In almost every state a nonprofit venture is statutorily authorized as a membership corporation and thus need not issue stock; the association thereby avoids

the problems of securities registration laws. Even if it does issue stock as a representation of membership rights to common properties and facilities, it does not appear to be subject to the registration laws (State v. Silberg, 166 Ohio St. 101, 139 N.E.2d 342 (1956)). The double tax liability of a corporation is also absent because the income of a homes association will generally be exempt from taxation under Internal Revenue Code Section 501 (c) (7) which classifies the association as a *club*. This section will exempt income obtained by the association *from its members* in the form of dues, assessments, admission fees or voluntary contributions subject to a strict requirement prohibiting the organization from allowing the net earnings to the benefit of the members. This restricts the association's ability to supplement the income obtained from outside sources except in cases of guest fees reasonably equal to the costs of the services received by the guests or any reasonable funds held in reserve for improvements or contingencies. *Clurman,* p. 222.

126. *Handbook,* p. x.

127. *Clurman,* p. 139.

128. *FHA Land Planning Bulletin #6,* p. 3.

129. *Clurman,* p. 223.

130. *Id.*

131. *Id.,* p. 225.

132. *Id.,* p. 226.

133. *FHA Land Planning Bulletin #6,* p. 4.

134. *Clurman,* p. 225.

135. *Handbook,* p. 214.

136. *Id.,* and *FHA Planning Bulletin #6.*

137. *Building the American City,* p. 134.

138. *Wall Street Journal,* April 13, 1970, p. 1, col. 8.

139. *Building the American City,* p. 140-41.

140. R. Burchell, J. Hughes, G. Sternlieb, *Housing Costs and Housing Restraints,* Chap. IV (1970).

141. *Teaford,* p. 257.

142. *Id.*

143. *Id.*

144. *Id.,* p. 258-59.

145. *Ramsey,* p. 52.

146. *Building the American City,* p. 139.

147. *Id.*

148. *Id.,* p. 137.

149. *Berger,* p. 1017.

150. *E.g.* Sec. 213 or 221 (d) (3), National Housing Act.

151. *Clurman,* p. 209.

152. *Berger,* p. 1017.

153. *Teaford,* p. 251.

10 Reforming the Landlord-Tenant Relationship

LONG RANGE REFORMATION

10.1   Increasing tenant hostility towards private and public land-lords tends to stem the flow of capital into the construction of private and public housing. Wholesale abandonment of properties by private land-lords and widespread deterioration of public housing aggravate the al-ready critical shortage of housing for low- and moderate-income tenants. Tenant dissatisfaction with the rental relationship foments into hostili-ty toward the landlord, not because of any isolated set of inequities but because the very nature and essence of the relationship is inconsistent with the economic, social and political principles of urban democracy. Chapters 1 through 8 have disclosed the pattern by which the sometimes subtle and often blatant inequities are woven into the fabric of the legal relationship of tenants of both private and public landlords. Chapter 9 describes the principles by which a mutual ownership landlord relation-ship may be created.

10.2   Our evaluation of the economic, social and political conse-quences of the present landlord-tenant relationship directs attention to the need for a complete transformation from private and public land-lords to mutual ownership landlords.

ECONOMIC REASONS FOR TRANSFORMATION

10.3

1. Tenants of private and public landlords have little incentive to preserve, protect and maintain the structures that contain their units. As long as all increases in value of the property inure to the benefit of the landlord, tenants of private and public landlords are unwilling contributors to the costs of repair. The tenants' attitude is reenforced by the realization that their interest in the premises may be terminated by the summary and often arbitrary determina-tion of the landlord. On the other hand, a mutual ownership tenant has an entreprenurial interest in the property. Expenditures for re-pair not only improve his present living conditions but also enhance the value and marketability of his proprietary interest.
2. The incentive of private landlords to make expenditures for re-pair and maintenance depends on the comparative rate of return of competing investment alternatives. Unless the rent can be raised sufficiently to provide a satisfactory return there is little incentive for the private landlord to increase his investment. The public land-lord has no economic incentive to enhance the value of the property and is usually severely restricted by fiscal and statutory limitations on expenditures. The incentive of the mutual ownership landlord to

227

repair and maintain the property is both direct and personal because of the improvement of his living conditions and his investment.
3. Construction of private rental units requires long-term investment of capital by investors who have become wary of the risks arising out of the increasing hostility and activism of tenants. Mutual ownership, on the other hand, permits the entrepreneur to limit his risks by short-term investment in development and construction and to recoup his investment quickly for continuing rapid turnover by sale of this interest to mutual ownership tenants. Mutual ownership thereby tends to encourage both the investment and turnover of capital required to overcome the underlying problem of an inadequate supply of housing.

SOCIAL REASONS FOR TRANSFORMATION
10.4

1. Tenants of private and public landlords tend to be the "have-nots" in our society. The lack of any proprietary interest in the community diminishes the tenant's willingness to support and preserve the existing social structure. Without such proprietary interest, tenants have little to lose but their hopes and aspirations, from proposals for drastic social change. On the other hand, mutual ownership tenants acquire a tangible and protectable interest in the community that provides a reason for maintaining social stability and tranquility.
2. Tenants live under a continuing threat that they may be deprived of their shelter security by the autocratic whim of a private landlord or by the impersonal institutional prescription of a public landlord. The insecurity that arises from the threat of eviction creates feelings of anguish and hostility toward the symbols of authority that support and perpetuate this threat. Mutual ownership tenants, on the other hand, become participants in the organizational structure that governs the conditions and tenure of their shelter security. They are thereby brought into the social system and the institutions that support it.

POLITICAL REASONS FOR TRANSFORMATION
10.5

1. Landlords and investors have become fearful of the potential political power that tenant constituencies may exert as their influence is consolidated by tenant organizations. Such fear becomes the basis of landlords' self-fulfilling prophecy that the increase of tenant political influence will dry up the flow of capital into multiple dwelling investment. Such fear and prophecy are completely eliminated by mutual ownership, where investors avoid all hostile and other relations with tenants by the sale of their interest to the mutual ownership tenants.

2. The growing awareness of the inequities in a legal system that favors the protection of property rights to the detriment of fundamental social needs has undermined tenants' political support for the governmental entity most closely associated with the landlord of tenants toward private and public landlords spills over and on to the governmental entity most closely associated with the landlord in issue. The inequities of landlordism become the inequities of government and the resulting antipathies are directed against the political system. A transformation from private and public landlordism to mutual ownership would stay this dangerous debilitation of governmental integrity by eliminating the entire pattern of inequity of the landlord relationship. Mutual ownership landlordism would substitute in its place an entirely new and different system that is more consistent with the realities and aspirations of an urban democracy.

SHORT RANGE REFORMATION

10.6   Until the time when it is possible to replace the private and public landlord tenant relationship with mutual ownership landlords, the law should be modified to ameliorate some of the gross abuses of the existing relationship. The proposals for reform which follow[1] have been classified into three categories: creation of the tenancy, duration of the tenancy and termination of the tenancy.

CREATION OF THE TENANCY

Effect of Failure To Sign and Deliver the Lease
10.7   *The rental agreement should be given the same force and effect as though signed and delivered where rent and possession are given and accepted without reservation.* If the landlord does not sign a written rental agreement that has been signed and tendered to him by the tenant, acceptance of rent without reservation by the landlord should give to the rental agreement the same force and effect as though it had been signed and delivered by the landlord. If the tenant does not sign a written rental agreement that has been signed and tendered to him by the landlord, acceptance of possession and payment of rent without reservation should give to the rental agreement the same force and effect as though it had been signed by the tenant. (*Model Code*, Sec. 1-301).

Specification of the Obligations of the Parties
10.8   *The landlord should be required to deliver and maintain the premises in habitable condition.* The landlord should be required to deliver the premises in such condition as will comply with minimum standards prescribed by housing codes and should make all repairs necessary to maintain the premises in said condition (*Model Code*, Sec. 2-203 (1)(c)).

229

10.9   *The tenant should be required to maintain the condition of his dwelling unit.* The tenant should be required to keep that part of the premises that he occupies and uses clean and sanitary. He should be responsible for any wilful or wanton destruction, damage or removal of any part of the dwelling unit or the facilities, equipment or appurtenances thereto (*Model Code,* Sec. 2-303 (1) and (5)).

10.10   *The tenant should be required to pay the agreed rent.* The parties may determine by agreement the amount of rent that the tenant shall pay in consideration for the use of the premises and the landlord's agreement to maintain same in habitable condition. In the absence of such agreement, the tenant should pay a reasonable sum for the use of the premises.

10.11   *Promises by either party should be considered as mutual and dependent covenants of the lease.* Material promises, agreements and covenants of any kind to be performed by either party to a rental agreement shall be interpreted as mutual and dependent conditions to the performance of material promises, agreements and covenants of the other party (*Model Code,* Sec. 2-102 (2)).

Specification of the Term of Agreement
10.12   *The rental agreement should specify the term of tenancy.* The landlord and tenant should specify in writing their agreement of the term of the tenancy. In the absence of such agreement, the tenancy shall be for a period of from month to month (*Model Code,* Sec. 2-309).

The Right To Full Possession at the Beginning of the Term
10.13   *The tenant's obligation to pay rent should be abated until he receives full possession.* If the landlord fails to provide the tenant with full possession, including substantial performance of all essential services at the beginning of the term, the obligation of the tenant should be abated until he receives full possession and substantial performance of all essential services. If the landlord wrongfully fails or refuses to provide full possession or essential services at the beginning of the term, the tenant should be entitled to recover reasonable expenditures necessary to secure adequate substitute housing (*Model Code,* Sec. 2-202).

DURATION OF THE TENANCY

The Right To Repair and Deduct
10.14   *The tenant should be permitted to subtract from his rent the costs of repairing the dwelling.* If the landlord fails to keep the premises in repair and fails to remedy a defect within a reasonable time after notice, the tenant may thereafter notify the landlord of his intention to remedy the defect at the landlord's expense. The tenant may then deduct from his rent a reasonable sum required to remedy the defect. In no event should a tenant be permitted to repair at the landlord's expense, a condition caused by the tenant's own lack of care (*Model Code,* Sec. 2-206).

Tenant's Remedies Upon Failure To Receive Essential Services
10.15 *The tenant should have a choice of remedies upon the landlord's failure to provide essential services.* If the landlord fails to provide water, heat or hot water when the building is equipped for such purposes, the tenant should at his option, be permitted to: procure substitute housing until the deficiency is corrected and abate the rent by the cost of that substitute housing; remain in the premises with rent abatement to the extent of the decreased value of the occupancy; terminate the rental agreement (*Model Code*, Sec. 2-207).

Exculpatory Provisions
10.16 *The landlord's waiver of liability should be forbidden.* Any agreement between a landlord and tenant exempting the landlord from liability for injuries to persons or property caused by the actions of the landlord or his agents should be unenforceable (*Model Code*, Sec. 2-406).

The Right To Sublet
10.17 *A tenant should be allowed to sublet the premises subject to reasonable conditions of the landlord.* A tenant should be permitted to sublet the premises except where the proposed substitute tenancy would be less favorable to the landlord for such reasons as insufficient financial responsibility, age, number of occupants or other significant differences in the terms or conditions of the tenancy. The burden of proving the reasonableness of the rejection of a substitute tenant should be placed upon the landlord (*Model Code*, Sec. 2-403).

Retaliatory Increases in Rent
10.18 *Retaliatory rent increases should be forbidden.* Landlords should not be permitted to increase the rent of (or evict) a tenant who has requested repairs or made complaints about the conditions of the premises to governmental authorities. The period of prohibition of retaliatory rent increases or eviction should be specified by statute (*Model Code*, Sec. 2-407).

TERMINATION OF THE TENANCY

Self-Help Evictions and Distraint
10.19 *Self-help evictions and distraint should be abolished.* All common law remedies by which a landlord was permitted to remove a tenant and to lay claim to the tenant's household and other property as security for the payment of unpaid rent, without the use of legal process, should be abolished. Violation of this principle by the landlord should subject him to punitive damages and all costs of a tenant's suit to recover possession (*Model Code*, Sec. 2-408).

Service of Process
10.20 *No default judgment should be issued unless the court is satisfied that the tenant has had actual notice.* In actions for summary

proceedings for eviction and rent the landlord should be required to provide any additional evidence necessary to satisfy the court that a defaulting tenant has had actual notice of the proceeding (*Model Code,* Sec. 3-213).

Tenants' Right To Terminate

10.21 *A tenant should have the right to terminate the tenancy upon the landlord's failure to maintain the premises in habitable condition.* If the landlord fails to maintain the premises in any way that deprives the tenant of a substantial benefit or enjoyment of the tenancy, the tenant should have the right to terminate if the landlord fails to remedy the situation within a reasonable time after written notice (*Model Code,* Sec. 2-204, 2-205, 2-207, (2) (a) 2-208).

Landlord's Right To Terminate

10.22 *A landlord should have the right to terminate the tenancy upon the tenant's failure to perform his responsibilities under the rental agreement or statute.* If the tenant fails to pay rent when due or fails to perform any responsibility of care or maintenance of the premises, required by statute or regulation, within a reasonable time after written notice, the landlord should have the right to terminate the tenancy (*Model Code,* Sec. 2-304).

The Right of Appeal

10.23 *Judgments involving eviction or money judgments for rent or damages should be subject to appeal without additional restrictions.* Either party to a judicial proceeding involving the landlord-tenant relationship should have the same right to appeal the judgment as is available in other civil actions (*Model Code,* Sec. 3-214).

The Security Deposit

10.24 *The security deposit should be preserved for the tenant and should be returned promptly upon termination of the tenancy.* Any advance or deposit of money to the landlord should be held for the benefit of the tenant. The landlord should be required to place the security deposit in a special interest earning bank account. The tenant's claim to that fund should be superior to the claim of any creditor of the landlord. The landlord's claim to such fund should be limited to such sum as is reasonably necessary to remedy the tenant's default and damage to the property. The remaining sum should be returned to the tenant within a reasonable time after the termination of the tenancy (*Model Code,* Sec. 2-401 (1) and (2)).

NOTES

1. *American Bar Foundation, Model Residential Landlord-Tenant Code* (Tent. Draft, 1969) (hereinafter cited as *Model Code*). Many provisions of the *Model Code* have been incorporated into the Uniform Landlord and Tenant Relationship Act.

APPENDIX

1 Model Residential Landlord-Tenant Code (Tentative Draft)

AMERICAN BAR FOUNDATION

Julian H. Levi, Philip Habutzel, Louis Rosenberg, James White

ARTICLE 1: GENERAL PROVISIONS

TITLE, PURPOSES AND APPLICATION

Section 1-101   Short Title

This Act shall be known and may be cited as the Residential Landlord-Tenant Code.

Section 1-102   Legislative Findings

The legislature hereby finds that a significant proportion of the rental housing in this State is substandard in structure, equipment, sanitation, and maintenance; that the condition of this housing has had and will continue to have, unless corrected, a deleterious effect on the residents of this housing; that poorly maintained and overcrowded housing contributes to the development and spread of disease, crime, infant mortality, juvenile delinquency, broken homes, and other physical, social, and psychological problems, and constitutes a menace to the health, safety, morals, and welfare of the residents of this State; that these conditions have necessitated excessive and disproportionate expenditures of public funds for crime prevention and punishment, for public health and safety, and for other public services and facilities, and have impaired the efficient and economic provision of government services by municipalities and the State. The legislature further finds that these conditions result in part from the often unequal bargaining power of landlords and tenants as well as from an ill-suited common law of landlord and tenant in which leases are interpreted as grants of the right of possession rather than mutual and dependent covenants; that this common law, which evolved in an agricultural setting, is inappropriate when applied to modern residential property; that in order to facilitate fair and equitable arrangements, to foster the development of housing which will meet the minimum standards of the present day, and to promote the health, safety, morals and welfare of the people, it is necessary and appropriate that the State specify certain minimum rights and remedies, obligations and prohibitions, for landlords and tenants of certain kinds of residential property.

Section 1-103   Purposes and Policies

This Act shall be liberally construed and applied to promote its underlying purposes and policies.

The underlying purposes and policies of this Act are:

(1) to simplify and clarify the law governing the rental of dwelling units;

(2) to encourage landlords and tenants to maintain and improve the quality of housing in this State; and

(3) to revise and modernize the law of landlord and tenant to serve more realistically the needs of an urban society.

Section 1-104   Applicability of Act

This Act shall regulate and determine all legal rights, remedies and obligations of the parties and beneficiaries of any rental agreement of a dwelling unit within this State, wherever executed. *Any agreement, whether written or oral, shall be unenforceable insofar as the agreement or any provision thereof conflicts with any provision of this Act and is not expressly authorized herein.* Such unenforceability shall not affect other provisions of the agreement which can be given effect without such void provision.

Cross-References:

Other agreements governed, see Sec. 1-401.

Scope of Article II, see Sec. 2-101.

"Dwelling unit," see Sec. 1-201.

"Rental agreement," see Sec. 1-207.

Permissible agreements generally, see Sec. 2-203 (3).

Permissible agreements with regard to single-family residence, see Sec. 2-203 (2).

Permissible agreements by "occasional" landlord. See Sec. 2-203 (4).

Rent provision, see Sec. 2-301.

Tenant's obligation to use and occupy, agreement, see Sec. 2-307.

Period of rental agreement, see Sec. 2-309.

Landlord's rule-making power, see Secs. 2-311, 2-312.

Permissible prohibition of assignment and limitation of sublease, see Sec. 2-403.

Security deposit authorized, see Sec. 2-401.

Section 1-105   Severability

If any provision or clause of this Act or application thereof to any person or circumstances is held invalid, such invalidity shall not affect other provisions or applications of the Act which can be given effect without the invalid provision or application, and to this end the provisions of this Act are declared to be severable.

Section 1-106   Jurisdiction

Any person, whether or not a citizen or resident of this State, who owns holds an ownership or beneficial interest in, uses, manages, or possesses real estate situated in this State, submits himself or his personal representative to the jurisdiction of the courts of this State as to any action or proceeding for the enforcement of an obligation arising under this Act.

Section 1-107   Personal Service of Process Outside State

(1)   Personal service of process may be made out of this state on any party to an action or proceeding arising under this Act if jurisdiction over the party has been conferred on the court by section 1-106 or in any other manner.

(2)   Such service shall be subject to all requirements pertaining to service inside the State, except that service may be made by any person over twenty-one years of age not a party to the action or proceeding. [An affidavit shall be filed by the server stating the time, place, and manner of service. The court shall on its own motion determine whether service has been properly made, on the basis of the affidavit and any other competent proofs.]

(3)   No default order or judgment shall be entered until the expiration of at least thirty days after service. A default order or judgment rendered on such service may be set aside only on a showing which would be timely and sufficient to set aside a default order or judgment rendered on personal service within this State.

Cross-References:
Personal jurisdiction under this Act, see Sec. 1-106.
Personal jurisdiction over out-of-State parties generally, see Secs. 1-106, 1-107.
Default judgments generally, see Sec. 1-107.
Personal service within State, see Sec. 1-107.
Service under summary proceeding, see Secs. 3-205, 3-206.
Default judgment in summary proceeding, see Sec. 3-214.

Section 1-108   Disclosure

(1)   On each written rental agreement, the lessor shall prominently disclose:

(a)   the names and usual addresses of all persons who are owners of the dwelling unit or the property of which the dwelling unit is a part (section 1-208); and

(b)   the names and usual addresses of all persons who are landlords of the dwelling unit (section 1-209).

(2)   In the case of an oral agreement, the lessor shall, on demand, furnish the tenant with a written statement containing the information required by subsection (1).

(3)   Any owner or landlord not dealing with the tenant as a lessor shall be responsible for compliance with this section by the lessor, and shall be estopped from any objection to a failure to serve process upon him in any proceeding arising under this Act when such failure is due to failure to comply with this section.

Cross-References:
Estopped in Tenant receivership petitions, see Sec. 3-302.
Separation of rents and responsibilities forbidden, see Sec. 1-401.

DEFINITIONS

Section 1-201   Person

Person includes an individual, corporation, government, or governmental agency, business trust, estate, trust, partnership or association, two or more persons having a joint or common interest, or any other legal or commercial entity.

Section 1-202   Dwelling Unit

A *dwelling unit* is a structure or that part of a structure which is used as a home, residence, or sleeping place by one person or by two or more persons maintaining a common household, to the exclusion of all others.

Section 1-203   Premises

Premises means a dwelling unit, appurtenances thereto, grounds and facilities held out for the use of tenants generally and any other area or facility whose use is promised to the tenants.

Definitional Cross-Reference:

"Dwelling unit," see Sec. 1-202.

Section 1-204   Roomer; Boarder

A *roomer* or *boarder* is a tenant occupying a dwelling unit

(1)   which lacks at least one major bathroom or kitchen facility, such as a toilet, refrigerator, or stove,

(2)   in a building

(a)   where one or more such major facilities are supplied to be used in common by the occupants of the roomer or boarder's dwelling unit and one or more other dwelling units; and

(b)   in which the landlord resides.

Definitional Cross-References:

"Tenant," see Sec. 1-210.

"Dwelling unit," see Sec. 1-202.

"Landlord," see Sec. 1-209.

Section 1-205   Single Family Residence

A *single family residence* is a structure maintained and used as a single dwelling unit.

Notwithstanding that a dwelling unit shares one or more walls with another dwelling unit, it shall be deemed a single family residence if it has direct access to a street or thoroughfare and shares neither heating facilities nor hot water equipment, nor any other essential facility or service, with any other dwelling unit.

Definitional Cross-Reference:

"Dwelling unit," see Sec. 1-202.

Section 1-206   Apartment Building

An *apartment building* is any structure containing one or more dwelling units except:

(1)   a single-family residence (section 1-205).

(2)   a structure in which all tenants are roomers or boarders (section 1-204).

Section 1-207   Rental Agreement

Rental agreement means and includes all agreements, written or oral, which establish or modify the terms, conditions, rules, regulations, or any other provisions concerning the use and occupancy of a dwelling unit.

Section 1-208   Owner

An *owner* means one or more persons, jointly or severally, in whom is vested:

(1)   all or any part of the legal title to property; or

(2)   (a)   part or all of the beneficial ownership; and

(b)   a right to present use and enjoyment of the property.

Section 1-209   Landlord

(1)   *Landlord* means the owner, lessor, or sub-lessor of the dwelling unit or the property of which it is a part and in addition means any person authorized to exercise any aspect of the management of the premises, including any person who, directly or indirectly receives rents or any part thereof, other than as a bona fide purchaser, and who has no obligation to deliver the whole of such receipts to another person.

(2)   Wherever *landlord* is used in this Code to signify the person to whom the tenant has a duty (including a condition to the exercise of a privilege), this duty may, at the tenant's election, be discharged in regard to:
    (a)   any person held out by any landlord as the appropriate party to accept performance, whether a landlord or not; or
    (b)   any person with whom the tenant normally deals as a landlord; or
    (c)   any person to whom the person specified in (1) or (2) is directly or ultimately responsible.
(3)   Wherever *landlord* is used in this Code to signify the person who is under a duty, whether to a tenant or to property, all persons specified in (a) shall be responsible for its performance and liable for its non-performance. Nothing in this subsection should be taken to forbid the allocation by agreement among multiple landlords of such duties although no such agreement shall be effective as against a tenant or other party with rights against the landlord under this Code.

Section 1-210   Tenant
    A *tenant* is any person who occupies a dwelling unit for living or dwelling purposes with the landlord's consent.

STATUTE OF FRAUDS
Section 1-301   Effect of Unsigned Rental Agreement
(1)   If the landlord does not sign a written rental agreement which has been signed and tendered to him by the tenant, acceptance of rent without reservation by the landlord shall give to the rental agreement the same effect as if it had been signed by the landlord.
(2)   If the tenant does not sign a written rental agreement which has been signed and tendered to him by the landlord, acceptance of possession and payment of rent without reservation shall give to the rental agreement the same effect as if it had been signed by the tenant.
(3)   Where the rental agreement which is given effect by the operation of this section provides by its terms for a term longer than one year, it shall operate to create only a one-year term.

SEPARATION OF RENTS AND OBLIGATIONS
Section 1-401   Separation of Rents and Obligations to Property Forbidden
    Any agreement, conveyance, or trust instrument which authorizes a person other than the beneficial owner to act as the landlord of a dwelling unit shall operate, regardless of its terms, to authorize and require such person to use rents to conform with this Act and any other law, code, ordinance, or regulation concerning the maintenance and operation of the premises.
    Cross-Reference:
Landlord defined, see Sec. 1-209.

ARTICLE 2: LANDLORD OBLIGATIONS AND REMEDIES
GENERAL PROVISIONS
Section 2-101   Exclusions from Application of Article
    The following arrangements are not intended to be governed by this Article, unless created solely to avoid the application of this Article.
(1)   residence at an institution, whether public or private, where residence is merely incidental to detention or the provision of medical, geriatric, educational, counseling, religious, or similar services, including (but not limited to) prisons,

student housing provided by the college or school, old age homes, nursing homes, homes for unwed mothers, monasteries and nunneries, and hospitals.

(2) occupancy under a bona fide contract of sale of the dwelling unit or the property of which it is a part, where the tenant is, or stands in the place of, the purchaser.

(3) residence by a member of a fraternal organization in a structure operated for the benefit of the organization.

(4) residence in a hotel, motel, cubicle hotel or other transient lodgings whose operation is subject to [cite State transient lodgings tax act].

Cross-References:
Applicability of Act, see Sec. 1-104.

Section 2-102   Promises in Rental Agreement Mutual and Dependent—
Interpretation

(1) Where a remedy is given to either party by this Article for a particular breach by the other party, this remedy shall be exclusive of any unmentioned remedy arising by operation of existing law or by operation of subsection (2) of this section.

(2) Material promises, agreements, covenants, or undertakings of any kind to be performed by either party to a rental agreement shall be interpreted as mutual and dependent conditions to the performance of material promises, agreements, covenants, and undertakings by the other party.

(3) A party undertaking to remedy a breach by the other party in accordance with this Article shall be deemed to have complied with the terms of this Article if his non-compliance with the exact instructions of this Article is non-material and non-prejudicial to the other party.

LANDLORD OBLIGATIONS AND TENANT REMEDIES

Section 2-201   Landlord to Supply Possession of Dwelling Unit
The landlord shall supply the dwelling unit bargained for at the beginning of the term and put the tenant into full possession.

Cross-Reference:
Tenant's remedy, see Sec. 2-202.

Section 2-202   Tenant's Remedies for Failure to Supply Possession
If the landlord fails to put the tenant into full possession of the dwelling unit at the beginning of the agreed term, the rent shall abate during any period the tenant is unable to enter, and:

(1) upon notice to the landlord, the tenant may terminate the rental agreement at any time he is unable to enter into possession; and

(2) if such inability to enter is caused wrongfully by the landlord or by anyone with the landlord's consent or license, the tenant may recover reasonable expenditures necessary to secure adequate substitute housing for up to one month, but no more than [½] the agreed rent for one month. Such expenditures may be recovered by appropriate action or proceeding or by deduction from the rent upon the submission of receipts totaling at least

    (a) the amount of abated rent; plus

    (b) the amount claimed against the rent; or

(3) if such inability to enter results from the wrongful holdover of a prior tenant, the tenant may maintain a summary proceeding for possession against such wrongful occupant. The expenses of such proceeding, including a reasonable attorney's fee, and substitute housing expenditures, as provided in subsection (2), may be claimed from the rent in the manner specified in subsection (2).

Cross-References:
Effect of termination, see Sec. 2-402.
Apportionability of rent, see Sec. 2-301(3).
Summary proceeding for possession against holdover tenant, see Secs. 3-202(1) and 3-203(3).

Section 2-203   *Landlord to Supply and Maintain Fit Dwelling Unit*

(1)   The landlord shall at all times during the tenancy:

(a)   comply with all applicable provisions of any State or local statute, code, regulation, or ordinance governing the maintenance, construction, use, or appearance of the dwelling unit and the property of which it is a part;

(b)   keep all areas of his building, grounds, facilities, and appurtenances in a clean and sanitary condition;

(c)   make all repairs and arrangements necessary to put and keep the dwelling unit and the appurtenances thereto in as good condition as they were, or ought by law or agreement to have been, at the commencement of tenancy;

(d)   maintain all electrical, plumbing, and other facilities supplied by him in good working order;

(e)   except in the case of a single family residence, provide and maintain appropriate receptacles and conveniences for the removal of ashes, rubbish, and garbage, and arrange for the frequent removal of such waste; and

(f)   except in the case of a single family residence, or where the building is not equipped for the purpose, supply water and hot water as reasonably required by the tenant and supply adequate heat between [October 1] and [May 1].

Where the duty imposed by clause (a) is incompatible with, or greater than, the duty imposed by any other clause of this subsection, the landlord's duty shall be determined by reference to clause (a).

(2)   The landlord and tenant of a single family residence may agree by a conspicuous writing independent of the rental agreement that the tenant is to perform specified repairs, maintenance tasks, alterations, or remodeling, but only if:

(a)   the work is not necessary to bring a non-complying dwelling unit into compliance with a building or housing code, ordinance, or the like; and remaining tenancy; or

(b)   adequate consideration apart from any provision of the rental agreement is exchanged for the tenant's promise. In no event under this subsection may the landlord treat performance of this agreement as a condition to any provision of the rental agreement.

(3)   The landlord and tenant of any other dwelling unit may agree by a conspicuous writing independent of the rental agreement that the tenant is to perform specified repairs, maintenance tasks, alterations, or remodeling, but only if:

(a)   the work is not necessary to bring a noncomplying dwelling unit into compliance with a building or housing code, ordinance, or the like; and

(b)   the agreement is supported by adequate consideration apart from the rental agreement. In no event under this subsection may the landlord treat performance of this agreement as a condition to any provision of the rental agreement.

(4)   Where a single family residence which is the owner's usual residence is rented during a temporary absence of the owner, the landlord and tenant may agree in writing that the tenant is to perform specified repairs, maintenance tasks, alterations, or remodeling.

Cross-References:
Dependence of covenants generally, see Sec. 2-102(2).
Remedy for defects at beginning of term, see Sec. 2-204.
Remedy for major defects, see Sec. 2-205.
Remedies for failure to supply heat, water, hot water, see Sec. 2-207.
Tenant's right to repair and deduct for minor defects, see Sec. 2-206.
Remedies for fire and casualty damage, see Sec. 2-208.
Tenant's duties generally, see Sec. 2-203.

Section 2-204   Tenant May Terminate at Beginning of Term

If the landlord fails to conform exactly to the rental agreement, or if there is a material non-compliance with any code, statute, ordinance, or regulation governing the maintenance or operation of the premises, the tenant may, on notice to the landlord, terminate the rental agreement and vacate the premises at any time during the first week of occupancy. The tenant shall retain this right to terminate beyond the first week of occupancy so long as he remains in possession in reliance on a promise, whether written or oral, by the landlord to correct all or any part of the condition or conditions which would justify termination by the tenant under this section.

Cross-References:
Effect of termination, see Sec. 2-402.
Landlord's duties generally, see Sec. 2-203.

Section 2-205   Tenant's Remedy of Termination at Any Time

(1) If there exists any condition which deprives the tenant of a substantial part of the benefit and enjoyment of his bargain, the tenant may notify the landlord in writing of the situation and, if the landlord does not remedy the situation within [one week], terminate the rental agreement. Such notice need not be given when the condition renders the dwelling unit uninhabitable or poses an imminent threat to the health or safety of any occupant. The tenant may not terminate for a condition caused by the want of due care of the tenant, a member of his family, or other person on the premises with his consent.

(2) If the condition referred to in subsection (1) was caused wilfully or negligently by the landlord, the tenant may recover any damages sustained as a result of the condition including, but not limited to, reasonable expenditures necessary to obtain adequate substitute housing.

Cross-References:
Effect of termination, see Sec. 2-402.
Apportionability of rent, see Sec. 2-301(3).

Section 2-206   Tenant's Remedy of Repair and Deduct for Minor Defects

(1) If the landlord of an apartment building or single family dwelling fails to repair, maintain, keep in sanitary condition, or perform in any other manner required by section 2-203 or as agreed to in a rental agreement, and fails to remedy such failure within [two weeks] after being notified by the tenant to do so, the tenant may further notify the landlord of his intention to correct the objectionable condition at the landlord's expense and immediately do or have done the necessary work in a workmanlike manner. The tenant may deduct from his rent a reasonable sum, not exceeding [fifty] dollars, for his expenditures by submitting to the landlord copies of his receipts covering at least the sum deducted. If the tenant submits a written estimate by a qualified workman at least [four weeks] before having the work done, and substitutes workmen and materials as the landlord may reasonably request in writing, the tenant may deduct

240

from his rent a reasonable sum not exceeding one month's rent by submitting to the landlord copies of his receipts covering at least the sum deducted.

(2)   In no event may a tenant repair at the landlord's expense when the condition complained of was caused by the want of due care of the tenant, a member of his family, or other person on the premises with his consent.

(3)   Before correcting conditions affecting facilities shared by more than one dwelling unit, the tenant shall notify all other tenants sharing such facilities of his plans, and shall so arrange the work as to create the least practicable inconvenience to such other tenants.

Section 2-207   *Tenant's Remedies for Failure to Supply Heat, Water, or Hot Water*

(1)   If the landlord fails to provide hot water to a roomer, boarder, or apartment building tenant, when the building is equipped for the purpose, for [one week] after the tenant notifies him of the failure, the tenant may:

    (a)   upon written notice to the landlord, immediately terminate the rental agreement; or

    (b)   upon notice to the landlord, keep [one-fourth] of the rent accrued during any period when hot water is not supplied. The landlord may avoid this liability by showing of impossibility of performance.

(2)   If the landlord fails to provide a reasonable amount of water or, between [October 1] and [May 1], heat to the roomer, boarder, or apartment building tenant, when the building is equipped for the purpose, the tenant may:

    (a)   upon written notice to the landlord, immediately terminate the rental agreement; or

    (b)   upon notice to the landlord, procure adequate substitute housing for as long as heat or water is not supplied, during which time the rent shall abate and the landlord shall be liable for any additional expense incurred by the tenant, up to [one-half] the amount of abated rent. This additional expense shall not be chargeable to the landlord if he is able to show impossibility of performance.

Cross-References:

Effect of termination of rental agreement, see Sec. 2-402.

Apportionability of rent, see Sec. 2-301(3).

Section 2-208   *Tenant's Remedies for Fire or Casualty Damage*

When the dwelling unit or any of the property or appurtenances necessary to the enjoyment thereof are rendered partially or wholly unusable by fire or other casualty which occurs without fault on the part of the tenant, a member of his family, or other person on the premises with his consent, the tenant may:

(1)   immediately quit the premises and notify the landlord of his election to quit within [one week] after quitting, in which case the rental agreement shall terminate as of the date of quitting. If the tenant fails to notify the landlord of his election to quit, he shall be liable for rent accruing to the date of the landlord's actual knowledge of the tenant's vacation or impossibility of further occupancy; or

(2)   if continued occupancy is otherwise lawful, vacate any part of the premises rendered unusable by the fire or casualty, in which case the tenant's liability for rent shall be no more than the market value of that part of the premises which he continues to use and occupy.

Cross-References:

Effect of termination, see Sec. 2-402.

241

Apportionability of rent, see Sec. 2-301(3).

Landlord right to possession to repair casualty damage, see Sec. 3-202(7).

TENANT OBLIGATIONS AND LANDLORD REMEDIES

Section 2-301   Rent

(1) The landlord and tenant may agree to any consideration as rent. In the absence of such agreement, the tenant shall pay to the landlord a reasonable sum for the use and occupation of the dwelling unit.

(2) Rent shall be payable at the time and place agreed to by the parties. Unless otherwise agreed, the entire rent shall be payable at the beginning of any term for one month or less, while one month's rent shall be payable at the beginning of each month of a longer term.

(3) Except for the purposes of payment, rent shall be uniformly apportionable from day to day.

Cross-References:

Effect of termination, see Sec. 2-402.

Security deposits, see Sec. 2-401.

Section 2-302   Remedy for Failure to Pay Rent

(1) A landlord or his agent may, any time after rent is due, demand payment thereof and notify the tenant in writing that unless payment is made within a time mentioned in such notice, not less than [10] days after receipt thereof, the rental agreement will be terminated. If the tenant remains in default, the landlord may thereafter bring a summary proceeding for possession of the dwelling unit (sections 3-201 through 3-218) or any other proper proceeding, action, or suit for possession.

(2) A landlord or his agent may bring an action for rent alone at any time after he has demanded payment of past due rent and notified the tenant of his intention to bring such an action.

Cross-References:

Waiver of landlord's right to terminate, see Sec. 2-313.

Landlord may join rent claim in summary proceeding for possession, see Sec. 3-208(5).

Landlord not estopped from rent action after judgment in summary proceeding for possession, see Sec. 3-213(2).

Remedies provided here are landlord's exclusive remedies, see Sec. 2-102.

Section 2-303   Tenant to Maintain Dwelling Unit

Each tenant shall comply with all obligations imposed upon tenants by applicable provisions of all municipal, county, and State codes, regulations, ordinances, and statutes, and in particular:

(1) keep that part of the premises which he occupies and uses as clean and sanitary as the conditions of the premises permit;

(2) Dispose from his dwelling unit all rubbish, garbage and other organic or flammable waste, in a clean and sanitary manner;

(3) keep all plumbing fixtures as clean and sanitary as their condition permits;

(4) properly use and operate all electrical and plumbing fixtures;

(5) not permit any person on the premises with his permission to wilfully or wantonly destroy, deface, damage, impair, or remove any part of the structure or dwelling unit or the facilities, equipment or appurtenances thereto, nor himself do any such thing; and

(6) comply with all covenants, rules, requirements, and the like which are in

242

accordance with section 2-311 and which the landlord can demonstrate are reasonably necessary for the preservation of the property and persons of the landlord, other tenants, or any other person.

Cross-References:
Remedy for tenant's breach, see Sec. 2-304.
Landlord to supply and maintain fit dwelling unit, see Sec. 2-203.

Section 2-304   Remedy for Tenant's Waste, Failure to Maintain, or Unlawful Use

(1)   If the tenant fails to carry out any responsibility in relation to his tenancy imposed by the preceding section, the landlord upon learning of such failure shall notify the tenant in writing of the lapse and allow a specified time, not less than [5] days from the receipt thereof, for the tenant to remedy such failure. Upon the expiration of this period,

(a) if the tenant's failure can be remedied by the landlord, as by cleaning, repairing, replacing a damaged item, or the like, the landlord may so remedy the tenant's failure and bill him for the actual and reasonable cost of such remedy. This bill shall be treated by all parties as rent due and payable on the next regular rent collection date or, if the tenancy has terminated, immediately upon receipt; or

(b) if the tenant's failure constitutes a breach of an obligation imposed upon tenants by a provision of a municipal, county, or State Code, ordinance, or statute, the landlord may terminate the rental agreement and bring a summary proceeding for possession.

No allowance of a period to correct a deficiency shall be required when a failure by the tenant causes or threatens to cause irremediable harm to any person or property.

(2)   Failure to remedy a deficiency within the specified time in the case of a roomer or boarder shall entitle the landlord to terminate the rental agreement and bring a summary proceeding for possession.

(3)   The landlord may bring an action or proceeding for waste or for breach of contract for damage suffered by the tenant's wilful or negligent failure to comply with his responsibilities under the preceding section.

Cross-References:
Duty to pay rent, see Secs. 2-301, 2-302.
Summary proceeding for possession, see Secs. 3-201 to 3-216.
Limitations on action for waste, see Sec. 3-401.
Tenant's duty to use and occupy, see Sec. 2-307.
Landlord's remedies for absence, misuse, and abandonment, see Sec. 2-308.
Tenant's duty to use properly, see Sec. 2-311.
Landlord's remedy for improper use, see Sec. 2-312.
Waiver of landlord's right to terminate, see Sec. 2-313.
Effect of termination by either party, see Sec. 2-402.

Section 2-305   Tenant's Responsibility to Inform Landlord

Any defective condition of the premises which comes to the tenant's attention, which he has reason to believe is unknown to the landlord, and which he has reason to believe is the duty of the landlord or of another tenant to repair, shall be reported by the tenant to the landlord as soon as practicable.

Cross-References:
Liability for failure to inform, see Sec. 2-306.
Landlord's duties generally, see Sec. 2-203.

Section 2-306   Liability for Failure to Inform

The tenant shall be responsible for any liability or injury resulting to the landlord as a result of the tenant's failure to carry out the duty imposed by the preceding section.

Section 2-307   Tenant to Use and Occupy

Unless otherwise agreed, the tenant shall occupy the rented premises as his abode and shall continue to occupy until the end of the agreed term. The land-lord may also require, in the rental agreement, that the tenant notify him of any anticipated extended absence from the premises no later than the first day of such absence.

This section shall have no effect except as between the parties.

Cross-Reference:

Landlord's remedy, see Sec. 2-308.

Section 2-308   Landlord's Remedies for Absence, Misuse, and Abandonment

(1) If the rental agreement provides for notification of the landlord by the tenant of an anticipated extended absence, and the tenant fails to make reasonable efforts to comply with such requirement, the tenant shall indemnify the landlord for any harm resulting from such absence.

(2) The landlord may, during any extended absence of the tenant enter the dwelling unit as reasonably necessary for inspection, maintenance, and safe-keeping.

(3) Unless otherwise agreed,

(a) use of the dwelling unit by the tenant for any other purpose than as his abode, or

(b) non-use of the dwelling unit shall constitute a breach of a rule under section 2-311 and entitle the landlord to proceed as specified in section 2-312.

(4) If the tenant wrongfully quits the dwelling unit and unequivocally indicates by words or deeds his intention not to resume tenancy, he shall be liable for the lesser of the following for such abandonment:

(a) the entire rent due for the remainder of the term: or

(b) all rent accrued during the period reasonable necessary to re-rent the premises at a fair rental, plus the difference between such fair rental and the rent agreed to in the prior rental agreement, plus a reasonable commission for the renting of the premises. This subsection shall apply if less than (a), notwithstanding that the landlord did not re-rent the premises.

Section 2-309   Term of Agreement

The landlord and tenant may agree in writing to any period as the term of the rental agreement. In the absence of such agreement, the tenancy shall be month to month, or in the case of a boarder, week to week.

Cross-References:

Effect of unsigned written rental agreement, see Sec. 1-301.

Termination of periodic tenancy, see Sec. 2-310.

Section 2-310   Termination of Tenancy; Holdover Remedies

(1) When the tenancy is month to month, the landlord or the tenant may terminate upon his notifying the other at least one month in advance of the anticipated termination.

(2) When the tenancy is less than month to month, the landlord or the tenant may terminate upon his notifying the other at least ten days before the anticipated termination.

(3) Whenever the term of the rental agreement expires, whether by passage of

time, by mutual agreement, by the giving of notice as provided in (1) or (2) above, or by the exercise by the landlord of a right to terminate given him under any section of this Act, if the tenant continues in possession of the premises after the date of termination without the landlord's consent, such tenant shall pay to the landlord a sum not to exceed twice the monthly rental under the previous agreement, computed and prorated on a daily basis, for each day he remains in possession for any period up to one month. If the tenant remains in possession for a period greater than one month, he shall be liable to the landlord for a sum equal to the average monthly rental under the previous rental agreement for each additional month or fraction thereof. The landlord may commence summary proceedings for the recovery of possession at any time during the first [60] days of holdover, except that the acceptance of rent in advance after the first month of holdover shall create a month-to-month tenancy absent an agreement between the parties to the contrary at the time of such acceptance.

Cross-References:
Termination of tenancy when landlord is employer, see Sec. 3-202(4).
Month-to-month tenancy presumed, see Sec. 2-209.
Summary proceeding for possession, see Secs. 3-201 to 3-218.
Effect of termination, see Sec. 2-402.
Rent, see Sec. 2-301.
Termination when there are material code violations, see Sec. 3-210.

Section 2-311   Tenant to Use Properly
(1)   The tenant shall obey all obligations or restrictions, whether denominated by the landlord as "rules" or otherwise, concerning his use, occupation and maintenance of his dwelling unit, appurtenances thereto, and the property of which the dwelling unit is a part if:

(a)   such obligations or restrictions are brought to the attention of the tenant at the time of his entry into the agreement to occupy the dwelling unit; or

(b)   such obligations or restrictions, if not so known by the tenant at the commencement of tenancy, are brought to the attention of the tenant and, if they work a substantial modification of his bargain, are consented to in writing by him.

(2)   No such restriction or obligation shall be enforceable against the tenant unless:

(a)   it is for the purpose of promoting the convenience, safety, or welfare of the tenants of the property, or for the preservation of the landlord's property from abusive use, or for the fair distribution of services and facilities held out for the tenants generally.

(b)   it is reasonably related to the purpose for which it is promulgated.

(c)   it applies to all tenants of the property in a fair manner.

(d)   it is sufficiently explicit in its prohibition, direction, or limitation of the tenant's conduct to fairly inform him of what he must or must not do to comply.

Section 2-312   Remedy for Improper Use
(1)   If the tenant breaches any rule, covenant, or the like under the preceding section, the landlord may notify the tenant of his breach and must allow [5] days after such notice for the remedy or correction of such breach. Such notice shall be in substantially the following form:

(Name and address of tenant)   (date)

Your are hereby notified that you have failed to perform according to the following rule, covenant, restriction, etc.:

(specify rule breached)

Be informed that if you [continue violating] [again violate] this [rule] after [a date not less than 5 days after this notice], the Landlord may terminate the lease and sue for possession of your dwelling unit.

(2) If the breach complained of continues or recurs after the date specified in the notice, the landlord may bring a summary proceeding for possession within [30] days after such continued or renewed breach.

Cross-References:

Misuse or non-use as a breach of rule, see Sec. 2-308(3).

Summary proceedings for possession, see Sec. 3-201 to 3-218.

Rule for preservation of person or property, see Sec. 2-304.

Waiver of landlord's right to terminate, see Sec. 2-313.

Section 2-313   Waiver of Landlord's Right to Terminate

Whenever the landlord accepts rent after learning of a breach or has accepted performance by the tenant which is at variance with the terms of the rental agreement or subsequent rules, he has waived his right to terminate the rental agreement on account of such breach or varying performance.

OTHER LIMITATIONS ON LANDLORDS AND TENANTS

Section 2-401   Security Deposit

(1) Any advance or deposit of money, regardless of its denomination, whose primary function is to secure the performance of a rental agreement or any part thereof, shall be governed by this section. This money shall be held and administered for the benefit of the tenant. The tenant's claim to such money shall be prior to that of any creditor of the landlord, including a trustee in bankruptcy, even if such security funds are commingled.

(2) The landlord may only claim such funds as are reasonably necessary to remedy tenant defaults covered by any of the following provisions: Secs. 2-301, 2-304(1) or 2-308. Remaining funds shall be returned to the tenant no later than two weeks after the time at which the rental agreement would have terminated, had all parties performed perfectly, except if, at the end of this period, the landlord is in the process of remedying tenant's defaults under Sec. 2-304(1), the landlord may retain the security deposit until he has been able to ascertain the cost of the remedy.

(3) Upon cessation of his interest in the dwelling unit, whether by sale, assignment, death, appointment of a receiver, or otherwise, the person in possession of the security deposit (landlord, his agent, or executor) shall within a reasonable time:

(a) transfer the funds, or any remainder after lawful deductions under subsection (2), to the landlord's successor in interest and notify the tenant by registered or certified mail of such transfer and of the transferee's name and address; or

(b) return the funds, or any remainder after lawful deductions under subsection (2), to the tenant.

In either case, the landlord shall be relieved of further liability.

(4) Upon receipt of transferred funds under subsection (3)(a), the transferee, in relation to such funds, shall be deemed to have all of the rights and obligations of a landlord holding the funds as a security deposit.

(5)   The wilful retention of a security deposit in violation of this section by a landlord whose interest has expired or terminated shall be a misdemeanor.

Cross-References:

Rent generally, see Sec. 2-301.

Advance payments of rent, see Sec. 2-301(2).

Landlord remedy for tenant waste or failure to maintain, see Sec. 2-304(1).

Landlord remedies for tenant absence, misuse, or abandonment, see Sec. 2-308.

Penalty for landlord misdemeanor, see Sec. 3-501.

Tenant to receive half of misdemeanor penalty, see Sec. 3-502.

Section 2-402   Effect of Termination by Either Party

Except as otherwise provided in this Code, whenever either party to a rental agreement rightfully elects to terminate, the duties of each party under the rental agreement shall cease and determine, and the parties shall thereupon discharge any remaining obligations as soon as practicable.

Cross-References:

Tenant's liability for rent generally, see Sec. 2-301.

Apportionability of rent, see Sec. 2-301(3).

Tenant's rights to terminate, see Secs. 2-304, 2-305, 2-207, 2-208, 2-403, 2-405(3).

Security deposit generally, see Sec. 2-401.

Section 2-403   Sublease and Assignments

(1)   Unless otherwise agreed in writing, the tenant may sublet his premises or assign the rental agreement to another without the landlord's consent.

(2)   A written rental agreement may restrict the tenant's right to assign the rental agreement in any manner. The tenant's right to sublease the premises may be conditioned on obtaining the landlord's consent, which shall be withheld upon reasonable grounds as specified in subsection (5); no further restriction on sublease shall be effective.

(3)   When the rental agreement requires the landlord's consent to sublease, the tenant may secure one or more persons who are willing to sublet the premises. Each such prospective subtenant shall make a formal, written, signed offer to the landlord, containing all of the following, except as the landlord may waive one or more items:

(a)   the prospective subtenant's full name and age.

(b)   the prospective subtenant's marital status.

(c)   the prospective subtenant's occupation, place of employment, and name and address of employer.

(d)   the names and ages and relationships to the prospective subtenant of all persons who would normally reside in the premises.

(e)   two credit references, or responsible persons who will confirm the financial responsibility of the prospective subtenant.

(f)   the names and addresses of all landlords of the prospective subtenant from whom he has leased or rented during the prior three years, [or, if more than three, any three of them].

(4)   Within [10] days, not including legal holidays, after such a written offer has been delivered or mailed [by certified mail] to the landlord, the landlord may reject the prospective subtenant by delivering or mailing [by certified mail] to the tenant a written reply signed by the landlord which shall contain one or more specific grounds for the rejection.

If the landlord fails to reply within the [10] days, or if his written reply fails to give reasonable grounds for rejecting the prospective subtenant, the tenant may, at his option, terminate the rental agreement by giving written notice to the landlord within [90] days following the lapse of the [10] day reply period or the receipt of the rejection reply which fails to state any reasonable ground for rejection.

[Thirty] days after such notice is delivered or mailed [by registered mail] to the landlord, the rental agreement shall terminate. The tenant shall be subject to no damages, penalty, or forfeiture of any part or all of his security deposit or any other payment for such termination.

(5)   Reasonable grounds for rejecting a proposed subtenant include any facts which reasonably indicate that the proposed tenancy would be less favorable to the landlord than the existing tenancy, including, but not limited to:

   (a)   insufficient credit standing or financial responsibility.

   (b)   number of persons in the proposed household.

   (c)   number of persons under 18 in the proposed household.

   (d)   unwillingness of the prospective tenant to assume the same terms as are included in the existing rental agreement.

   (e)   proposed maintenance of pets.

   (f)   proposed commercial activity.

   (g)   written information signed by a previous landlord, which shall accompany the rejection, setting forth abuses of other premises occupied by the prospective subtenant.

No consideration of race, creed, sex, religion, political opinion or affiliation, or national origin may be relied on by the landlord as reasonable grounds for rejection.

(6)   In any proceeding in which the reasonableness of the landlord's rejection shall be in issue, the burden of showing reasonableness shall be on the landlord.

   Cross-References:

Effect of termination, see Sec. 2-402.

Section 2-404   Access

(1)   The tenant shall not unreasonably withhold his consent to the landlord to enter into the dwelling unit in order to inspect the premises, make necessary repairs, decorations, alterations, or improvements, supply services as agreed, or exhibit the dwelling unit to prospective purchasers, mortgagees, or tenants.

(2)   The landlord shall not abuse this right of access nor use it to harass the tenant. Insofar as it is practicable to do so, the landlord shall give the tenant at least two days notice of his intent to enter, and shall enter only during normal business hours.

Section 2-405   Landlord and Tenant Remedies for Abuse of Access

(1)   The tenant shall be liable to the landlord for any harm proximately caused by the tenant's unreasonable refusal to allow access.

(2)   The landlord shall be liable to the tenant for any theft, casualty, or other harm proximately resulting from an entry into the dwelling unit by him or with his permission or license:

   (a)   when the tenant is absent and has not specifically consented to the entry.

   (b)   without the tenant's actual consent when he is present and able to consent.

(c)   in any other case, when the harm suffered by the tenant is due to the landlord's negligence.

(3)   Repeated demands for unreasonable entry, or any entry which is unreasonable and not consented to by the tenant, may be treated by the tenant as grounds for termination of the rental agreement. Any court of competent jurisdiction may issue an injunction against this manner of harassment on behalf of one or more tenants.

(4)   Every agreement or understanding between a landlord and a tenant which purports to exempt the landlord from any liability imposed by this section, except consent to a particular entry, shall be null and void.

Cross-References:

Effect of termination, see Sec. 2-402.

Tenant's remedies for unlawful ouster or exclusion, see Sec. 2-408.

Section 2-406   Landlord's Waiver of Liability Forbidden

Every agreement between landlord and tenant in or in connection with a rental agreement of residential property exempting the landlord from liability for damages for injuries to persons or property caused by or resulting from the acts or omissions of the landlord, his agrents, servants or employees, in the operation or maintenance of the dwelling unit or the property of which it is a part shall be unenforceable.

Section 2-407   Retaliatory Evictions and Rent Increases Prohibited

(1)   Notwithstanding that the tenant has no written rental agreement or that it has expired, so long as the tenant continues to tender the usual rent to the landlord or proceeds to tender receipts for rent lawfully withheld under part 2 of this Article, no (A) action or proceeding to recover possession of the dwelling unit may be maintained against the tenant, nor shall the landlord (B) otherwise cause the tenant to quit the dwelling unit involuntarily, nor (C) demand an increase in rent from the tenant, nor (D) decrease the services to which the tenant has been entitled, within six months after:

(a)   the tenant has complained in good faith of conditions in or affecting his dwelling unit which constitute a violation of a building, housing, sanitary, or other code or ordinance, to a body charged with the enforcement of such code or ordinance; or

(b)   such a body has filed a notice or complaint of such a violation; or

(c)   the tenant has in good faith requested repairs under sections 2-205, 2-206, or 2-207.

(2)   Notwithstanding subsection (1), the landlord may recover possession of the dwelling unit if:

(a)   the tenant is committing waste, or a nuisance, or is using the dwelling unit for an illegal purpose or for other than living or dwelling purposes in violation of his rental agreement; or

(b)   the landlord seeks in good faith to recover possession of the dwelling unit for immediate use as his own abode; or

(c)   the landlord seeks in good faith to recover possession of the dwelling unit for the purpose of substantially altering, remodeling, or demolishing the premises; or

(d)   the landlord seeks in good faith to recover possession of the dwelling unit for the purpose of immediately terminating for at least six months use of the dwelling unit as a dwelling unit; or

(e)   the complaint or request of subsection (1) relates only to a condition or conditions caused by the lack of ordinary care by the tenant or another person in his household or on the premises with his consent; or

(f) the dwelling unit and other property and facilities used by or affecting the use and enjoyment of the tenant were on the date of filing of such complaint or request in full compliance with all codes, statutes, and ordinances; or

(g) the landlord has in good faith contracted to sell the property, and the contract of sale contains a representation by the purchaser corresponding to (b), (c), or (d) above; or

(h) the landlord is seeking to recover possession on the basis of a notice to terminate a periodic tenancy, which notice was given to the tenant previous to the complaint or request of subsection (1).

(3) Any tenant from whom possession has been recovered or who has been otherwise involuntarily dispossessed, in violation of this section, shall be entitled to recover three months' rent or threefold the damages sustained by him, whichever is greater, and the cost of suit, including a reasonable attorney's fee.

(4) Notwithstanding subsection (1), the landlord may increase the rent if:

(a) the dwelling unit and other property and facilities used by and affecting the use and enjoyment of the tenant were on the date of filing of such complaint or request of subsection (1) in full compliance with all codes, statutes, and ordinances; or

(b) the landlord has become liable for a substantial increase in property taxes, or a substantial increase in other maintenance or operating costs not associated with his complying with the complaint or request, not less that four months prior to the demand for an increase in rent; and the increase in rent does not exceed the prorated portion of the net increase in taxes or costs; or

(c) the landlord has completed a substantial capital improvement of the dwelling unit or the property of which it is a part not less than four months prior to the demand for increased rent, and the increase in rent does not exceed the amount which may be claimed for Federal Income Tax purposes as a straightline depreciation of the improvement, prorated among the dwelling units benefited by the improvements; or

(d) the complaint or request of subsection (1) relates only to a condition or conditions caused by the want of due care by the tenant or another person of his household or on the premises with his consent; or

(e) the landlord can establish, by competent evidence, that the rent now demanded of the tenant does not exceed the rent charged other tenants of similar dwelling units in his building or, in the case of a single family residence or where there is no similar dwelling unit in the building, does not exceed the market value of the dwelling unit.

Section 2-408   Tenant's Remedies for Landlord's Unlawful Ouster or Exclusion

If removed from the premises or excluded therefrom by the landlord or his agent except under color of a valid court order so authorizing, the tenant may recover possession or terminate the rental agreement and, in either case, recover three months' rent or threefold the damages sustained by him, and the cost of suit, including a reasonable attorney's fee.

Cross-References:

Summary proceeding for possession, see Sec. 3-203(3).

Effect of termination, see Sec. 2-402.

250

ARTICLE 3: ACTIONS AND PROCEEDINGS

APPOINTED COUNSEL FOR TENANTS

Section 3-101   *Court to Appoint Counsel for Indigent Tenants*

(1) In any proceeding brought by or for a landlord against a tenant to recover possession of his dwelling unit, the court shall inform the tenant of his right to counsel, and if the tenant is unable to afford his own, the court shall appoint counsel [designate appropriate source].

(2) A tenant shall be deemed unable to afford a private attorney when the expenditure therefore would work untoward hardship on the tenant or his family.

(3) [Provide for payment in accordance with State practice.]

SUMMARY PROCEEDINGS FOR POSSESSION

Section 3-201   *Jurisdiction and Venue*

(1) A summary proceeding to recover the possession of residential real property may be maintained in [specify court or courts].

(2) The place of trial of the summary proceeding shall be [specify as appropriate].

Sections 3-202   *Grounds for Summary Proceeding*

Unless otherwise agreed in written rental agreement, a special proceeding may be maintained under this part on one or more of the following grounds:

(1) The tenant continues in possession of any part of the premises after the expiration of the rental agreement (except expiration at the landlord's election on breach of rule or condition subsequent or the equivalent) without the permission of the landlord or, where a new tenant is entitled to possession, without the permission of the new tenant.

(2) The tenant has wrongfully failed to pay the agreed rent (section 2-302).

(3) The tenant has breached a lawful obligation relating to his use of the premises (sections 2-304(2), 2-308(3), 2-312).

(4) The defendant, an employee, servant, or agent of the petitioner, holds over for more than five days after dismissal when the housing supplied by petitioner was a part of the compensation for labor or services.

(5) The defendant, a buyer of the dwelling unit or the property of which it is a part, holds over for more than five days after the property has been duly sold upon the foreclosure of a mortgage, and the title under the mortgage has been duly perfected.

(6) The defendant has wrongfully ousted the petitioner, who is the rightful tenant of the dwelling unit.

(7) The tenant refuses to yield possession of a dwelling unit rendered partially or wholly unusable by fire or casualty, and the landlord requires possession for the purpose of effecting repairs of the damage in accordance with plans which have been duly filed with any appropriate authorities.

Cross-References:

Termination of tenancy, see Sec. 2-310.

Right of new tenant to sue holdover for possession, see Secs. 2-202, 3-203.

Rent, see Secs. 2-301, 2-302.

Tenant's obligations, generally, see Secs. 2-303 to 312.

Waiver of landlord's right to terminate, see Sec. 2-313.

Section 3-203   *Who May Maintain Proceeding*

The proceeding may be initiated by:

(1) the landlord.

(2)   the owner.

(3)   the tenant who has been wrongfully put out or kept out.

(4)   the next tenant of the premises, whose term has begun.

Cross-References:

Grounds for summary proceeding, see Sec. 3-202.

Next tenant may sue holdover for possession, see Sec. 2-202.

Section 3-204   Commencement of Action and Notice of Petition

(1)   The proceeding shall be commenced by service of petition and a notice of petition. A notice of petition may be issued only by a lawyer, judge, or the clerk of the court.

(2)   The notice of petition shall state the time and place of the hearing on the petition and state that if respondent shall fail at such time to appear and defend against such petition, he may be precluded from afterwards raising any defense or a claim based on such defense in any other proceeding or action.

Section 3-205   Service and Filing of Notice

(1)   The notice of petition and petition shall be served at least [5] and not more than [12] days before the time at which the petition is to be heard.

(2)   The notice of petition and petition together with proof of service thereof shall be filed with the court before which the petition is to be heard prior to the hearing, and in no event later than [3] days after service. [If service has been made by mail, the return receipt with respondent's signature shall be filed at or before the hearing.]

Section 3-206   Manner of Service

Service of the notice of petition and petition shall be made in the same manner as personal service of a summons in an action.

If service cannot be made in such manner, it shall be made by leaving a copy of the notice and petition personally with a person of suitable age and discretion who resides or is employed in the dwelling unit.

If no such person can be found after a reasonable effort, service may be made by:

(a)   affixing a copy of the notice and petition upon a conspicuous part of the dwelling unit; and

(b)   within one day thereafter, if tenant is a natural person, sending by certified mail an additional copy of each document to the dwelling unit and to any other address known to the person seeking possession as reasonably chosen to give actual notice to respondent; and

(c)   if tenant is a corporation or other unnatural person, by sending by certified mail within one day after affixation additional copies of each document to the dwelling unit and to the principal place of business of such tenant, if known, or to any other place of business of such tenant, if known, or to any other place known to the party seeking possession as reasonably chosen to effect actual notice.

Section 3-207   Necessary Parties Defendant

In addition to the party in possession of the property, the petitioner shall name and join any person under whom the possessor claims, when such other person's claim to possession is inconsistent with petitioner's.

Section 3-208   Contents of Petition Generally

The petition shall:

(1)   state the interest of the petitioner in the dwelling unit from which removal is sought.

(2) state the defendant's interest in the dwelling unit and his relationship to petitioner with regard thereto.

(3) describe the dwelling unit from which removal is sought.

(4) state the facts upon which this proceeding is based.

(5) state the relief sought. The relief may include a judgment for rent due if the notice of petition contains a conspicuous notice that such demand has been made.

Sample Petition

I

John Doe, hereinafter petitioner, is a real estate agent licensed in the city of Chicago, Illinois.

II

Irving Max, hereinafter owner, is the owner in fee simple absolute of property located at 2001 East Seventy-second Place in the city of Chicago, Illinois, of which apartment 3-B, hereinafter the dwelling unit, is a part.

III

Irving Max, on the 4th of April, 1954, entered into an agreement with petitioner whereby petitioner was and continues to act as owner's manager in all affairs with regard to the dwelling unit and the property of which it is a part.

IV

Louis Moe, hereinafter defendant first, is in full and exclusive possession of the dwelling unit, and has been since at least July 15, 1968.

V

Petitioner's information and belief is that defendant first is the tenant or guest of Seward Poe, hereinafter defendant second.

VI

Seward Poe entered into a lease agreement with petitioner whereby he was to use and occupy the dwelling unit from November 1, 1967 to October 31, 1968, subject to the payment of rent and other conditions.

VII

Petitioner demanded possession of the dwelling unit from defendant first on November 1, 1968, and said defendant first thereupon denied petitioner's right to possession and referred petitioner to defendant second.

VIII

Petitioner demanded of defendant second that possession of the dwelling unit be relinquished by him and all claiming under him on November 2, 1968, whereupon defendant second denied petitioner's right to possession and referred petitioner to defendant first.

IX

The lease agreement described in paragraph sixth above has expired, and petitioner has not agreed nor acquiesced to the continued tenancy of the dwelling unit by either of said defendants.

X

Therefore, petitioner prays that this court award him possession and such other relief as the court deems meet and just.

Section 3-209   *Additional Contents of Certain Petitions*

If possession of the dwelling unit is sought on the grounds that the tenant has violated or failed to observe a lawful obligation in relation to his use and enjoyment of the dwelling unit (sections 2-304(2), 2-308(3), 2-311, 2-312), the petition shall in addition to the requirements of the foregoing section:

253

(1) set forth the rule, condition, or the like allegedly breached, together with the date and manner in which the rule or the like was made known to the tenant.
(2) allege with specificity the facts constituting a breach of the rule, and that notice or warning as required by law was given to the tenant.
(3) set forth the facts constituting a continued or recurrent violation of the rule.
(4) set forth the purpose served by the rule breached, and that the rule promotes the convenience, safety, or welfare of other tenants of the property, or preserves the property and appurtenances thereto from abusive use by tenants or others, or seeks to distribute services and facilities held out for common use in an equitable manner.
(5) allege that the rule, if not a part of the rental agreement or any understanding of the landlord and tenant at the time of the formation of the rental agreement, does not work a substantial modification of the tenant's bargain; or, if it does, that the tenant consented knowingly in writing to the rule.
(6) if the rule breached is for the benefit of other tenants only, allege that all the tenants for whose benefit the rule purports to be, or if more than three, any three of them, are in favor of the rule.

Sample Petition

I

John Doe, hereinafter petitioner, is the owner in fee simple absolute, of certain property, namely a single-family detached dwelling, at 11625 Denny Road, city of Sunset Hills, Saint Louis County, Missouri.

II

Louis Poe, hereinafter defendant, is the occupant and resident of said property under a month to month tenancy which began on 1 September 1966.

III

Petitioner orally informed defendant at the commencement of tenancy, and thereafter delivered in writing to him, certain rules respecting defendant's use and enjoyment of the property.

IV

Among such rules, as is well known to defendant, was the following: "Defrost refrigerator every month. Do not use sharp instruments."

V

The refrigerator on the property and used by defendant is the property of petitioner.

VI

On November 6, 1968, defendant complained that said refrigerator did not function properly. Upon examination thereof, petitioner discovered that the malfunction was due solely to an accumulation of ice and frost, indicating to petitioner that at least three months had elapsed since the refrigerator had been defrosted.

VII

Petitioner thereupon called the situation to the attention of the defendant, and averred that at least three months must have passed since the refrigerator had been defrosted. Defendant confessed that this was so, and explained that he did not know how to defrost a refrigerator.

VIII

Petitioner thereupon defrosted the refrigerator and explained to defendant each step of the process. Defendant expressed gratitude at petitioner's instruction. All of the events described in paragraphs sixth, seventh, and eighth occurred on the afternoon of November 6, 1968.

IX

On November 7, 1968, petitioner delivered to defendant in person the following written notice:

"Louis Poe
11625 Denny Road   7 November, 1968
Sunset Hills, Mo. 63126

You are hereby notified that you have failed to comply with the following rule:
'Defrost refrigerator every month...'
Be informed that if you again fail to comply with this rule after 20 November 1968 the landlord may terminate the lease and proceed to recover possession of your dwelling unit."

X

Petitioner inspected the refrigerator on the 20th of November, the 27th of November, the 4th of December, and the 11th of December, 1968. On each occasion, petitioner reminded defendant orally of his duty to defrost the refrigerator. At no time during this period did defendant defrost the refrigerator.

XI

The rule mentioned in paragraphs fourth and ninth above is for the purpose of protecting petitioner's refrigerator from excessive wear and abuse.

XII

Therefore, the petitioner prays that this court award him full and exclusive possession of the property, and such other relief as the court deems just.

Cross-References:

Waiver of landlord's right to terminate, see Sec. 2-313.

Landlord's right to terminate when boarder fails to repair, see Sec. 2-304 (2).

Misuse or non-use of the dwelling unit, see Sec. 2-308(3).

Improper use, rules, see Secs. 2-311, 2-312.

Section 3-210   Answer

At the time when the petition is to be heard, the defendant, or any person in possession or claiming possession of the dwelling unit, may answer, orally or in writing. If the answer is oral the substance thereof shall be endorsed on the petition. The answer may contain any legal or equitable defense, or counterclaim.

Section 3-211   Trial

Where triable issues of fact are raised, they shall be tried by the court [unless, at the time the petition is to be heard, a party demands a trial by jury, in which case the trial shall be by jury notwithstanding any waiver of jury trial contained in any lease]. At the time when issue is joined, the court, in its discretion at the application of either party and upon proof to its satisfaction by affidavit or orally that an adjournment is necessary to enable the applicant to procure necessary witnesses or evidence, or by consent of all the parties who appear, may adjourn the trial of issue, but not more than ten days, except by consent of all parties.

Section 3-212   Judgment

(1) The court shall direct that a final judgment be entered determining the rights

of the parties. The judgment shall award to the successful party the costs of the special proceeding.

(2) The judgment shall not bar an action to recover the possession of real property. [The judgment shall not bar an action, proceeding or counterclaim, commenced or interposed within [60] days of entry of judgment, for affirmative equitable relief which was not sought by counterclaim in the proceeding because of the limited jurisdiction of the court.]

(3) If the proceeding is founded upon an allegation of forcible entry or forcible holding out, the court may award to the successful party a fixed sum as damages, not exceeding [50] dollars, in addition to his costs.

(4) If the proceeding is founded upon an allegation that tenant has wrongfully failed to pay rent, costs shall be no more than [25] dollars.

> *Cross-References:*
> Landlord may join rent claim in summary proceeding for possession, Sec. 3-208(5).
> Landlord not estopped from rent action after summary proceeding judgment, Sec. 3-213(2).

Section 3-213   Default Judgment

No judgment for the petitioner shall be entered unless the court is satisfied, upon competent proof, that the respondent has received actual notice of the proceeding, or, having abandoned the dwelling unit, cannot be found within the jurisdiction of the court after the exercise of reasonable diligence. Where the respondent cannot be found, no claim for rent due shall be allowed to be joined in this proceeding.

Section 3-214   Stay of Proceedings on Appeal or Certiorari

If either party shall feel aggrieved by the judgment rendered in such proceeding he may appeal or apply for a writ of certiorari within 10 days to [specify court or courts]. No such appeal or application by tenant shall stay proceedings on such judgment unless the tenant shall, within said 10 days, execute and file with the [trial court] his undertaking to the petitioner, with such bond or other assurances as may be required by the court, to the effect that the tenant will pay all costs of such appeal or proceedings on certiorari which may be awarded against him, and abide the order of the court therein, and pay all rent and other damages justly accruing to the plaintiff during the pendency of such proceedings. All further proceedings in execution of the trial court judgment shall thereupon be stayed.

Section 3-215   Execution of Judgment

(1) Upon rendering a final judgment for petitioner, the court shall issue a warrant directed to [the sheriff of the county] in which the property is located, describing the property and commanding the officer to remove all persons and put the petitioner into full possession.

(2) The officer to whom the warrant is directed and delivered shall give at least twenty-four hours' notice to the person or persons to be removed and shall execute it between the hours of sunrise and sunset.

(3) The issuing of a warrant for the removal of a tenant cancels the agreement under which the person removed held the premises, and annuls the relation of landlord and tenant. Petitioner may recover by action any sum of money which was payable at the time when the special proceeding was commenced and the reasonable value of the use and occupation to the time when the warrant was

issued, for any period of time with respect to which the agreement does not make any provision for payment of rent.

Section 3-216   Stay of Proceedings by Tenant

When a final judgment is rendered in favor of petitioner in a proceeding brought against a tenant for failure to pay rent, and the default arose out of a good faith dispute, the tenant may stay all proceedings on such judgment by paying all rent due at the date of the judgment and the costs of the proceeding, or by filing with the court his undertaking to the petitioner, with such assurances as the court shall require, to the effect that he will pay such rent and costs within ten days. At the expiration of said period, the court shall issue a warrant of execution unless satisfactory proof of payment is produced by the tenant.

APARTMENT BUILDING TENANTS' RECEIVERSHIP

Section 3-301   Petition for Receivership: Grounds, Notice, and Jurisdiction

Any tenant occuping an apartment building [located in   ] may petition for the establishment of a receivership in [specify court] upon the grounds that there has existed, for [5] days or more after notice to the landlord, in such building or any part thereof; a lack of heat, or of running water, or of light, or of electricity, or of adequate sewage facilities; or any other condition dangerous to the life, health, or safety of the petitioner; or any combination of such conditions. In the case of the existence of an infestation of rodents or other vermin, the tenant may file a petition for the establishment of a receivership immediately upon notifying the landlord.

Section 3-302   Necessary Parties Defendant

(1)   Petitioners shall join as defendants:

(a)   all parties duly disclosed to any of them in accordance with section 1-108; and

(b)   all parties whose interest in the property is (i) a matter of public record and (ii) capable of being protected in this proceeding.

(2)   Petitioners shall not be prejudiced by a failure to join any other interested parties.

(3)   Nothing in this section shall preclude a municipality from intervening in the proceeding.

Section 3-303   Defenses

It shall be sufficient defense to this proceeding, if any defendant of record establishes that:

(1)   the condition or conditions described in the petition do not exist at the time of trial; or

(2)   the condition or conditions alleged in the petition have been caused by the wilful or [grossly] negligent acts of one or more of the petitioning tenants or members of his or their families or by other persons on the premises with his or their consent; or

(3)   such condition or conditions would have been corrected, were it not for the refusal by any petitioner to allow reasonable access.

Cross-Reference:

Access generally, see Sec. 2-404.

Section 3-304   Stay of Judgment by Defendant

(1)   If, after a trial, the court shall determine that the petition should be granted, the owner or any mortgagee or lienor of record or other person having an interest n the property may apply to the court to be permitted to remove or remedy the

257

conditions specified in the petition. If such person (A) demonstrates the ability to perform promptly the necessary work and (B) posts security for the performance thereof within the time, and in the amount and manner, deemed necessary by the court, then the court may stay judgment and issue an order permitting such person to perform the work within a time fixed by the court and requiring such person to report to the court periodically on the progress of the work. The court shall retain jurisdiction over the matter until the work is completed.

(2) If, after the issuance of an order under the foregoing provision but before the time fixed in such order for the completion of the work prescribed therein, there is reason to believe that the work will not be completed pursuant to the court's order or that the person permitted to do the same is not proceeding with due diligence, the court or the petitioners, upon notice to all parties to the proceeding, may move that a hearing be held to determine whether judgment should be rendered immediately as provided in the following subsection.

(3) (a) If, upon a hearing authorized in the preceding subsection, the court shall determine that such party is not proceeding with due diligence, or upon the actual failure of such person to complete the work in accordance with the provisions of the order, the court shall appoint a receiver as authorized by sections 3-305 and 3-306.

(b) Such judgment shall direct the receiver to apply the security posted to executing the powers and duties described in section 3-306.

(c) In the event that the amount of such security should be insufficient to accomplish the above objectives, such judgment shall direct the receiver to collect the rents, profits and issues, to the extent of the deficiency. In the event that the security should exceed the amount necessary to accomplish the above objectives, such judgment shall direct the receiver to return the excess to the person posting the security.

Section 3-305   Appointment of a Receiver

A court may appoint any suitable person as a receiver.

Definitional Cross-Reference:

Person, Sec. 1-201.

Section 3-306   Powers and Duties of the Receiver

(1) The receiver shall have all the powers and duties accorded a receiver foreclosing a mortgage on real property and all other powers and duties deemed necessary by the court. Such powers and duties shall include, but are not necessarily limited to, collecting and using all rents, issues, and profits of the property, prior to and despite any assignment of rent, for the purposes of:

(a) correcting the condition or conditions alleged in the petition;

(b) materially complying with all applicable provisions of any State or local, statute, code, regulation, or ordinance governing the maintenance, construction, use or appearances of the building and surrounding grounds;

(c) paying all expenses reasonably necessary to the proper operation and management of the property including insurance, taxes and assessments, and fees for the services of the receiver and any agent he should hire;

(d) compensating the tenants for whatever deprivation of their rental agreement rights resulted from the condition or conditions alleged in the petition; and

(e) paying the costs of the receivership proceeding, including attorney fees.

258

(2) (a) The court may authorize the receiver to cover the costs of the above subsection by the issuance and sale of notes, bearing such interest as the court may fix. Such notes may be negotiable.

(b) Such notes shall be superior to all prior assignments of rent and all prior and existing liens and encumbrances except taxes and assessments, provided that within [sixty days] of such sale or transfer by the receiver of the note, the holders shall file notice of the lien in the office of the [Recorder of Deeds] in the county in which the real estate is located.

(c) The court may further authorize the receiver to enter into such agreements and to do such acts as may be required to obtain first mortgage insurance on the receiver's notes from an agency of the Federal government.

Section 3-307   Discharge of the Receiver

(1) The receiver shall be discharged when:

(a) the condition or conditions alleged in the petition have been remedied;

(b) the property materially complies with all applicable provisions of any State or local statute, code, regulation, or ordinance governing the maintenance, construction, use, or appearance of the building and the surrounding grounds;

(c) the costs of the above work and any other costs authorized by section 3-306 have been paid or reimbursed from the rents, issues and profits, or notes of the property; and

(d) the surplus money, if any, has been paid over to the owner.

(2) Upon clauses (a) and (b) of the preceeding subsection being satisfied, the owner, mortgagee, or any lienor may apply for the discharge of the receiver after paying to the latter all monies expended by him and all other costs which have not been pair or reimbursed from the rent, issues, profits, or notes of the property.

(3) If the court determines that future profits of the property will not cover the costs of satisfying clauses (a) and (b) of subsection (1), the court may discharge the receiver or order him to take such action as would be appropriate in the situation, including but not limited to demolishing the building. In no case shall the court permit repairs which cannot be paid out of the future profits of the property.

LIMITATIONS ON OTHER PROCEEDINGS

Section 3-401   Action for Waste

(1) It shall be a complete defense to an action, suit, or proceeding for waste if the tenant allege and establish that he notified the landlord a reasonable time in advance of the repair, alteration, or replacement and the repair, alteration, or replacement:

(a) is one which a prudent owner of an estate in fee simple absolute of the affected property would be likely to make in view of the conditions existing on or in the neighborhood of the affected property; or

(b) has not reduced the market value of the reversion or other interest of the plaintiff.

(2) The court shall deny a petition for an injunction against a tenant who contemplates any repair, alteration, or replacement if the tenant:

(a) alleges and establishes that the proposed repair, alteration, or replacement is one which a prudent owner of the fee of the property would be likely to make in view of the conditions existing on or in the neighborhood of the affected property; or

(b) alleges and establishes that the proposed repair, alteration, or replacement will not reduce the market value of the reversion or other interest of the petitioner; and

(c) having satisfied the court as to either of the above, upon demand by the petitioner, posts such security as the court shall direct to protect the petitioner against a failure to complete the proposed work, and against any responsibility for expenditures incident to the making of such proposed repairs, alterations, or replacements.

(3) This section shall not be interpreted to bar an action for damages for breach of a written rental agreement nor an action or summary proceeding based on breach of a written rental agreement, nor an injunction against the breach of a condition contained in a written rental agreement.

Section 3-402   Attorney's Fees

No provision in a rental agreement providing for the recovery of attorney's fees by either party in any suit, action, or proceeding arising from the tenancy shall be enforceable.

Section 3-403   Landlord Liens; Distress for Rent

(1) No lien on behalf of the landlord in the tenant's chattels shall be enforceable unless perfected before the effective date of this Act.

(2) The common law right of the landlord of distress for rent is hereby abolished.

Section 3-404   Confession of Judgment

(1) A provision of a written rental agreement authorizing a person other than the tenant to confess judgment against the tenant is void and unenforceable.

(2) The inclusion by the landlord in a written rental agreement of such a clause shall be a misdemeanor.

Cross-Reference:

Misdemeanor penalty, see Sec. 3-501.

PENALTIES

Section 3-501   Penalty for Landlord's Misdemeanors

Any person found guilty of any of the misdemeanors enumerated in this Act shall be punished by a fine of not more than [200] dollars.

Cross-References:

Inclusion of confession of judgment form in rental agreement a misdemeanor, see Sec. 3-404(2).

Wilful retention of security deposit a misdemeanor, see Sec. 2-401(5).

Tenant to receive half of fine, see Sec. 3-502.

Section 3-502   Tenant to Receive Half of Penalty

Upon the successful prosecution of any landlord for a misdemeanor under this Act, the clerk of the [specify court] shall forward one-half of any fines collected to the tenant or tenants whose complaint or information resulted in such prosecution.

2 Standard Form of Apartment Lease

The Real Estate Board of New York, Inc.

Agreement of lease, made this _____ day of _____ 19___ , between party of the first part, hereinafter referred to as Landlord and _____ party of the second part, hereinafter referred to as Tenant,

WITNESSETH: That Landlord hereby leases to Tenant and Tenant hereby hires from Landlord, the apartment known as Apartment on the _____ floor, in the building known as _____ in the Borough of _____ , City of New York, for the term of
(or until such term shall sooner cease and expire, as hereinafter provided), to commence on the _____ day of _____ nineteen hundred and _____ and to end on the _____ day of _____ nineteen hundred and _____ both dates inclusive, at an annual rental of _____

which Tenant agrees to pay in lawful money of the United States, which shall be legal tender in payment of all debts and dues, public and private, at the time of payment, in equal monthly installments in advance on the first day of each month during said term, at the office of Landlord or such other place as Landlord may designate, without any set-off or deduction whatsoever, except that Tenant shall pay the first monthly installment on the execution hereof (unless this lease be a renewal).

It is understood and agreed that if the demised premises are rented from the 15th day of the month, Landlord may serve a notice in such manner and under such circumstances as Landlord alone may determine requiring Tenant to pay one-half month's rent in advance on the 25th day of any following month and that thereafter the rent shall become due and payable on the 1st day of each and every month in advance.

In the event that, at the commencement of the term of this lease, Tenant shall be in default in the payment of rent to Landlord pursuant to the terms of a prior lease with Landlord or with Landlord's predecessor in interest, Landlord may at Landlord's option and without notice to Tenant add the amount of such arrearages to any monthly installment of rent payable hereunder, and the same shall be payable to Landlord as additional rent hereunder.

The parties hereto, for themselves, their heirs, distributees, executors, administrators, legal representatives, successors and assigns, hereby covenant, as follows:

RENT   1. Tenant shall pay the rent as above and as hereinafter provided.

OCCUPANCY   2. The demised premises and any part thereof shall be occupied only by Tenant and the members of the immediate family of Tenant, and as a strictly private dwelling apartment and for no other purpose.

ASSIGNMENT,   3. Tenant, and Tenant's heirs, distributees, executors, representatives, successors and assigns, shall not assign, mortgage or encumber this agreement, nor underlet, or use or permit the demised premises of any part thereof to be used by others, without the prior written consent of Landlord in each instance. If this lease be assigned, or if the demised premises or any part thereof be underlet or occupied by anybody other than Tenant, Landlord may, after default by Tenant, collect rent from the assignee, under-tenant or occupant, and apply the net amount collected to the rent herein reserved, but no such assignment, underletting, occupancy or collection shall be deemed a waiver of this covenant, or the acceptance of the assignee, under-tenant or occupant as tenant, or a release of Tenant from the further performance by Tenant of covenants on the part of the Tenant herein contained. The consent by Landlord to an assignment or underletting shall not in any wise be construed to relieve Tenant from obtaining the express consent in writing of Landlord to any further assignment or underletting.

ALTERATIONS   4. Tenant shall make no alterations, decorations, additions or improvements in or to demised premises without Landlord's prior written consent, and then only by contractors or mechanics approved by Landlord. All such work shall be done at such times and in such manner as Landlord may from time to time designate. All alterations, additions or improvements upon demised premises, made by either party, including all panelling, decorations, partitions, railings, mezzanine floors, galleries and the like, shall, unless Landlord elect otherwise (which election shall be made by giving a notice pursuant to the provisions of Article 25 not less than 3 days prior to the expiration or other termination of this lease or any renewal or extension thereof), become the property of Landlord, and shall remain upon, and be sur-

262

rendered with said premises, as a part thereof, at the end of the term hereof. Any mechanic's lien filed against the demised premises, or the building, of which the same form a part, for work claimed to have been done for, or materials claimed to have been furnished to, Tenant, shall be discharged by Tenant within 10 days thereafter at Tenant's expense, by filing of the bond required by law.

REPAIRS　　　　5. Tenant shall take good care of demised premises and fixtures therein and, subject to provisions of Article 4 hereof shall make, as and when needed, as a result of misuse or neglect by Tenant, all repairs in and about demised premises necessary to preserve them in good order and condition, which repairs shall be in quality and class equal to the original work. However, Landlord may repair, at the expense of Tenant, all damage or injury to demised premises, or to the building, of which the same form a part, or to its fixtures, appuretnances or equipment, done by Tenant or Tenant's servants, employees, agents, visitors or licensees, or caused by moving property of Tenant in and/or out of the building, or by installation or removal of furniture or other property, or resulting from air-conditioning unit or system, short circuits, overflow or leakage of water, steam, illuminating gas, sewer gas, sewerage or odors, or by frost or by bursting or leaking of pipes or plumbing works, or gas, or from any other cause, due to carelessness, negligence, or improper conduct of Tenant, or Tenant's servants, employees, agents, visitors or licensees. Except as provided in Article 11 hereof, there shall be no allowance to Tenant for a diminution of rental value, and no liability on the part of Landlord by reason of inconvenience, or annoyance arising from the making of any repairs, alterations, additions or improvements in or to any portion of the building or demised premises, or in or to fixtures, appurtenances or equipment, and no liability upon Landlord for failure to make any repairs, alterations, additions, or improvements in or to any portion of the building or demised premises, or in or to fixtures, appurtenances or equipment.

WINDOW　　　　6. Tenant will not clean, nor require, permit, suffer or
CLEANING　　　allow any window in the demised premises to be cleaned, from the outside in violation of Section 202 of the Labor Law or of the rules of the Board of Standards and Appeals, or of any other board or body having or asserting jurisdiction.

REQUIREMENTS　7. Tenant shall comply with all laws, orders and regu-
OF LAW　　　　lations of Federal, State, County and Municipal Authorities, and with any direction of any public officer or officers, pursuant to law, which shall impose any duty upon Landlord or Tenant with respect to demised premises, or the use or occupation thereof; and shall not do or permit to be done, any act or thing upon said premises, which will invalidate or be in conflict with fire insurance policies covering the building, of which demised premises are a part, and fixtures and property therein, and shall not do or permit to be done, any act or thing upon said premises which shall or might subject the Landlord to any liability or responsibility for injury to any person or persons or to any property by reason of any business or operation being carried on upon said premises; and shall comply with all rules, orders, regulations or requirements of the New York Board of Fire Underwriters, or any other similar body, and shall not do, or permit anything to be done, in or upon said premises, or bring or keep anything therein,

FIRE　　　　　which shall increase the rate of fire insurance on the build-
INSURANCE　　ing, of which demised premises form a part, or on property located therein. If by reason of failure of Tenant to comply with the provisions

of this paragraph, the fire insurance rate shall at any time be higher than it otherwise would be, then Tenant shall reimburse Landlord, as additional rent hereunder, for that part of all fire insurance premiums thereafter paid by Landlord which shall have been charged because of such violation by Tenant, and shall make such reimbursement upon the first day of the month following such outlay by Landlord. In any action or proceeding wherein Landlord and Tenant are parties, a schedule or "make up" of rate for the building or demised premises issued by the New York Fire Insurance Exchange, or other body making fire insurance rates for said premises, shall be conclusive evidence of the facts therein stated and of the several items and charges in the fire insurance rates then applicable to said premises.

SUBORDINATION 8. This lease is subject and subordinate to all ground or underlying leases and mortgages which may now or hereafter affect the real property, of which demised premises form a part, and to all renewals, modifications, consolidations, replacements and extensions thereof. In confirmation of such subordination, Tenant shall execute promptly any certificate that Landlord may request. Tenant hereby constitutes and appoints Landlord the Tenant's attorney in fact to execute any such certificate or certificates for and on behalf of Tenant.

RULES AND REGULATIONS 9. Tenant and Tenant's family, servants, employees, agents, visitors, and licensees shall observe faithfully and comply strictly with, the Rules and Regulations set forth on the back of this lease, and such other and further reasonable Rules and Regulations as Landlord or Landlord's agents may from time to time adopt. Notice of any additional rules or regulations shall be given in such manner as Landlord may elect. In case Tenant disputes the reasonableness of any Rule or Regulation hereafter made or adopted by Landlord or Landlord's agents, the parties hereto agree to submit the question of the reasonableness of such Rule or Regulation for arbitration to the Chairman for the time being of the Board of Directors of the Management Division of The Real Estate Board of New York, Inc., or to such person or persons as he may designate, whose determination shall be final and conclusive upon the parties hereto. No dispute of the reasonableness of any rule or regulation shall be deemed a compliance upon Tenant's part with the foregoing provisions of this article unless the same shall have been raised by service of a notice in writing upon Landlord within ten days after the adoption of any such rule or regulation. Landlord shall not be liable to Tenant for violation of any of said Rules and Regulations, or the breach of any covenant or condition in any lease, by any other tenant in the building.

PROPERTY-LOSS, DAMAGE 10. Landlord or Landlord's agents shall not be liable for any damage to property entrusted to employees of the building, nor for the loss of any property by theft or otherwise. Landlord or Landlord's agents shall not be liable for any injury or damage to persons or property resulting from falling plaster, steam, gas, electricity, water, rain or snow which may leak from any part of said building or from the pipes, appliances or plumbing works of the same or from the street subsurface or from any other place or by dampness or any other cause of whatsoever nature, unless caused by or due to the negligence of Landlord, Landlord's agents, servants or employees; nor shall Landlord or Landlord's agents be liable for any such damage caused by other tenants or persons in said building, or for interference with the light or other incorporeal hereditaments, or caused by operations in construction of any public or quasi public work; nor shall Landlord be liable for any latent defect in the building. If at any time any windows of the demised premises become closed or darkened, for any reason whatever, Landlord shall not be liable for any damage that Tenant may sustain thereby and Tenant shall not be entitled to any compensation or abatement of rent or release from any of the obligations of Tenant hereunder because of such closing or darkening. Landlord or Landlord's agents shall not be liable for the presence of bugs, vermin or insects, if any, in the premises, nor shall their presence affect this lease. If Landlord shall furnish to Tenant any storeroom, use of laundry or any other facility outside of the demised premises, the same shall be furnished gratuitously, and any such storeroom shall be used by Tenant for the storage of trunks, bags, suitcases and packing cases only, all of which shall be empty, and the use of any such laundry, storeroom or other facility shall be at the risk of the person using the same and Landlord or Landlord's agents shall not be liable for any injury to person or loss by theft or otherwise or damage to property, whether due to negligence of Landlord or Landlord's agents or otherwise. Tenant shall reimburse Landlord as additional rent for all expenses, damages or fines incurred or suffered by Landlord by reason of any breach, violation or non-performance by Tenant, or Tenant's family, servants, employees, agents, visitors or licensees of any covenant or provision of this lease, or by reason of damage to persons or property caused by moving property in and/or out of the building or by the installation or removal of furniture or other property of or for Tenant, or by reason of or arising out of the occupancy or use by Tenant of demised premises or of the building of which demised premises form a part, or any part of either thereof, or from any other cause due to the carelessness, negligence or improper conduct of the Tenant or the Tenant's family, servants, employees, agents, visitors or licensees. Tenant shall give immediate notice to Landlord in case of fire or accidents to or defects in any fixtures or equipment of the building.

DESTRUCTION- 11. If the demised premises shall be partially damaged
FIRE OR by fire or other cause without the fault or neglect of Ten-
OTHER CAUSE ant, Tenant's servants, employees, agents, visitors or licensees, the damages shall be repaired by and at the expense of Landlord, and the rent until such repairs shall be made shall be apportioned according to the part of the demised premises which is usable by Tenant. No penalty shall accrue for reasonable delay which may arise by reason of adjustment of fire insurance on the part of Landlord and or Tenant, and for reasonable delay on account of "labor troubles," or any other cause beyond Landlord's control. But if the demised premises are totally damaged or are rendered wholly untenantable by fire or other cause, and Landlord shall decide not to rebuild the same, or if the building shall be so damaged that Landlord shall decide to demolish it or to rebuild it, then or in any of such events Landlord may, within ninety (90) days after such fire or other cause, give Tenant a notice in writing of such decision, which notice shall be given as in Article 25 hereof provided, and thereupon the term of this lease shall expire by lapse of time upon the third day after such notice is given, and Tenant shall vacate the demised premises and surrender the same to Landlord.

EMINENT 12. If the whole or any part of demised premises shall
DOMAIN be taken or condemned by any competent authority for any public or quasi public use or purpose, then, and in that event, the term of this lease shall cease and terminate from the date when the possession of the part

265

so taken shall be required for such use or purpose, and without apportionment of the award. The current rental, however, shall in any such case be apportioned.

SERVICES   13. As long as Tenant is not in default under any of the provisions of this lease Landlord covenants to furnish, insofar as the existing facilities provide, the following services: (a) Elevator service; (b) Hot and cold water in reasonable quantities at all times; (c) Heat at reasonable hours during the cold seasons of the year. Interruption or curtailment of any such services shall not constitute a constructive or partial eviction nor, unless caused by the gross negligence of Landlord, entitle Tenant to any compensation or abatement of rent. Mechanical refrigeration equipment, if provided, is for the accommodation of Tenant, and the Landlord shall not be responsible for any failure of refrigeration or for leakage or damage caused by or as the result of such mechanical refrigeration or failure thereof for any reason whatsoever. If Landlord maintains a telephone switchboard connected with the demised premises, Tenant may use such service at the rates charged to other tenants of the building. The amount charged shall be deemed to be and be paid as additional rental. Landlord may discontinue such service upon 30 days written notice to the Tenant, without in any way affecting the obligations of the parties hereunder. If the building, of which the demised premises are a part, supplies manually operated elevator service, Landlord may discontinue such service upon ten (10) days notice to Tenant without in any way affecting the obligations of Tenant hereunder, provided that within a reasonable time after the expiration of said ten (10) day period Landlord shall commence the substitution of an automatic control type of elevator in lieu of the manually operated elevator, and with due diligence pursue to completion the installation of such automatic control elevator or elevators. It is understood, however, that due allowance shall be made by Tenant for reasonable delay caused by strikes or any other cause beyond Landlord's control. If electric current be supplied by Landlord, Tenant covenants and agrees to purchase the same from Landlord or Landlord's designated agent at the rates charged to residential consumers by any electric corporation subject to jurisdiction of the Public Service Commission and serving the part of the city where the building is located; bills therefor shall be rendered at such times as Landlord may elect and the amount, as computed from a meter installed by Landlord, or Landlord's agent, shall be deemed to be and be paid as additional rental. Landlord may discontinue such service upon thirty (30) days notice to Tenant without being liable therefor or in any way affecting the liability of Tenant hereunder. In the event that Landlord gives such notice, Landlord shall permit Tenant to receive such service from any other person or corporation and shall permit Landlord's wires and conduits to be used for such purpose. Tenant shall make no alteration or additions to the electric equipment and/or appliances without the prior written consent of Landlord in each instance. It is expressly understood and agreed that any covenants on Landlord's part to furnish any service pursuant to any of the terms or provisions of this lease, or to perform any act or thing for the benefit of Tenant shall not be deemed breached if Landlord is unable to perform the same by virtue of a strike or labor trouble or any other cause whatsoever beyond Landlord's control. If any tax be imposed upon Landlord's receipts from the sale or resale of electrical energy or gas or telephone service to Tenant by any Municipal, State or Federal agency, Tenant covenants and agrees that, where permitted by law, Tenant's pro-rata share of such taxes shall be passed on to and included in the bill of and paid by Tenant to Landlord.

ACCESS TO   14. Tenant shall permit Landlord to erect, use and
PREMISES   maintain pipes and conduits in and through the demised
premises. Landlord or Landlord's agents shall have the right to enter the demised premises during reasonable hours, to examine the same, and to show them
to prospective purchasers or lessees of the building, and to make such decorations, repairs, alterations, improvements or additions as Landlord may deem
necessary or desirable, and Landlord shall be allowed to take all material into and
upon said premises that may be required therefor without the same constituting
an eviction in whole or in part, and the rent reserved shall in no wise abate while
said decorations, repairs, alterations, improvements or additions are being made,
because of the prosecution of any such work, or otherwise. For a period of seven
months prior to the termination of this lease, Landlord shall have the right, during
reasonable hours, to enter said premises for the purpose of exhibiting the same to
persons desiring to rent or buy the same. If, during the last month of the term,
Tenant shall have removed all or substantially all of Tenant's property therefrom, Landlord may immediately enter and alter, renovate and redecorate the
demised premises, without elimination or abatement of rent, or other compensation, and such acts shall have no effect upon this lease. If Tenant shall not
be personally present to open and permit an entry into said premises, at any
time, when for any reason an entry therein shall be necessary or permissable
hereunder, Landlord or Landlord's agents may enter the same by a master
key, or may forcibly enter the same, without rendering Landlord or such agents
liable therefor (if during such entry Landlord or Landlord's agents shall accord
reasonable care to Tenant's property), and without in any manner affecting the
obligations and covenants of this lease.

BANKRUPTCY   15. (a) If at any time *prior* to the date herein fixed as
     the commencement of the term of this lease there shall be
filed by or against Tenant in any court pursuant to any statute either of the United
States or of any State a petition in bankruptcy or insolvency or for reorganization
or for the appointment of a receiver or a trustee of all or a portion of Tenant's
property, or if Tenant make an assignment for the benefit of creditors, this lease
(a) Prior to Term   shall *Ipso Facto* be cancelled and terminated
     and in which event neither Tenant nor any per-
son claiming through or under Tenant or by virtue of any statute or of an order of
any court shall be entitled to possession of demised premises and Landlord, in
addition to the other rights and remedies given by (c) hereof and by virtue of any
other provision herein or elsewhere in this lease contained or by virtue of any statute or rule of law, may retain as liquidated damages any rent, security, deposit
or moneys received by him from Tenant or others in behalf of Tenant upon the
execution hereof.

     (b). If at the date fixed as the commencement of the term of this lease
or if at any time during the term hereby demised there shall be filed by or against
Tenant in any court pursuant to any statute either of the United States or of any
State a petition in bankruptcy or insolvency or for reorganization or for the
appointment of a receiver or trustee of all or a portion of Tenant's property or
if Tenant make an assignment for the benefit of creditors, this lease, at
(b) During Term   the option of the Landlord, exercised within a reasona-
     ble time after notice of the happening of any one or more
of such events, may be cancelled and terminated and in which event neither
Tenant nor any person claiming through or under Tenant by virtue of any stat-

ute or of an order of any court shall be entitled to possession or to remain in possession of the premises demised but shall forthwith quit and surrender the premises and Landlord, in addition to the other rights and remedies Landlord has by virtue of any other provision herein or elsewhere in this lease contained or by virtue of any statute or rule of law, may retain as liquidated damages any rent, security, deposit or moneys received by him from Tenant or others in behalf of Tenant.

(c). It is stipulated and agreed that in the event of the termination of this lease pursuant to (a) or (b) hereof, Landlord shall forthwith, notwithstanding any other provisions of this lease to the contrary, be entitled to recover from Tenant as and for liquidated damages an amount equal to the difference between the rent reserved hereunder for the unexpired portion of the term demised and the rental value of the demised premises, at the time of termination, for the unexpired term or portion thereof, both discounted at the rate of four *(c) Measure* per centum (4%) per annum to present worth; nothing *of Damages* herein contained shall limit or prejudice the right of the Landlord to prove for and obtain as liquidated damages by reason of such termination, an amount equal to the maximum allowed by any statute or rule of law in effect at the time when, and governing the proceedings in which, such damages are to be proved, whether or not such amount be greater, equal to, or less than the amount of the difference referred to above. In determining rental value of the demised premises the rental realized by any reletting, if such reletting be accomplished by Landlord within a reasonable time after termination of this lease, shall be deemed prima facie to be the rental value.

DEFAULT 16. (1) If Tenant shall make default in fulfilling any of the covenants of this lease other than the covenants for the payment of rent or additional rent, or if the demised premises become vacant or deserted, Landlord may give Tenant three days notice of intention to end the term of this lease and thereupon, at the expiration of said three days (if said default continues to exist) the term under this lease shall expire as fully and completely as if that day were the day herein definitely fixed for the expiration of the term, and Tenant will then quit and surrender the demised premises to Landlord but Tenant shall remain liable as hereinafter provided; or (2) if Landlord or Landlord's agents shall deem objectionable or improper any conduct on the part of Tenant or occupants, or visitors or licensees, or shall deem Tenant or occupants, or visitors or licensees objectionable, Landlord may in like manner give to Tenant three days notice of intention to end the term of this lease and tender therewith or offer to tender the rent paid on account of the unexpired term, and thereupon at the expiration of said three days the term under this lease shall expire as fully and completely as if that day were the day herein definitely fixed for the expiration of the term, and Tenant will then quit and surrender the demised premises to Landlord.

(3) If the notice provided for in (1) or (2) hereof shall have been given, and the term shall expire as aforesaid; or (3a) if Tenant shall make default in the payment of the rent reserved herein or any item of additional rent herein mentioned or any part of either or in making any other payment herein provided; or (3b) if any execution or attachment shall be issued against Tenant or any of Tenant's property whereupon the demised premises shall be taken or occupied or attempted to be taken or occupied by someone other than Tenant; or (3c) if Tenant shall make default with respect to any other lease between Landlord and

268

Tenant; of (3d) if Tenant shall fail to move into or take possession of the premises within fifteen (15) days after commencement of the term of this lease of which fact Landlord shall be the sole judge; then and in any of such events Landlord may without notice, re-enter the demised premises either by force or otherwise, and dispossess tenant by summary proceedings or otherwise, and the legal representative of Tenant or other occupant of demised premises, and remove their effects and hold the premises as if this lease had not been made, and Tenant hereby waives the service of notice of intention to re-enter or to institute legal proceedings to that end. If Tenant shall make default hereunder prior to the date fixed as the commencement of any renewal or extension of this lease, Landlord may cancel and terminate such renewal or extension agreement by written notice as hereinafter provided.

REMEDIES OF In case of any such default, re-entry, expiration and/or **LANDLORD** dispossess by summary proceedings or otherwise, (a) the rent shall become due thereupon and be paid up to the time of such re-entry, dispossess and/or expiration, together with such expenses as Landlord may incur for legal expenses, attorneys' fees, brokerage and/or putting the demised premises in good order, or for preparing the same for re-rental; (b) Landlord may re-let the premises or any part or parts thereof, either in the name of Landlord or otherwise, for a term or terms which may at Landlord's option be less than or exceed the period which would otherwise have constituted the balance of the term of this lease and may grant concessions or free rent; and/or (c) Tenant or the legal representatives of Tenant shall also pay Landlord as liquidated damages for the failure of Tenant to observe and perform said Tenant's covenants herein contained, any deficiency between the rent hereby reserved and/or covenanted to be paid and the net amount, if any, of the rents collected on account of the lease or leases of the demised premises for each month of the period which would otherwise have constituted the balance of the term of this lease. In computing such liquidated damages there shall be added to the said deficiency such expenses as Landlord may incur in connection with re-letting, such as legal expenses, attorneys' fees, brokerage and for keeping the demised premises in good order or for preparing the same for re-letting. Any such liquidated damages shall be paid in monthly installments by Tenant on the rent day specified in this lease and any suit brought to collect the amount of the deficiency for any month shall not prejudice in any way the rights of Landlord to collect the deficiency for any subsequent month by a similar proceeding. Landlord at Landlord's option may make such alteration and/or decorations in the demised premises as Landlord in Landlord's sole judgment considers advisable and necessary for the purpose of re-letting the demised premises; and the making of such alterations and/or decorations shall not operate or be construed to release Tenant from liability hereunder as aforesaid. Landlord shall in no event be liable in any way whatsoever for failure to re-let the demised premises, or in the event that the demised premises are re-let for failure to collect the rent thereof under such re-letting. In the event of a breach or threatened breach by Tenant of any of the covenants or provisions hereof, Landlord shall have the right of injunction and the right to invoke any remedy allowed at law or in equity as if re-entry, summary proceedings and other remedies were not herein provided for. Mention in this lease of any particular remedy, shall not preclude landlord from any other remedy, in law or in equity. Tenant hereby expressly waives any and all rights of re-

WAIVER OF demption granted by or under any present or future laws **REDEMPTION** in the event of tenant being evicted or dispossessed for

any cause, or in the event of Landlord obtaining possession of demised premises, by reason of the violation by Tenant of any of the covenants and conditions of this lease or otherwise.

FEES AND EXPENSES 17. If Tenant shall default in the performance of any covenant on Tenant's part to be performed by virtue of any provision in any article in this lease contained, Landlord may immediately, or at any time thereafter, without notice, perform the same for the account of Tenant. If Landlord at any time is compelled to pay or elects to pay any sum of money, or do any act which will require the payment of any sum of money by reason of the failure of Tenant to comply with any provision hereof, or, if Landlord is compelled to incur any expense including reasonable attorney's fees in instituting, prosecuting and/or defending any action or proceeding instituted by reason of any default of Tenant hereunder, the sum or sums so paid by Landlord with all interest, costs and damages, shall be deemed to be additional rent hereunder and shall be due from Tenant to Landlord on the first day of the month following the incurring of such respective expenses.

NO REPRESENTATIONS BY LANDLORD 18. Landlord or Landlord's agents have made no representations or promises with respect to the said building, the land upon which it is erected or demised premises except as herein expressly set forth and no rights, easement or licenses are required by Tenant by implication or otherwise except as expressly set forth in the provisions of this lease. The taking possession of the demised premises by Tenant shall be conclusive evidence, as against Tenant, that Tenant accepts same "as is" and that said premises and the building of which the same form a part were in good and satisfactory condition at the time such possession was so taken.

END OF TERM 19. Upon the expiration or other termination of the term of this lease, Tenant shall quit and surrender to Landlord the demised premises, broom clean, in good order and condition, ordinary wear excepted. Tenant shall remove all property of Tenant as directed by Landlord. If the last day of the term of this lease or any renewal thereof falls on Sunday, this lease shall expire on the business day immediately preceding. Tenant's obligation to observe or perform this covenant shall survive the expiration or other termination of the term of this lease.

QUIET ENJOYMENT 20. Landlord covenants and agrees with Tenant that upon Tenant paying said rent, and performing all the covenants and conditions aforesaid, on Tenant's part to be observed and performed, Tenant shall and may peaceably and quietly have, hold and enjoy the premises hereby demised, for the term aforesaid, subject, however, to the terms of the lease, and of the ground leases, underlying leases and mortgages hereinbefore mentioned.

FAILURE TO GIVE POSSESSION 21. If Landlord shall be unable to give possession of the demised premises on the date of the commencement of the term hereof by reason of the fact that the premises are located in a building being constructed and which has not been sufficiently completed to make the premises ready for occupancy or by reason of the fact that a certificate of occupancy has not been procured or for any other reason, Landlord shall not be subject to any liability for the failure to give possession on said date. Under such circumstances the rent reserved and covenanted to be paid herein shall not commence until the possession of demised premises is given or the premises are available for occupancy by Tenant, and no such failure to give possession on the date of commencement of the term shall in any wise affect the validity of this lease or the obligations of Tenant hereunder, nor shall same be construed in any wise to extend the term of this lease. If the building in which the demised premises are located is not in course of construction, and Landlord is unable to give possession of the demised premises on the date of the commencement of the term hereof by reason of the holding over of any tenant or tenants or for any other reason; or if repairs, improvements or decorations of the demised premises or of the building in which said premises are located, are not completed, no abatement or diminution of the rent to be paid hereunder shall be allowed to Tenant under such circumstances. If permission is given to Tenant to enter into the possession of the demised premises or to occupy premises other than the demised premises prior to the date specified as the commencement of the term of this lease, Tenant covenants and agrees that such occupancy shall be deemed to be under all the terms, covenants, conditions and provisions of this lease, except as to the covenant to pay rent. In either case rent shall commence on the date specified in this lease.

NO WAIVER 22. If there be any agreement between Landlord and Tenant providing for the cancellation of this lease upon certain as provisions or contingencies, and/or an agreement for the renewal hereof at the expiration of the term first above mentioned, the right to such renewal or the execution of a renewal agreement between Landlord and Tenant prior to the expiration of such first mentioned term shall not be considered an extension thereof or a vested right in Tenant to such further term, so as to prevent Landlord from cancelling this lease and any such extension thereof during the remainder of the original term hereby granted; such privilege, if and when so exercised by Landlord, shall cancel and terminate this lease and any such renewal or extension previously entered into between said Landlord and Tenant or the right of Tenant to any such renewal; any right herein contained on the part of Landlord to cancel this lease shall continue during any extension or renewal hereof; any option on the part of Tenant herein contained for an extension or renewal hereof shall not be deemed to give Tenant any option for a further extension beyond the first renewal or extended term. No act or thing done by Landlord or Landlord's agents during the term hereby demised shall constitute an eviction by Landlord, nor shall be deemed an acceptance of a surrender of said premises, and no agreement to accept such surrender shall be valid unless in writing signed by Landlord. No employee of Landlord or of Landlord's agents shall have any power to accept the keys of said premises prior to the termination of the lease. The delivery of keys to any employee of Landlord or of Landlord's agents shall not operate as a termination of the lease or a surrender of the premises. In the event of Tenant at any time desiring to have Landlord sublet the premises for Tenant's account, Landlord or Landlord's agents are authorized to receive said keys for such purposes without releasing Tenant from any of the obligations under this lease, Tenant hereby relieves Landlord of any liability for loss of any of Tenant's effects or the happening of any other event in connection with such subletting. The failure of Landlord to seek redress for violation of, or to insist upon the strict performance of any covenant or condition of this lease, or any of the rules and regulations set forth on the back of this lease or hereafter adopted by Landlord, shall not prevent a subsequent act, which would have originally constituted a violation, from having all the force and effect of an original violation. The receipt by Landlord of rent with knowledge

271

of the breach of any covenant of this lease, shall not be deemed a waiver of such breach. The failure of Landlord to enforce any of the rules and Regulations set forth on the back of this lease, or hereafter adopted, against Tenant and/or any other tenant in the building shall not be deemed a waiver of any such Rules and Regulations. No provision of this lease shall be deemed to have been waived by Landlord, unless such waiver be in writing signed by Landlord. No payment by Tenant or receipt by Landlord of a lesser amount than the monthly rent herein stipulated shall be deemed to be other than on account of the earliest stipulated rent, nor shall any endorsement or statement on any check nor any letter accompanying any check or payment as rent be deemed an accord and satisfaction, and Landlord may accept such check or payment without prejudice to Landlord's right to recover the balance of such rent or pursue any other remedy in this lease provided. This lease contains the entire agreement between the parties, and any executory agreement hereafter made shall be ineffective to change, modify or discharge it in whole or in part unless such executory agreement is in writing and signed by the party against whom enforcement of the change, modification or discharge is sought.

WAIVER OF 23. It is mutually agreed by and between Landlord and
TRIAL BY JURY Tenant that the respective parties hereto shall and they
hereby do waive trial by jury in any action, proceeding
or counterclaim brought by either of the parties hereto against the other on any matters whatsoever arising out of or in any way connected with this lease, the Tenant's use or occupancy of said premises, and/or any claim of injury or damage.

INABILITY TO 24. This lease and the obligation of Tenant to pay rent
PERFORM hereunder and perform all of the other covenants and
agreements hereunder on part of Tenant to be performed
shall in nowise be affected, impaired or excused because Landlord is unable to supply or is delayed in supplying any service expressly or impliedly to be supplied or is unable to make, or is delayed in making any repairs, additions, alterations or decorations or is unable to supply or is delayed in supplying any equipment or fixtures if Landlord is prevented or delayed from so doing by reason of governmental preemption in connection with the National Emergency declared by the President of the United States or in connection with any rule, order or regulation of any department or subdivision thereof of any governmental agency or by reason of the conditions of supply and demand which have been or are affected by the war.

BILLS AND 25. Except as otherwise in this lease provided, a bill,
NOTICES statement, notice or communication which Landlord may
desire or be required to give to Tenant, including any notice of expiration, shall be deemed sufficiently given or rendered if, in writing, delivered to Tenant personally or sent by registered mail addressed to Tenant at the building of which the demised premises are a part or left at said premises addressed to Tenant, and the time of the rendition of such bill or statement and of the giving of such notice or communication shall be deemed to be the time when the same is delivered to Tenant, mailed, or left at the premises as herein provided. Any notice by Tenant to Landlord must be served by registered mail addressed to Landlord at the address where the last previous rental hereunder was paid.

26. The Captions are inserted only as a matter of convenience and for reference and in no way define, limit or describe the scope

of this lease nor the intent of any provision thereof.

DEFINITIONS   27. The term "Landlord" as used in this lease means only the owner or the mortgagee in possession for the time being of the land and building (or the owner of a lease of the building) of which the demised premises form a part, so that in the event of any sale or sales of said land and building or of said lease, or in the event of a lease of said building, the said Landlord shall be and hereby is entirely freed and relieved of all covenants and obligations of Landlord hereunder, and it shall be deemed and construed without further agreement between the parties or their successors in interest, or between the parties and the purchaser, at any such sale, or the said lessee of the building, that the purchaser or the lessee of the building has assumed and agreed to carry out any and all covenants and obligations of Landlord hereunder. The words "re-enter" and "re-entry" as used in this lease are not restricted to their technical legal meaning.

28. The covenants, conditions and agreements contained in this lease shall bind and inure to the benefit of Landlord and Tenant and their respective heirs, distributees, executors, administrators, successors, and, except as otherwise provided in this lease, their assigns.

ADDITIONAL ARTICLES NOT PROVIDED IN STANDARD FORM OF LEASE OF APARTMENT, BUT FORMING A PART HEREOF

IN WITNESS WHEREOF, the Landlord and Tenant have respectively signed and sealed this lease as of the day and year first above written.

Witness for Landlord:

_____[L.S.]

_____

_____[L.S.]

Witness for Tenant:

_____[L.S.]

_____   Tenant's Signature.

STATE OF NEW YORK,]
County of New York   ]SS:

On this _____ day of _____ in the year one thousand nine hundred and _____ before me personally came _____ to me known and known to me to be the individual described in and who executed the foregoing instrument, and duly acknowledged that he executed the same for the purpose mentioned therein.

_____ [Seal]
Notary Public, Number ____ , County of New York.

GUARANTY

FOR VALUE RECEIVED, and in consideration for, and as an inducement to Landlord making the within Lease with Tenant, the undersigned guarantees to Landlord, Landlord's successors and assigns, the full performance and observance of all the covenants, conditions and agreements, therein provided to be performed and observed by Tenant, including the "Rules and Regulations" as therein provided, without requiring any notice of non-payment, non-performance, or non-observance, of proof, or notice, or demand, whereby to charge the undersigned therefor, all of which the undersigned hereby expressly waives and expressly agrees that the validity of this agreement and the obligations of the guarantor hereunder shall in nowise be terminated, affected or impaired

273

by reason of the assertion by Landlord against Tenant of any of the rights or remedies reserved to Landlord pursuant to the provisions of the within lease. The undersigned further covenants and agrees that this guaranty shall remain and continue in full force and effect as to any renewal, modification or extension of this lease. As a further inducement to Landlord to make this lease and in consideration thereof, Landlord and the undersigned covenant and agree that in any action or proceeding brought by either Landlord or the undersigned against the other on any matters whatsoever arising out of, under, or by virtue of the terms of this lease or of this guaranty that Landlord and the undersigned shall and do hereby waive trial by jury.

Dated, New York City _____ 19 ___ _____ [L.S.]
WITNESS:

RESIDENCE _____

BUSINESS _____

ADDRESS _____

FIRM NAME _____

RULES AND REGULATIONS

1. The sidewalks, entrances, passages, courts, elevators, vestibules, stairways, corridors and halls must not be obstructed or encumbered or used for any purpose other than ingress and egress to and from the demised premises.

2. No sign, advertisement, notice or other lettering shall be exhibited, inscribed, painted or affixed by any Tenant on any part of the outside or inside of the demised premises or building without the prior written consent of the Landlord.

3. No awnings or other projections shall be attached to the outside walls of the building, and no blinds, shades, or screens shall be attached to or hung in, or used in connection with, any window or door of the demised premises, without the prior written consent of the Landlord.

4. No baby carriages, velocipedes, or bicycles shall be allowed in passenger elevators, if service elevator is provided, nor allowed to stand in the halls, passageways, areas or courts of the building.

5. Unless automatic, the passenger and service elevators, if any, shall be operated only by employees of the Landlord, and must not in any event be interfered with by the Tenant, his family, servants, employees, agents, visitors or licenses. Elevators will be operated only during such hours as the Landlord may from time to time determine.

6. Children shall not play in the public halls, stairways, or elevators, if any, nor be permitted in the service elevators.

7. The service elevators, if any, shall be used by servants, messengers and trades people for ingress and egress, and the passenger elevators, if any, shall not be used by them for that purpose, if service elevator is provided, except that nurses with children may use the passenger elevators, if any.

8. Supplies, goods and packages of every kind are to be delivered at the entrance provided therefor, through service elevators, or dumb-waiters, to the Tenant, or in such manner as the Landlord may provide and the Landlord is not responsible for the loss or damage of any such property, notwithstanding such

274

loss or damage may occur through the carelessness or negligence of the employees of the building.

9. Unless the building is equipped with an incinerator, all garbage and refuse must be sent down to the basement in such manner and at such times as the superintendent may direct.

10. The laundry and drying apparatus if any, shall be used in such manner and at such times as the superintendent may direct. If the Landlord provides clothes dryers in other parts of the premises, the Tenant shall not dry or air clothes on the roof.

11. The Landlord may retain a pass key to the premises. No Tenant shall alter any lock or install a new lock or a knocker on any door of the demised premises without the written consent of the Landlord, or the Landlord's agent. In case such consent is given the Tenant shall provide the Landlord with an additional key for the use of the Landlord pursuant to the Landlord's right of access to the demised premises.

12. No servants or employees of the Landlord shall be sent out of the building by any Tenant at any time for any purpose.

13. No Tenant shall allow anything whatever to fall from the window or doors of the demised premises, nor shall sweep or throw from the demised premises any dirt or other substance into any of the corridors, or halls, elevators, light shafts, dumb-waiter shafts, ventilators or elsewhere in the building.

14. No garbage cans, coal holder, woodbox, supplies, ice, milk bottles, or other articles shall be placed in the halls or on the staircase landings, nor shall anything be hung from the windows, or balconies, or placed upon the window sills. Neither shall any linens, cloths, clothing, curtains, rugs or mops be shaken or hung from any of the windows or doors. No fire escapes shall be obstructed in any manner.

15. No Tenant shall make or permit any disturbing noises in the building by himself, his family, servants, employees, agents, visitors and licensees, nor do or permit anything by such persons that will interfere with the rights, comforts or convenience of other Tenants. No Tenant shall play upon, or suffer to be played upon, any musical instrument or operate or suffer to be operated a phonograph or radio in the demised premises between the hours of elevel o'clock P.M. and the following eight o'clock A.M. if the same shall disturb or annoy other occupants of the building. No Tenant shall conduct or permit to be conducted, vocal or instrumental practice, nor give nor permit to be given vocal or instrumental instruction at any time.

16. No radio installation shall be made without the written consent of the Landlord. Any aerial erected on the roof or exterior walls of the building without the consent of the landlord, in writing, is liable to removal without notice.

17. No animals of any kind shall be kept or harbored in the demised premises, unless the same in each instance be expressly permitted in writing by the Landlord, and such consent, if given, shall be revocable by the Landlord at any time. In no event shall any dog be permitted on any passenger elevator or in any public portion of the building unless carried or on leash, nor in any grass or garden plot under any condition.

SPECIAL RULES AND REGULATIONS NOT PROVIDED IN STANDARD FORM OF LEASE OF APARTMENT, BUT FORMING A PART HEREOF.

275

3 Proposed Model Rental Agreement[1]

This monthly agreement is made duplicate original this _____ day of _____ , 19 ____ by and between _____ hereinafter called landlord and _____ hereinafter called tenant.

The landlord rents to the tenant premises known as _____ in the District of Columbia, by the month commencing on the _____ day of each month.

The landlord and tenant hereby agree as follows:

1. The landlord covenants and warrants that at the time of the signing of this agreement or at the time of delivery of possession the premises are in compliance with the Housing Regulations of the District of Columbia, in a clean, safe and sanitary condition, in repair and free from rodents and vermin, as well in compliance with all other applicable laws and regulations of the District of Columbia relating to health and safety.

2. The landlord covenants and agrees to maintain said premises in such condition for the duration of this agreement and in accordance therewith; provided, however, that the creation other than through normal wear and tear, of unclean, unsafe, and unsanitary or rodent or vermin infested conditions by the negligence of the tenant shall be the responsibility of the tenant and not the landlord to correct.

3. It is further agreed that if the landlord breaches any of the covenants or warranties herein regarding the condition and maintenance of these premises after the tenancy has commenced, and the tenant gives notice of the need for repairs, restoration of said premises or replacement of certain parts thereon,

and a reasonable time passes without the repair, restoration, or replacement having been made by the landlord, the stipulated rent payable by the tenant for these premises shall be reduced by 50% until said repairs, restoration, or replacement have been made. "Reasonable time" means reasonable in the circumstances but in no event shall be longer than the maximum Allotted Time allowed for similar repairs under the Housing Division Procedural Manual of the District of Columbia Department of Licenses and Inspection. Full rent shall begin to be due on the day repairs, restoration, or replacements are completed; and only 50% of the stipulated rent shall be due for the interval between the expiration of time for the repairs to have been completed and the time when they are actually completed. At the option of the tenant, the landlord shall either credit the amount of the reduction under this paragraph toward the succeeding month's rent, or shall refund said amount in cash to the tenant within two weeks of the date of completion of repairs, restoration or replacement.

4.   The tenant shall not waive any rights or remedies under this agreement or under the laws of the District of Columbia by taking possession of the premises when one or more conditions of the premises violate the warranties and covenants of this agreement.

5.   The landlord agrees specifically among his other warranties to the following: To maintain in operable condition a water heating facility; plumbing facilities; kitchen sink and heating facility; to furnish sufficient heat to maintain a minimum of 68 degrees F. between the hours of 6:30 A.M. and 11:00 P.M. whenever temperatures fall below this level regardless of the time of year; to furnish hot water of at least 120 degrees F. continuously to kitchen and bathroom sink and bathtub in amounts sufficient for normal demands; to furnish water, gas and electricity for airconditioning when these or any of them are supplied as part of the consideration for the payment of rent; to maintain in operable condition the refrigerator and cooking stove when furnished by the landlord; to maintain the roof in good repair; to maintain interior wall surfaces free of moisture, loose or peeling paint or paper, or cracked plaster, unless the need for repairs or correction results from the misuse or abuse by the tenant or his invitees of the facilities. The landlord agrees to complete repairs for which he is responsible in accordance with Paragraph 3 of this contract. The landlord further agrees to provide at the outset of the lease one complete set of screens for all windows and outer doors.

6.   The tenant covenants that all statements made by him in his applications for the renting of these premises are true; that the actual occupants will be ————————————————; that he wll not use any portion of the premises in which there is a furnace, water heater, or gas meter for sleeping purposes, nor permit them to be used by his invitees. The tenant further agrees to conserve the heat and to avoid waste of hot water. The tenant agrees to keep the premises under his control in a clean, safe and sanitary condition including but not limited to floors and floor coverings, and other walking surfaces. The tenant further agrees to keep walls, ceilings, windows, and doorways clean and free of any unsanitary matter. The tenant agrees to keep plumbing fixtures in a clean and sanitary condition and agrees to use care in the proper use and operation of the plumbing facilities. The tenant agrees to use the premises for residential purposes only. It is understood by the parties that not more than ———— persons may lawfully reside on these premises.

7.   The landlord recognizes his continuing obligation to maintain this property. The landlord agreed that he or his duly appointed agent will inspect the prem-

ises subject of this agreement at least twice yearly during daylight hours or by special appointment, to note conditions and to arrange for the immediate correction of those conditions which fall within the landlord's responsibility in accordance with this agreement. The tenant hereby agrees to permit the inspection of these premises twice yearly and as well when emergency requires, and to arrange and pay for the immediate correction of those conditions which have been caused by his negligence or that of his invitees. The tenant further agrees to notify the landlord of conditions which require correction.

8. In the event the landlord requires a security deposit or any additional monies to be paid by the tenant as a condition to the completing of this agreement the landlord agrees to hold such monies in a separate interest bearing bank account and to pay any accumulated interest for the period for which the monies are held as security and not used for the purpose of defraying unpaid rent or paying for repairs which were the duty of the tenant to make in accordance with his agreement. The landlord further agrees that he will not use such security deposit or additional rent money for any other purpose.

The landlord agrees without demand to refund to the tenant within fifteen days of the expiration of this tenancy the security deposit and any additional deposits, and any accumulated interest thereon, paid by the tenant as a condition of his tenancy and in addition to the stipulated rent, or within such fifteen-day period to notify the tenant, by personal service or certified mailing to the tenant's last known address, of his intention to withhold and apply such monies toward defraying the cost of repair which under the terms of this agreement should have been made by the tenant. Failure to give the tenant such timely notice shall be a bar to the landlord's right to withhold and apply these funds in whole or in part. Within 30 days after the landlord has properly notified the tenant of his intention to withhold such monies he shall give the tenant an itemized and signed statement of the use to which such monies were applied, including names, addresses and fees of the persons making repairs, and he shall refund the balance. Failure to submit such an itemized accounting within the time allowed will render the landlord liable for the entire sum withheld. The landlord is authorized to incur reasonable costs in effecting repairs. In the event the landlord himself effects such repairs he shall within 30 days from the giving of notice of intention to withhold provide an itemized statement of the cost of material and the reasonable value of his services.

9. The tenant hereby waives notice to quit in the event he fails to pay rent within five days after the due date. In the event the landlord seeks to recover possession for any breach of this contract, he agrees prior to the filing of any legal action to notify the tenant by either certified mail or personal service of his intention to commence suit in the District of Columbia Court of General Sessions; provided, however, that, provisions of the law to the contrary notwithstanding failure by the landlord to so notify the tenant, if timely pleaded by the tenant, shall constitute a complete defense to the suit for possession.

10. The landlord hereby waives notice to quit from the date he receives notice from the tenant, under paragraph three (3) of this agreement, of the need for repairs or restoration of the premises or replacement of certain parts thereon. Under any other circumstances both the landlord and the tenant agree to give each other written notice to quit in accordance with this agreement when either of them shall wish to bring this agreement to an end. Said notice to quit when given by the landlord shall be accompanied by a statement of reasons therefor and shall

278

be given thirty (30) days in advance and at such time as to expire on the day
_____ the tenancy commenced to run. Not less than fifteen (15) days notice
shall be given by the tenant and such notice may be given at any time. If such
notice is given and the tenant vacates these premises in accordance with such
notice, the tenant shall be liable for rent or for use and occupancy for the period
during which the notice runs, but not for longer. Where the period during which
the tenant's notice to quit runs will expire in a new monthly rental period the
tenant at the usual time shall pay an amount equal to the number of days for
which the notice thereafter runs multiplied by 1/30 of the agreed monthly rental
figure.

Where the tenant's notice expires and the tenant vacates in advance of the
expiration of rental period for which the tenant has already paid rent in full,
the landlord shall refund an amount equal to the number of days between the expiration date of the monthly rental period, including the latter day but not the
former, multiplied by 1/30 of the monthly rental figure.

11. The landlord and the tenant hereby agree that the conditions and agreements contained herein are binding on, and may be legally enforced by the parties hereto, their heirs, executors, administrators, successors and assigns respectively. Feminine and neuter nouns shall be substituted for the masculine
form and the plurals shall be substituted for the singular number in any place
herein in which the context may require such substitution.

12. At the execution of this agreement the tenant shall pay the sum of
_____ dollars for the first month's rent in advance beginning _____ the day
of _____ 19 _____ , and shall be given a separate rental receipt for such
payment.

13. The landlord agrees to provide receipts in writing for all money paid
as rent by the tenant and to state on each receipt the amount received, the date
the money is received by him and the period for which the money pays the rent
on these premises. In the event the landlord fails to provide receipts in accordance with this agreement, and a dispute over rent arises, the landlord shall
be obligated to refer to and to pay the cost of an accountant for an accounting.

14. The landlord agrees to accept rental money without regard to any other
obligation owed by the tenant to the landlord and to seek separate legal remedies for other debts which may accrue to the landlord from the tenant. Where a
landlord's refusal of cash payments for rent requires the tenant to purchase a
money order or other cash equivalent, any service charge or other expense incurred in securing said money order or other cash equivalent may be deducted,
along with any postage, from succeeding rental payments.

15. The tenant agrees to return all keys to the landlord at the time of the
termination of this agreement and, except for changes due to normal wear and
tear, to return the premises in the same condition as when he received them.

16. In the event these premises become uninhabitable as a result of fire,
flood, civil disorder or other cause beyond the control of either the landlord
or the tenant the obligation to pay rent shall cease immediately and the tenant
agrees to vacate said premises within a reasonable time.

In testimony whereof, the landlord and the tenant have signed this agreement this _____ day of _____ 19 _____ . The tenant herewith
acknowledges receipt of the duplicate copy of this agreement.

| _____ | _____ |
| Tenant | Landlord |

Index